W. D. L'Estrange

Under Fourteen Flags

Being the Life and Adventures of Brigadier-General MacIver

W. D. L'Estrange

Under Fourteen Flags
Being the Life and Adventures of Brigadier-General MacIver

ISBN/EAN: 9783337136703

Printed in Europe, USA, Canada, Australia, Japan

Cover: Foto ©ninafisch / pixelio.de

More available books at **www.hansebooks.com**

UNDER FOURTEEN FLAGS

BEING

THE LIFE AND ADVENTURES OF
BRIGADIER-GENERAL MACIVER, A SOLDIER OF FORTUNE

BY

CAPTAIN W. D. L'ESTRANGE

AUTHOR OF "MARMADUKE INGLEBY," "CLAUGHTON ABBEY," ETC., ETC.

LONDON
SPENCER BLACKETT
(Successor to J. & R. Maxwell)
MILTON HOUSE, 35, ST. BRIDE STREET, LUDGATE CIRCUS, E.C.

CONTENTS.

CHAPTER I.
The Parentage and Education of Ronald MacIver—Receives his Commission and gains his first Experience of War . **1**

CHAPTER II.
A great Chief—A Highland Volunteer—Life on Shipboard—A daring Act **13**

CHAPTER III.
The celebrated Countess de la Torre—Quarrels in Camp—MacIver in Love **22**

CHAPTER IV.
Strange Friendship formed with the famous General Wheat—MacIver's first Duel and its Consequences . . . **28**

CHAPTER V.
Dangerous Ground—A startling Adventure—And a narrow Escape **35**

CHAPTER VI.
A Sequel to the attempted Assassination—A projected Elopement **43**

CHAPTER VII.
A rash Promise, and a foolish Expedition—Falls amongst Rogues; but not discourteous ones—A Night amongst the Brigands **48**

CHAPTER VIII.
MacIver receives the Cross of Savoy—A Lover's Stratagem . **58**

CHAPTER IX.
An intercepted Elopement—Home again . . . **66**

CHAPTER X.

The Outbreak of the Civil War in America—MacIver arrives in Washington and refuses to take service under the Federals — Imprisoned at Alexandria (Virginia) as a Secessionist 72

CHAPTER XI.

Amongst the Federals—Another fortunate Escape—Borrowed Plumage 78

CHAPTER XII.

Crossing the Confederate Lines—Meeting with Colonel Scott —Proceeds to Richmond 86

CHAPTER XIII.

Jackson's Campaign in the Valley of Virginia—An Irishman for the first time under Fire—The Battle of Fort Royal . 93

CHAPTER XIV.

The Battles of Cross Keys and Fort Republic—The Death of Turner Ashby 100

CHAPTER XV.

Capture of Percy Wyndham—Jackson's Opinion of Turner Ashby—The March on Richmond—The Battle of Gaines's Mills, and the Death of Wheat 108

CHAPTER XVI.

The Seven Days' Fighting round Richmond—The Fighting at Savage Station, Frazer Farm, and Malvern Hill—The Battles of Cedar Run and Manassas—MacIver wounded and taken Prisoner 114

CHAPTER XVII.

Lieutenant MacIver taken to Alexandria—Meets and is recognised by his former Jailer—Lee's Operations in the Enemy's Territory 122

CHAPTER XVIII.

Camp Life at Winchester—The end of the Sixty-two Campaign —A Night Adventure on the Mississippi—The Confederate Batteries and the Yankee Gunboats 129

CHAPTER XIX.

An unfortunate Accident—Captain MacIver receives orders to proceed to Europe with Despatches—Running the Blockade —Arrival in England 138

CHAPTER XX.

A nice little Plot interrupted—The end of the American War —MacIver starts for Mexico—Another fatal Duel . . 144

CONTENTS

CHAPTER XXI.
Another Duel—Anecdotes of MacIver—A Fight with the Indians 152

CHAPTER XXII.
A desperate Defence—an attempted Escape, and Capture by the Indians—Life among the Red Men 159

CHAPTER XXIII.
The Major made into an Indian Chief—A successful Attempt to Escape—Crosses the Mexican Frontier and falls into the hands of the Republicans—Robbing a Robber . . 166

CHAPTER XXIV.
MacIver joins the Mexican Royalist Army—Receives the Order of Guadaloupe—The end of the War, and the Death of the Emperor Maximilian—Colonel MacIver endures great Privations, and escapes at last 170

CHAPTER XXV.
Joins the Brazilian and Argentine Armies—Commissioned to form a Foreign Legion—Two Attempts on MacIver's Life defeated 176

CHAPTER XXVI.
MacIver fights two more Duels—A Mutiny in the Foreign Legion—The Outbreak of the Cholera in Buenos Ayres, and its Consequences 184

CHAPTER XXVII.
At Death's Door—The End of the Foreign Legion—Leaves the Argentine Service, and receives a Commission from the Cretan Provisional Government 190

CHAPTER XXVIII.
Colonel MacIver's Sojourn at Athens—Joins the Greek Service, and serves under Corroneus—Brigand-hunting on the Frontier of Thessaly—Returns to America . . 196

CHAPTER XXIX.
The Cuban Expedition—Appointed to the Command of a Corps of Officers—Failure of the first Attempt to reach Cuba . 205

CHAPTER XXX.
Seizure of the *Lilian*—Taken to Nassau—MacIver Sick unto Death—Leaves for Cuba—An order for his Arrest, and a narrow Escape 210

CHAPTER XXXI.
Cuba and her Claims—The Insurrection—Disaster . . 218

CHAPTER XXXII.

Friends in Need—A Love Affair and a Quarrel—Flight and a lucky Escape 225

CHAPTER XXXIII.

Lost in the Forest—Dangerous Neighbours—Alone on the wide Atlantic in an open Boat 231

CHAPTER XXXIV.

A Dreary Voyage—Ghastly Companions—Picked up by a Steamer 237

CHAPTER XXXV.

An Agreement with Ismail Pasha—MacIver receives his Commission as Colonel of Cavalry—Joins the Egyptian Army . 244

CHAPTER XXXVI.

The Climate affects Colonel MacIver's Health, and he resigns his Commission—Leaves for Constantinople—Intention of joining the French in the War against Germany . . 252

CHAPTER XXXVII.

The Close of the Franco-German War—Arrival of MacIver in France—Joins General Chanzy, and is wounded at the Battle of Orleans—The Battle of St. Quintin—Life in Paris after the Commune 257

CHAPTER XXXVIII.

Colonel MacIver presented to the Wife of Don Carlos in Switzerland—Returns to England and establishes the Carlist League—Joins Don Carlos on the Spanish Frontier . . 271

CHAPTER XXXIX.

A new Love Affair—A Rival and a Quarrel at the Café Riche—A Fatal Duel—The Herzegovinian Struggle . . . 285

CHAPTER XL.

Colonel MacIver leaves England for Servia—Receives his Commission, and raises a Foreign Legion of Cavalry . . 294

CHAPTER XLI.

Appointed to the Staff of the Commander-in-Chief—Receives the Order of the Takavo—Mission to England—The End of the War 315

CHAPTER XLII.

General Tchernaieff in London—MacIver returns to Servia—Receives a Commission under the Greek Government, with Instructions to form a Foreign Legion . . . 327

UNDER FOURTEEN FLAGS

CHAPTER I.

THE PARENTAGE AND EDUCATION OF RONALD MACIVER—RECEIVES HIS COMMISSION AND GAINS HIS FIRST EXPERIENCE OF WAR

ONE evening in the year eighteen hundred and forty, amongst the guests assembled at one of the principal mansions in the city of Edinburgh was a young lady named Anna Douglas, who was comparatively a stranger in the Scottish capital, having but recently arrived from America. Her advent had caused quite a sensation in the fashionable world of Scott's "ain romantic toon," and from her beauty and elegance she was the acknowledged belle of the season.

This lovely girl, although not a native of Scotland, was one of an old Cavalier family, and possessed all the pride and dignity of the ancient house of Douglas.

A Virginian by birth, she was descended from a scion of this old Scottish clan, who had formed one of that gallant company of gentlemen adventurers which, in sixteen hundred and seven, in the reign of our first James, colonised "His Majesty's Plantations of Virginia." In that beautiful and fruitful spot, those of the little band who survived the first hardships of a new life became lords and seigniors of the soil. Proud of their lineage, these gentlemen adventurers, many of whom were married, established amongst themselves and their families a society as aristocratic, as accomplished, and as exclusive as that of the most refined Court in the Old World.

Such did Virginian society continue from generation to generation, and of this select coterie Miss Anna Douglas was one of the brightest ornaments.

When nearly twenty-two, however, this fair daughter of the sunny Southern State evinced a delicacy of constitution which caused grave alarm to her friends. After consultation, her medical advisers determined that she must travel abroad for the benefit of her health.

Her father, Mr. Douglas, was unable at the time to leave his large plantations, but arrangements having been made for his daughter to visit a branch of his family then residing in Edinburgh, Miss Douglas left for Europe accompanied by two attendants.

The sea voyage was so beneficial that the fair Virginian arrived in the Scottish capital restored to health, where her beauty, her vivacity, and her amiability won not only admiration, but the regard of many friends.

On this particular night on which our chapter opens, Miss Douglas was to meet for the first time her future husband. As she came out of the supper-room, leaning on the arm of her host, there stood by the door a stalwart, broad-shouldered, manly young fellow, who was introduced to the fair American as Mr. Ronald MacIver.

In those days there were few handsomer or more distinguished-looking men amongst those who strolled up or down Prince's Street than this young Highlander, who now bowed low before Miss Douglas. He was a Ross-shire gentleman, a son of the chief of the clan MacIver, and was well known in the upper circles of Edinburgh.

After this casual introduction the young couple met frequently, and liked each other's company. They had much in common, too, in taste and feeling. She, with her old Cavalier instincts, and he, with the strong Jacobite proclivities of his forefathers, had one theme upon which they were ever in thorough unison.

Friendship soon ripened into mutual affection, and few were surprised when it was whispered that Ronald MacIver was deeply in love with the beautiful Miss Douglas, nor was the surprise heightened when it was more than suspected that his devotion was returned.

The courtship was a brief one. The young Highlander was a bold and ardent lover, and as soon as the sanction of the lady's father to the union had been obtained, they were married.

The happy pair, with a host of good wishes, proceeded to the bridegroom's home in Ross-shire, there to spend the honeymoon, and with the promise and the intention of returning to Edinburgh for the next season.

This promise, however, was not fated to be fulfilled, for, after a few months of happiness at their Highland retreat, there came sad tidings to mar their bliss. One morning brought a letter from Virginia announcing the severe illness of Mrs. MacIver's father, her only surviving parent. It was an attack, which it was feared would terminate fatally, although the end *might be prolonged, and Mr. Douglas had expressed an earnest desire to see his daughter and her husband.

It was a terrible shock to the youthful wife, for she had no other near relative except her father. The following day Ronald MacIver and his wife were on their way South, and took ship for America with as little delay as possible. Their voyage was a protracted one. Storms and contrary winds, and other causes delayed them long beyond the usual time, and before they reached land Mrs. MacIver was a mother.

Their son, Henry Ronald MacIver, the hero of this true story, was born at sea on Christmas morning, in the year eighteen hundred and forty-one, but within a league of the old State of Virginia, and in sight of her romantic and beautiful scenery.

Mr. Douglas lived to see his daughter restored to him and to welcome her husband and his baby grandson. On the death of her father Mrs. MacIver was his sole heiress, and the happy couple decided to settle down on their Virginian plantation. The lady was in the midst of her old friends, and the new life was one that just suited the young Highlander. There was plenty of fishing, shooting, and hunting, and the supervision of the estates found occupation for other spare hours.

Ten pleasant, uneventful years wore smoothly on, and Henry Ronald MacIver grew apace into an active, bright-eyed, curly-haired boy, who, young as he was, could run and jump, and ride and shoot with the best.

Braced by the pure sweet air of what might be called his native State, by the time he was a little turned ten he had filled out into a handsome, stalwart youngster, tall for his age, and already giving promise of that strength and stature which were to distinguish his manhood.

Before he had reached his eleventh year it was decided to send the boy to Scotland, to be placed under the guardianship of a foster-brother of his grandfather, one Donald Graham, an old retired general officer. This gentleman had offered to superintend his education for a few years, especially as to a course of military training, as it was intended that young Ronald MacIver's profession should be that of arms.

When he reached Scotland the old General was delighted with his youthful *protégé*, who soon became his almost constant companion. Ronald, too, was equally attached to his guardian, and the twain became fast and firm friends. Although, of course, he studied elsewhere as well as under this gentleman, to General Graham was young MacIver chiefly indebted for the rudiments of his military education, and for a discipline that in after life was to prove of infinite service.

It had been purposed by Mr. MacIver, that after his son had remained for a while with General Graham, he should, when old enough, return to

America to be entered at the military academy of West Point, with a view to his subsequently joining the United States Service.

When the time came, however, General Graham was loth to part with his young companion, and both the old man and the boy pleaded so earnestly, that at length the latter was allowed to finish his studies in Scotland.

Had destiny willed it that Ronald MacIver was to join the United States Army, there can be little question, from his career as a soldier under other flags, that he might have risen to be an eminent commander of the great Republic. Fortune or chance, however, did not so decide, and the youth who had been intended to serve under the "Stars and Stripes" was to live to fight against that banner.

Still, it was only the question of a year or two before the old General had to part with his *protégé*. When he was of sufficient age to receive a commission in the army, young MacIver, through the interest of influential friends of his father's family, combined with that of General Graham, received his appointment under the Honourable East India Company, and was ordered to proceed to Calcutta to join his regiment.

This was at the time of the Mutiny, and Ronald was then about sixteen, but was tall and powerfully built, and not only manly in stature, but in appearance. Besides being muscular, he was very active, and excelled in all athletic sports and exercises. Accustomed to riding, too, from his childhood, he was a capital horseman.

When young MacIver arrived in India, the rebellion was at its height. The history of the great Mutiny of our Sepoy troops is known and realised, alas, too well! Over and over again has it been told by able pens. To recapitulate a tithe of the vile atrocities that were perpetrated by the natives in that terrible war of race against race is not our province.

The story of the young soldier's adventures would be incomplete, however, without a record of his individual bravery at the siege of Jhansi, where his career had very nearly been nipped in the bud.

A skirmish was at its height, and during the *mêlée* MacIver got separated from his troop. Whilst he was urging his horse forward and trying to rejoin his comrades, he was attacked by two Sowars, who set upon him fiercely, and against whom he had to defend himself as best he could.

Although but a lad of sixteen, the rebels had more than met their match, for General Graham had not failed to make him a perfect master of the sword. The young Highlander with a cut of his sabre slew one of his swarthy enemies quickly, and then engaged the other—a big, burly fellow—in a hand-to-hand fight.

Now that the odds were equal, it was only an affair of a few brief moments before MacIver's sabre was run through the chest of his second foe. But before he could give the wrench in the recover and withdraw his blade, the Sowar seized MacIver's sabre with both hands, forcing the hilt against his own breast so as to bring himself close to his opponent, and then *spat* in the face of his enemy, exclaiming :

"Tum Feringhee Soor Walla!" (You European Pig!)

The next instant the Sowar released his hold of MacIver's sabre, threw up his arms in his death agony, and fell back from his horse dead, thus evincing even with his latest breath the spirit of hatred to the detested Christian.

Striking his spurs into his charger, the young soldier again dashed into the midst of the fray, and the next minute he was attacked by no less than seven well-mounted Sowars. Not a friend was at hand to help him, for each white man near had as much as he could do to hold his own, and at the moment Ronald MacIver saw nothing but death before him. He came, however, of a race that proverbially die hard, and he determined to fight to the last and sell his life as dearly as might be.

His Highland blood was up and he defended himself with such persistent obstinacy and bull-dog courage, yet so coolly and adroitly, that he not only kept his enemies at bay, but speedily reduced their number. One after another he managed to empty three of the saddles, cutting down or unhorsing his men, when the remaining four Sowars, probably realising that unless they made a united attack they were likely to get the worst of it, suddenly spurred in a body upon their youthful, but determined foe.

As the Sowars, their tulwars raised, made their rush, instinctively the lad's sabre went up to protect his head. Unfortunately, at the same moment, a pistol bullet struck him on the sword hand, ploughing its way along the palm, breaking down his guard, and leaving him defenceless and at the mercy of his exasperated enemies. Quick as lightning a tulwar flashed through the air, cutting clean through the young officer's *topee*, and down into his skull, and MacIver rolled out of the saddle and fell upon the earth apparently dead.

But Providence interposed, and though sorely wounded in the hand and head, the youthful soldier was still living. Shortly before the battle, as a protection from the fierce heat of the sun, MacIver had placed a damp towel under his felt helmet, and this no doubt was the means of saving his life. Yet so keen had been the steel, and so well-directed the hand which wielded the weapon, that the sharp blade had divided helmet and towel and cut down into the skull, although fortunately without serious injury to the brain. Yet what a ghastly wound must that have been, the vivid scar from which still remains, and will be carried through life!

Hours after the fight was over, and the battle won, young MacIver was found lying amongst the dead and wounded. More than once had he been passed by as one beyond all earthly help, but at length some of his own men recognised him, and discovered that there was still life in the apparently inanimate body. With all speed the wounded officer was conveyed to the field hospital, where his case was promptly attended to, but the surgeons had little, if any, hope of his recovery.

For three days the world was a blank to him, and for as many weeks it was doubtful whether he would survive. But in the end youth and a strong constitution, combined with great medical skill on the part of the doctor who attended him, pulled him through. It was months, however, before he was again reported fit for duty and ready for the saddle.

But fate seemed against MacIver ever leaving India alive, for scarcely had he recovered from his terrible wounds, when he was attacked by a foe as deadly in its effect as the human—or inhuman—enemies that had desolated the land and butchered helpless women and innocent children. The recent injury to his head and his bodily weakness marked him out too surely as a ready victim to sunstroke. He was struck down on the march, and had to be invalided to Calcutta.

The month of September, 'fifty-eight, saw the great East India Company abolished, and all the vast territories hitherto under its sole control transferred to the British Crown. The year which witnessed the end of the powerful English association of traders, which, from the reign of Queen Elizabeth in sixteen hundred, had continued to govern a country as large —excluding Russia—as the whole of Europe, was memorable for the suppression of the revolted Sepoys. The terrible Mutiny might then be said to be virtually stamped out. Cawnpore had been avenged, Delhi had fallen, and Lucknow had been relieved.

But, alas! at the sacrifice of how many gallant British hearts had the victory been achieved. Anson, Barnard, Henry Lawrence, John Nicholson, Havelock, Niell, and a host whose glorious deeds are household words, were no more, and their long list of names enrolled on the scroll of heroes who had died for their country.

But, though war and its attendant horrors had given place to peace and industry over a greater part of the land, yet like a foul plague spot that still festers, the arch-fiend, Nana Sahib, at the head of thousands of the more desperate rebels, fought obstinately on.

With a persistency worthy of a better cause, that human tiger, who had been the prime mover in the Mutiny, and the inciter and plotter of massacres, contested foot by foot each unsubdued spot, until that memorable Christmas Day, when he made his last stand within sight of the snowy range of the giant mountains of Nepaul.

At length his reign of terror was at an end. On New Year's Day, more than eighteen months after the first outbreak at Meerut, the final battle was fought and the last band of mutineers scattered to the winds. The war was over, and the arch-traitor and murderer, Nana Sahib, flying for his life into the fastnesses of the gloomy passes of Nepaul.

What stirring memories yet linger with a vivid freshness of those later months of the great Mutiny; memories that are written on the roll of fame and which must endure for all time! Stout-hearted old Colin Campbell, Outram, the Bayard of India, dauntless Peel, with his gallant blue-jackets, and scores of other brave men, the recollection of whose deeds of valour makes the pulse throb faster, and each and every British heart prouder of the birthland.

Unfortunately Ronald MacIver could take no share in the fighting under his countryman Sir Colin. Month after month he lay ill in Calcutta, too weak even to be moved. At length when he was able to get about, the East India Company being at an end, and the Mutiny suppressed, the youthful subaltern, like many others, left the Service and sailed for Europe. He was still ill and feeble, but hoped that the sea voyage would renew his strength.

That hope was granted, for the passage home from India restored him to his former robust health. On his arrival in England he at once proceeded to Edinburgh, where, unhappily, bad news awaited him. On reaching the Scottish capital, his mind filled with joyous anticipations at the thought of once more meeting his guardian, he found that his dear old friend, General Graham, was dead.

As may well be imagined, the shock which he experienced was great, for the deceased General had been to him like a second parent. It was Donald Graham who had first instilled into his youthful thoughts the desire for a soldier's life; he who had taught him the rudiments of his military education; and the one being, who, next to those who gave him life, he had learned to look up to as his best and dearest friend.

Even a deeper sorrow was at hand, and when he knew all what he had to bear it was indeed a dreary "home coming" to this youth but a few months turned eighteen. As he was being told of his guardian's decease, and ere he could scarcely realise that it was true, a letter was handed to him from America, which announced that death had claimed one nearer and dearer still. The epistle bore his mother's well-remembered superscription, and informed him that his father had been killed by a fall from his horse whilst engaged in a hunting expedition.

It was indeed a sad and pitiful letter. It might have been that the unfortunate lady had a presentiment that these were the last words which she was to write to her dearly-beloved son, from the solemnity that pervaded the whole of the lines. Whilst she laid bare, as it were, all the tenderness of her woman's heart for her absent boy, she exhorted him to follow the noble example of his late father's life, and told her son that, much as she loved him, she would rather that he, too, were dead, than that he should live to dishonour the name which he bore.

MacIver never forgot, nor ever will forget, those dying words of his mother; for dying words, alas! they were to prove. It was the last letter he ever received from those dear hands. Too soon came the news that the sorrowing wife had died of grief for the loss of her husband.

The lad's trouble had been heavy enough to bear before, but with this last death came the ineffable sorrow which only a man can realise when he loses a loving mother.

CHAPTER II.

A GREAT CHIEF — A HIGHLAND VOLUNTEER — LIFE ON SHIPBOARD — A DARING ACT

It has been often and perhaps truly remarked, that the feelings and impressions of youth are very elastic, and that the sense of joy or grief is quickly effaced from the minds of young people. If this be correct in the abstract, young MacIver was an exception, as for many months after the death of his parents and his guardian he was, so to speak, brooding over his sorrow for those dear friends.

Unfortunately, perhaps, for him in his then desponding mood, he had no incentive to exertion in a pecuniary point, his funds being ample. It had been the practice of the late Mr. MacIver to remit a liberal quarterly allowance for his son to General Graham, and during Ronald's absence in India these sums had been accumulating at the banker's.

Mrs. MacIver, too, had been, as the reader already knows, an heiress, and by the death of both his parents, her son was the owner of large plantations in the State of Virginia, and of considerable wealth, but he showed no inclination to be the possessor of his inheritance.

At length, however, the time came when his memories were less sad, and he began to long for some change of scene or new excitement. The restless spirit craving for occupation, ever the great motive power of his chequered career, was burning fiercely within his breast for an escape from what appeared to him a mere humdrum existence; a life wasted unless spent in a world of action. The escape for which he yearned was soon to come in the struggle for Italian liberty

On the night of the sixth of May, eighteen hundred and sixty, the moon was shedding a soft light on the port of Genoa; that city whose marble churches and palaces have long given to it the title of Genoa the Superb.

There was a calm sea, and the clocks were just striking nine, as thirty men embarked in two boats at La Marina, in this same port of Genoa, and rowed quietly out of the harbour in the direction of two steamers, named the *Piedmonte* and the *Lombardo*, which lay some distance away.

These boats rapidly boarded the vessels, and the men in them seized the steamers, and made prisoners of and confined the masters and the crews in the fore cabins.

On the same night, but about an hour later, a number of armed men came out of the Villa Spinola, the residence of Signor Vecchi, the well-known historian. One man amongst them was evidently the chief, and the others were his officers.

Proceeding by a narrow pathway which led from the villa to the sea, they moved silently down to the beach, where they found a large body of men assembled, and a flotilla of boats waiting to embark them.

The muster roll was called, and the number was found to be one thousand and eighty. Then as quickly as the boats were filled they were rowed out to sea, until thirty boats had left the shore, and none remained. One by one these boats were relieved of their passengers by the *Piedmonte* or the *Lombardo,* until the whole had been transferred to the decks of the steamers.

At the call of a great chieftain, these men had sprung to arms, and were ready to give their lives for the cause in which they had enlisted. And who was the leader, who had awakened these men's hearts, and at whose word or gesture were multitudes roused or calmed? GIUSEPPE GARIBALDI, who, with the battle cry of "Italy and Victor Emmanuel" on his lips, was about to liberate a down-trodden nation.

That very night, those two steamers, poorly equipped, and anything but warlike in appearance, left Genoa behind them, and with all steam up stood direct for Sicily. Soon all Europe was ringing with the news that Garibaldi had seized the ammunition and cannon at Talamone, and that six days after sailing from Genoa he had landed at Marsala. Next, how gallantly he had liberated the fortified Sicilian capital, Palermo, with a mere handful of men; followers that were not tried men-at-arms, but undisciplined volunteers, and who had opposed to them a whole fleet and twenty thousand soldiers.

What wonder that men's blood was brought to a fever heat when they heard of the fight at Milazzo, and of the surrender of Messina! Was it surprising that enthusiasm reigned paramount when it was known that the "Liberator" — uniting with his Garibaldians the volunteers organised by Bertani— had sailed for the mainland and disembarked his troops in spite of the broadsides of the Neapolitan fleet?

Three months and but a few days had elapsed since Garibaldi had landed at Marsala, yet Sicily had been freed. On the sixth of May he had embarked at Genoa with a trifle over a thousand followers all told, and on the nineteenth of August the hero of the day was about to commence his triumphal march on Naples.

But the Sicilian campaign of the great "Liberator," however brilliant, and however much it might have won his admiration, could scarcely be expected to enlist the sympathy of Ronald MacIver. He, whose father had been so staunch a Jacobite, whose mother was a Douglas, and whose early training by General Graham had been so utterly opposed to all the principles of a cause such as that in which

Garibaldi was engaged, might well be excused from drawing his sword for Italian liberty.

Young MacIver, however, was moved to enthusiasm by the glorious deeds of valour of which he read. The spirit of the great Italian chieftain stirred him as strongly as it did thousands and thousands of older and wiser heads, and he determined to join the expedition.

MacIver was staying in Glasgow at the time, and having made up his mind, he was not the one to delay in carrying out his arrangements. When he left Scotland he was not alone, having induced several of his youthful friends to accompany him to the seat of war.

In Calabria, each hour added fresh strength to General Garibaldi's ranks, and one morning brought a batch of sturdy young Scotchmen as volunteers. Amongst them was a handsome lad, with gray-blue eyes, short curly auburn hair, and easy, graceful carriage.

He was young in years, but he stood over six feet, with broad shoulders, deep chest, and long limbs. His form was lithe and active, but well set up, as though he had already seen service as a soldier. He had muscles of steel, too, and a heart as fearless as that of the great chief with whom he had come to link his fate.

This youth's name was Henry Ronald MacIver, and when enrolled as a volunteer he was attached to the Legion de Flotte. This celebrated band was then commanded by Major Pogam, the gallant De Flotte having fallen at the battle of Milazzo.

MacIver entered Naples with the "Liberator"

in September. General Garibaldi was quick to detect merit, and shortly entrusted him with a mission to Scotland for the purpose of organising a Scottish company. The youthful soldier left Italy to pay this flying visit, and was so successful as to be able to return to the seat of war with a small contingent.

A ship called the *Milazzo*, commanded by Captain Lionel Campbell Goldsmid, was the vessel employed to convey the British Legion to Italy, and Ronald MacIver was in time to join her. In the Legion, as might probably have been expected, there happened to be a large proportion of very unruly and turbulent spirits.

These men, being newly enlisted, had not been trained to that strict discipline necessarily enforced amongst soldiers, and on board ship was perhaps the worst place to have to control them. For a few days all went well, but presently these undesirable companions on a sea voyage found amusement for their leisure moments in picking quarrels, or trying to do so, with their more respectable and well-behaved fellow passengers.

Many, no doubt, who under other circumstances would have resented the impertinences of these black sheep, submitted to them for the sake of peace and order.

Unfortunately, however, for some of these quarrelsome fellows, they one day, presuming on his youth, selected MacIver as one amongst others to insult, and they caught a Tartar for their pains. They little knew the avalanche they were about to bring upon their heads. Not being blessed with too amiable a temper, and being of an exceedingly hasty disposition, their intended victim turned upon them like lightning. In a few minutes his strong arms had inflicted upon the aggressors a chastisement that they did not very easily nor soon forget.

Amongst the quarrelsome passengers was a Captain Hoskins, who, from his education and from the position which he held, ought, one would have imagined, to have known how to conduct himself better. This gentleman subsequently tried to avenge in another way a severe thrashing which he received from the young Highlander whilst on board the good ship *Milazzo*.

These troublesome members of the British Legion must have been a source of continual annoyance to Captain Goldsmid, the commander of the ship, who was a very gentlemanly man, and, like most of his profession, a most excellent fellow. He was as fine and smart a specimen of a sailor as ever trod a deck, and was liked by every one who knew him.

The Legion was landed safely at its destination, but shortly after the ship's arrival a fatal accident nearly occurred. One of the seamen fell overboard, and being unable to swim, would probably have been drowned but for the captain instantly jumping after him and effecting a rescue at great risk to himself. Besides bringing out for Garibaldi his British contingent, Captain Goldsmid afterwards assisted him in another way, for this gallant sailor went to the front with the Legion, fighting with great courage and distinction.

Ronald MacIver was now also attached to the British Legion, and took part with it in the bombardment of Capua. Being an excellent marksman, he did good service with the rifle, frequently being told off for duty behind the advanced breastworks to shoot down any of the enemy who ventured to show in front.

It was about this time that he became known familiarly by the sobriquet of Henri d'Ecosse, whilst many spoke of him as "Le brave Ecossais." His acts of cool daring and of individual courage when before the enemy soon became the talk of soldiers of every nationality engaged in the war. Wherever danger most threatened, there young MacIver was sure to be found. How he escaped death was a wonder to many. Some few, more superstitious than the rest, whispered that he bore a charmed life, and they might be excused, for nothing seemed to harm where he stood.

One desperate, foolhardy act of daring of his at the bombardment of Capua, we should scarcely dare to record, had it not been told to us by two Garibaldian officers who were present. Undertaken at the spur of the moment for a trifling bet, it seemed a temptation of that very Providence which had so long watched over and protected him. It was witnessed, we understand, by hundreds, and will, perhaps, be remembered by some old Garibaldians who were there.

The British Legion was occupying the advanced breastworks under a very heavy fire. The enemy were pouring in a perfect spray of bullets, and not a Garibaldian cared to show himself for an instant from under cover. Whilst the fire was yet at its hottest, Captain Davidson, one of the officers of the Legion, turned to MacIver, and said, more in jest than earnest, for he never for a moment imagined that his offer would be accepted :

"Come, now, MacIver, we all know by this that you are a regular dare-devil; I challenge you for a basket of wine to show yourself over those breastworks for one short minute!"

Without a moment's hesitation, but with great coolness, and speaking as quietly as though he were about to perform some ordinary duty, Ronald replied :

"Done, Captain. I take your bet."

The next moment, rifle in hand, the daring young soldier sprang on to the parapet, where he was fully exposed to the enemy's shots. Zip—zip—zip—zip, whistled the bullets around him, and there he stood as calmly as if on parade, firing and reloading, firing and reloading, and still without cessation the zip—zip—zip of the leaden messengers of death sighing around him and even striking near him, like a fierce storm of hail.

Ere long, his loose red Garibaldian shirt was perforated, his body actually grazed in many places, and yet he kept his stand. Each instant his comrades expected to see him fall back dead or mortally wounded, but he never flinched nor stirred excepting to discharge or load his rifle. Most of the officers were almost paralysed at his temerity, but at length one of them called out :

"For Heaven's sake, MacIver, come down! You have tempted Providence too long."

Thus adjured, the young Highlander fired a parting shot from his rifle, and then coolly lighted a cigar with his face still to the enemy. Then he turned deliberately round and jumped down amongst his astonished companions, from the parapet. When he was once more safely under cover, he said to Captain Davidson:

"That was rather hot work, Captain, and I am thirsty. I should like to go to Santa Maria to drink some of your wine, which I think I have fairly won."

The day following this extraordinary episode, Ronald MacIver was transferred from the British Legion to that of De Flotte, in which he had previously served, and now received his commission as a lieutenant.

Hitherto he had been but a simple volunteer, but General Garibaldi had been quick to notice the soldierly aptitude and intrepid courage of young Henri d'Ecosse, and now at the first opportunity—backed by the recommendation of Major Pogam—he made him one of his officers.

CHAPTER III.

THE CELEBRATED COUNTESS DE LA TORRE—QUARRELS IN CAMP—MACIVER IN LOVE

AFTER the surrender of Capua, several of the defenders were very anxious to know the name of the young soldier who had stood so coolly on the breastworks, defying, as it were, their marksmen. One officer especially, a captain, mentioned subsequently, that when he witnessed this act of daring, he was so struck with the wonderful nerve and coolness displayed that he immediately gave the command to the men of his company not to fire in the direction of MacIver, or rather of the bold stranger of whose name and nationality he was, of course, then in ignorance.

Shortly after he received his commission, MacIver was introduced by General Garibaldi to the beautiful and celebrated Countess de la Torre. This lady had made herself conspicuous in many ways during the Neapolitan war. She was nearly constantly in the saddle, stimulating the patriotism of the troops by her impassioned addresses, or exciting their admiration and enthusiasm by her quiet courage.

But though Madame la Comtesse devoted her time and energies, as it seemed, to Garibaldi, there were many who distrusted her. Indeed, there is now, we are told, but little doubt, however much good she may have done to the cause she appeared so warmly to espouse, that she was a woman of dangerous character and not to be relied upon.

This modern Circe did not disdain to try her wiles on the handsome young Highlander, Ronald MacIver, who was then much talked about from his exploit before Capua. The young lieutenant was no doubt considerably flattered by the attention shown to him by so notable a character, and subsequently blindly fell into a snare prepared for him by this fascinating lady. Little, however, did he imagine, when he was friendly with the Countess, in Italy, that they would meet in after years in another country and under very strange circumstances.

The war was being rapidly pushed forward towards a successful termination, but it was not its perils alone —the bullets and bayonets of the enemy—which threatened the followers of Garibaldi. Amongst an army composed of so many nationalities, it was, perhaps, natural that there should be disagreements. These differences of opinion unfortunately, however, too often expanded into serious encounters.

In fact, quarrels were of daily, nay, hourly occurrence, and duels were constantly taking place, many of which terminated fatally. From these embroilments it would indeed have been a wonder if young MacIver—with his impetuous temper, and keen sense of feeling as to his own personal honour—had escaped free, and it was not long before he had two or three duels on his hands.

After the surrender of Capua, MacIver had been ordered with a portion of the troops to Salerno, where also was the British Legion. Several of the officers of the Legion were overbearing in their manner, or at least Lieutenant MacIver fancied so, and that speedily brought about a coolness which ended in a quarrel.

He challenged more than one, but there seemed a disinclination to fight. Amongst those against whom he conceived himself aggrieved was a quartermaster named Deburgh, who, as far as words were concerned, took a very prominent position in the dispute. But he declined to mix himself up in any other way, contriving cleverly to keep from actual quarrel with the belligerently-inclined Scotchman.

One day, however, Mr. Deburgh went so far as to use some insulting words in reference to MacIver when the latter was present. Probably he imagined he was speaking in a tone which would not be heard, but the Lieutenant's quick ears caught the words, and turning round he struck the offending quartermaster on the face, exclaiming:

"Now, sir, that you have felt my hand, do you feel inclined to risk my steel? There is no law here to shelter cowards."

The gallant quartermaster, however, thus brought to the test, thought better of it, and refused to fight.

MacIver's quarrels with members of the British Legion were not confined to the subaltern officers. He believed that he had a just ground of offence against Colonel Peard, its Commandant. Very shortly after the affair at Salerno between the quartermaster and himself, he happened to meet Colonel Peard in Naples, who at the time was accompanied by another officer named Edenborough, a lieutenant.

This was an opportunity that the touchy young Highlander would not let pass, having heard, in addition to his former grievance, that the Colonel had recently made a statement reflecting upon his, MacIver's, reputation. Walking up to the British Commandant, he said:

"Colonel Peard, you insulted me on one occasion in your own camp at Santa Maria. You stated that I tried to cause dissensions amongst your men, and endeavoured to induce them to join other commands. I then informed you to your face that it was a base and cowardly slander. I now repeat it."

Colonel Peard looked steadily at MacIver, but did not answer, and the Lieutenant continued:

"You have the reputation, sir, of being a good marksman. Now that we are outside your own camp, I should like to exchange shots with you; or I will meet you in any way you choose to name, so that you afford me that satisfaction which one gentleman has a right to ask from another."

"MacIver," replied Colonel Peard gallantly, "you are but a youth, and, although I know you to be a brave fellow, it would be no honour for me to fight with you. What I said I regret, as I now feel that I was wrong. Is that enough? I apologise."

MacIver assented with a nod.

"There is my hand," continued the Colonel. "Come and dine with me to-night at the 'Hotel Victoria.'"

MacIver readily accepted the apology and the hand of Colonel Peard, but he was too proud to partake of that gentleman's dinner.

Having hitherto escaped an embroilment in any serious quarrel, it might have been hoped that he would have kept clear of further scrapes; but now MacIver must fall in love. His too susceptible heart was taken captive by the charms of a very beautiful English girl whom he happened to meet at the house of a friend.

This young lady was the daughter of a late British consul, who was residing in Naples with her mother. As might have been expected, perhaps, from her beauty, accomplishments, and position, she had a number of admirers besides her young countryman, but had shown no decided preference so far for any of her suitors.

Amongst the most attentive of her followers was a gentleman supposed to be an Italian-Frenchman, who was a noted duellist. He was an expert swordsman, and enjoyed the somewhat unenviable reputation of having invariably killed his antagonist in these so-called encounters of honour. He was known to be a most dangerous man to offend, and but few cared to give him cause for enmity. For reasons which the reader will afterwards understand, we shall call him Monsieur Blanc.

One evening MacIver was a guest at a ball, where he met the lady whom he so much admired. Up to that night, in words, he had not revealed his affection; but on this particular occasion, after dancing several times with the fair and fascinating Englishwoman, he found an opportunity to make a passionate declaration of his love.

The lady, who was a year or two older than Lieutenant MacIver, was probably not unprepared for the avowal, and, whilst not exactly binding herself by words, she gave considerable encouragement to her handsome young lover, which led him to hope that his passion was returned.

Elated by the apparent success of his suit, and proud of his conquest, the thoughtless young Lieutenant cared little for the glances of jealousy cast upon him, from time to time, that night by more than one pair of envious eyes. In truth, he was rather pleased by these confirmatory signs of his being favoured, and continued his assiduous attentions to the lady of his heart.

Towards the close of the ball, when he was again dancing with the late consul's daughter, she suddenly turned pale, and trembled. Then she whispered to her lover:

"Mr. MacIver, I beg that you will take care of yourself, for I have noticed that Monsieur Blanc is regarding you with glances of bitter hatred. Pray do not let him pick a quarrel with you, for he is a noted duellist, and I fear for the result."

The warning was well meant, for a deadly fear had seized the fair girl as she caught the malignant glare of the foreigner fixed upon MacIver. The latter, however, somewhat assured her by his light, fearless laugh; and the ball being nearly over, no further conversation passed between them on the subject.

After the Lieutenant had seen his partner and her mother to their carriage, he returned to his quarters, his heart full of sweet hopes, and but little dreaming —spite of the warning which he had received—of the fierce hatred and thirst for vengeance burning in his rival's breast.

Monsieur Blanc in his own mind had already condemned the audacious young Scotchman to death, having determined that he should die by his hand, as had many others who had given him offence or stood in his way as an obstacle to some end in view.

CHAPTER IV

STRANGE FRIENDSHIP FORMED WITH THE FAMOUS GENERAL WHEAT — MACIVER'S FIRST DUEL AND ITS CONSEQUENCES

AN angry meeting was fated to occur a few days after the ball between Ronald MacIver and his fiery Italian-Franco rival. The same time and place also was to be the scene of a serious quarrel between MacIver and a celebrated Garibaldian commander, which latter disagreement, however, oddly enough was to end in a lasting and most intimate friendship —a friendship which was to be severed only by death.

One afternoon Lieutenant MacIver strolled into one of the numerous *cafés* in Naples, and amongst a number of Garibaldian officers assembled there, found Monsieur Blanc, who was in company with the famous General Wheat, a Virginian officer, the second in command under General Walker in the Nicaraguan Expedition. There were also present Colonel Dunn and several other well-known men of the British Legion, most of whom were known to him.

Young MacIver, shortly after entering, asked, as was customary, those with whom he was acquainted to take wine with him. Amongst others who accepted this invitation was a Lieutenant Scott, who, turning to General Wheat and the gentleman whom we have called Monsieur Blanc, asked:

"Won't you join us?"

In a most insolent and offensive tone Blanc replied: "No, I will not drink with Monsieur MacIver."

"Then," said MacIver, "you can go to Jericho!"

Instantaneously, and without further parley, Monsieur Blanc's sword flashed from its scabbard. MacIver, who was in the uniform of the Zouaves of the Legion de Flotte, and armed with a short thick-bladed Roman sword, as quickly drew his weapon, saying:

"Come on, monsieur, I am ready for you!"

The bystanders, however, interfered, pushing between the would-be combatants, and insisted upon the swords being put up, remarking, very properly, that a public *café* was not a place for an encounter between gentlemen.

Thus for the moment, the brawl seemed ended; but MacIver had scarcely sheathed his sword when General Wheat stepped forward and accused him of having wantonly insulted his, the General's, friend, Monsieur Blanc.

"Pardon me, sir," replied MacIver, "he was the first to insult me, and I happen to know the reason why."

"Name it, sir," said the General, imperiously.

"I decline to drag a lady's name into an affair of this description," answered as haughtily the Lieutenant. "Besides, I should deny your right to ask me such a question, even if you were my commanding officer, which you are not."

General Wheat, excited by anger, and, as some afterwards said, by wine, advanced a step towards MacIver, and made a threatening gesture, as if about to strike him. The latter prepared to defend himself, when Wheat, with a sneer, pointed to the Lieutenant's sword, saying:

"You see I am unarmed; hence your valour."

Instantly unbuckling his belt, MacIver threw his sword from him, exclaiming:

"Now, General, we are on equal terms!"

So suddenly did all this occur that the bystanders and friends of both officers had scarcely realised what was about to take place. Before any one could interfere General Wheat had rushed forward, and the two were grappling together in a fierce struggle for mastery. Wheat was a strong, burly man, but his strength was more than matched by the activity of his young opponent, and when, after a brief wrestle, they both fell to the floor, the General was undermost.

Releasing himself from the grasp of General Wheat, MacIver was the first to rise; but as he stepped back the American, mad with rage, sprang up, and drawing a knuckle dagger, as it is called, from his right boot, rushed upon his unarmed foe.

The young Highlander neither drew back nor tried to arrest the blow, but, looking Wheat full in the eyes, said :

"Strike! but if you do you are a coward!"

General Wheat, however, did not take advantage of his opportunity, but paused, dropped his arm, and then threw the dagger from him, exclaiming :

"No, MacIver, you are too brave a fellow to die in an unseemly brawl like this. It was I who was in the wrong, and I beg you to forgive me. I ought to have known better. Let us be friends in the future."

These kindly words touched MacIver at once, and found an echo in his own generous nature.

General Wheat and he shook hands cordially, and strange as it may seem, the friendship commenced in this remarkable manner lasted without interruption up to the death of the brave American officer, who was fated to fall during the seven days' fighting around Richmond, Virginia.

To further cement this new-formed friendship between the two, Lieutenant MacIver, on the evening after the quarrel with the Franco-Italian, was entertained at dinner by General Wheat, at the latter's hotel. Oddly enough, whilst they were yet at the dinner-table, a challenge was received by the guest from Monsieur Blanc.

It is scarcely necessary to say that this hostile message met a ready response from the fiery Highlander. A friend and countryman of MacIver's, Lieutenant Robert Scott, an officer whose name we have before mentioned, at once offered to be his second, and his services were gladly accepted. General Wheat advised MacIver to choose pistols as the weapons to be used in the duel; but the latter replied:

"No, General, I shall fight this braggart with the weapon of his own selection."

Doubtless General Wheat's advice was good, for Monsieur Blanc was known to be one of the most expert swordsmen amongst a nation of men who have always been celebrated for their dexterity in the use of that weapon. However, MacIver having made his choice, there was no drawing back, but the General took care to give him several useful hints for his guidance. Wheat was no stranger to matters of this kind, but in spite of his numerous quarrels, this was the Lieutenant's first affair of honour.

It was a lovely morning, shortly after sunrise, when the two principals and their seconds and surgeons met in the King's Garden at Naples. All Nature was smiling and peaceful. There was not a sound to break the solemn silence that reigned in those deserted grounds, once devoted to the use of Royalty

The great city, encircled with its amphitheatre of hills, had not yet awoke into daily life, whilst calm and quiet as an inland lake sparkled the famous bay, blue as the cloudless heavens above. Further away, but sharp and clearly defined, Vesuvius showed his lofty head, and here and there the white sail of a passing barque seemed like a bird upon the waters.

But the men who sought this secluded spot in

the early morn had but little thought for the beauties that surrounded them. They were too intent upon carrying out the preliminaries of the deadly encounter which was about to take place—deadly, as more than one present thought, for the stalwart young Highlander, scarcely yet in his manhood.

As the two duellists were about to cross swords, the Franco-Italian involuntarily, as it seemed, asked his opponent if he was prepared to die. The question would have been startling enough under the circumstances to most men, but from the undaunted MacIver, who was coolly testing the temper of his blade, it only extorted the reply:

"That, sir, is in the hands of Providence."

The next moment there was a ring of steel as their swords crossed. MacIver was the taller and more muscular man of the two, but very fine swordsman as he undoubtedly was, he would have probably fared very badly against the superior skill of Monsieur Blanc had the latter kept his temper.

MacIver, following the instructions which his new friend General Wheat had given him, commenced by acting on the defensive, hoping to tire out his enemy by the mere strength of his arm, and in the end to get a chance of finishing the fight. Whether Monsieur Blanc lost his temper at finding a cool swordsman, where probably he had expected a rash and passionate antagonist, or whether his jealousy of his rival made him reckless of the consequences, it is impossible to say, but certainly his hand lost its usual deadly cunning.

Much to the astonishment of the witnesses of the tragedy—for tragedy it proved to be—who had anticipated a far different result, young MacIver, after a very short encounter, ran his sword through the Franco-Italian's body, who fell back into the arms of his second. Unhappily the end of this was the death of Monsieur Blanc.

It was owing to the fatal termination of the duel that we have concealed this gentleman's real name, especially as many persons in Naples considered that Lieutenant MacIver had done society a service in ridding the world of so noted a duellist.

The survivor, however, was very sorry for the result. He left Naples shortly after the duel, and proceeded once more to the front. There he remained for a while, although warlike operations had ceased for the time being. He wrote to the young English lady on his arrival in camp, and received a very kind letter in reply, in which the writer expressed her thankfulness that the duel had not terminated fatally to him.

We believe that these were the first and last letters which passed between the young people. Like many other love affairs, their sweethearting was but brief, and ended in nothing but some pleasant recollections, mingled, perchance, with a few regrets.

Amongst the numberless good qualities which Ronald MacIver undoubtedly possessed, we are afraid, however, that constancy in love could not be reckoned as one, for very shortly after the duel he had withdrawn his affection from his fair countrywoman, and bestowed his a little too susceptible heart upon another lady.

CHAPTER V

DANGEROUS GROUND—A STARTLING ADVENTURE—AND A NARROW ESCAPE

THE sudden breach of allegiance to the ex-consul's daughter was owing to the appearance on the scene of a very beautiful Italian girl, who had come to Santa Maria to visit a wounded brother.

To the charms of this youthful and fair Neapolitan MacIver at once became a ready victim.

This fascinating young lady on her return to Naples was followed a week later by her admirer, who, on a previous occasion, having met and having been introduced to her parents, made that an excuse to call at their house, ostensibly for resuming his acquaintance with the father, but in reality to make love to the daughter.

The Lieutenant was again treading on dangerous ground, for the young lady had already a lover—one of her own countrymen. MacIver's visits to the house soon came to the knowledge of this Italian, who, when he saw—or fancied—that his *fiancée* began to look with some favour upon Ronald, at once conceived a most bitter antipathy to the daring stranger.

This Italian lover's vengeance — had MacIver known it—was all the more to be dreaded, that he did not appear inclined to call him to account publicly, being either wanting in courage or preferring to vent his hate covertly on his rival.

MacIver, however—either in happy ignorance, or not caring—went on paying the most persistent attentions to the fair object of his new affection, little dreaming of the plot which was being hatched against him. The young lady, too, appeared to encourage her British lover, although what was transpiring was unknown to the parents, who saw in the Garibaldian officer only a casual visitor, who seemed to enjoy their society.

One evening, shortly after dark, MacIver was strolling through the city, and although he did not notice it, a little boy had been following for some time in his footsteps. As he arrived opposite the Grand Opera House, where there was a strong light, the lad touched him gently, and in a soft, youthful voice asked:

"Siete Inglese, Signor?"

"No, sono Scozzese," replied MacIver, also speaking in Italian.

"E'lo stesso," said the little Neapolitan. "I was to give this to the first Englishman I could find," and the boy handed a folded paper to the Lieutenant.

On opening the note MacIver found that it was written in English, and was to the effect that an Englishman, in sore distress and poverty, was lying sick and helpless amongst strangers. The writer implored the aid of any countryman into whose hands the note might by chance fall, and further stated that the bearer would conduct such good Samaritan to the unfortunate man who claimed his pity.

There was no signature to the letter, nor could the Lieutenant learn anything from the boy except that a poor English Signor was very ill. The lad being unable or unwilling to give any definite information might have roused many persons' suspicions; but without giving much thought about it, MacIver determined to accompany the boy and give what assistance he could to this stranger in a foreign land.

Bidding the boy to lead the way, MacIver followed him, and fortunately had not gone very far when he met Lieutenant Scott of the British Legion, the same young officer who had acted as his second in the duel with Blanc. Stopping for a moment to speak to Scott, he asked:

"What do you think of this letter, Bob?" at the same time handing to him the epistle.

"Wait until I can see to read it, Harry," said Scott, laughing, as he walked along by his friend's side.

Presently they came to a spot where there was light enough for Lieutenant Scott to decipher the writing, and he not only read it carefully but examined it closely. Then he glanced at the messenger, but the boy was waiting patiently, and looked innocent enough to have disarmed the most suspicious.

"What do you think of it?" again asked MacIver, getting impatient at his friend's delay in giving an opinion.

"I believe it is a trap to draw you into some mischief, Harry," said Scott, "and I advise you to be very careful what you are about. I feel convinced, in the first place, that although this letter is worded in good English, it was written by an Italian. If it were genuine, too, why did not this pretended

Englishman—for pretender I am sure he is—sign his name?"

"As he knew not into whose hands it would fall," suggested MacIver, "that is perhaps not so surprising."

Lieutenant Scott shook his head dubiously.

"I am afraid, Harry," he said, "that your headstrong impulsiveness is again about to lead you into danger; if, however, you are determined to follow up this foolish affair, I am ready to stand by you."

"I shall certainly go now and see the end, Bob," replied MacIver, "for you have quite raised my curiosity by your doubts."

"Well, a wilful man will have his own way, but I am with you."

It was then agreed that Scott should pretend to leave MacIver, but in reality should follow him at a distance near enough to be within hearing. In case of danger arising to the latter he was to shout "Scott" at the top of his voice, as a signal.

Whilst the two gentlemen had been conversing and arranging their plan of operations, the little Italian waited patiently. He did not understand a word of what was being spoken, but it is doubtful if he did not, with the cunning of his class and his nation, suspect that something was wrong. Whatever his thoughts, he evinced no suspicions by his manner, and smiled pleasantly, showing his white, even teeth, when MacIver again bade him to lead the way, at the same time parting from Scott with the usual "Good-night" and hand-shaking.

Lieutenant MacIver followed his youthful guide through several streets, and as yet had seen nothing to arouse his suspicions. Spite his love of adventure, however, which enjoyed an enterprise like the present, he had the precaution to have his sword ready to his hand, and to keep his eyes well about him to guard against a surprise.

The part of the city which they had reached was not much frequented by passengers, and there were but few people about. The streets, too, were ill-lighted, but it was not what could be called a low quarter of the town.

Finally they came to an archway, down which the lad turned, and then the two entered a large court-yard with a house of some size standing before them. Crossing the yard the boy led the way up a staircase, which was dimly lighted with a small oil lamp, and halted on the first floor.

There appeared to be but one door on the landing, which, on a low knock being given by the boy, instantly sprang open, as though a visitor had been expected. Standing within the portal was an old woman, with her finger raised to her lip, as if to enjoin silence, but who motioned to MacIver with her other hand to enter.

When the Lieutenant crossed the threshold, he found himself in a large room almost bare of furniture. It was not badly lighted, although the illumination came from a single lamp. In one corner was a bed, on which apparently lay the figure of a man, covered over with the bed clothes. Near to the bed, but more towards the centre of the wall, was a second door.

MacIver's first impulse naturally was to approach the couch upon which, as he presumed, lay the sick man; but as the figure did not move he paused, and asked in a somewhat loud voice, and in Italian:

"Where is the Englishman whom I have come to visit?"

"Hist!" replied the old woman, again raising her finger to her lip. "He will come to you immediately." And at the same time she glided softly from the room by the door by which the Lieutenant had entered, closing it after her.

He could scarcely have told why, but at that moment MacIver suspected treachery, and drawing his sword he sprang into the corner of the room, placing his back to the wall, and standing on the defensive. Scarcely had he availed himself of this point of vantage, when a man fully dressed jumped from the bed and extinguished the lamp.

Although it had been, no doubt, the intention of the late occupant of the couch to leave the room in sudden darkness, there was still light enough from a lamp in the courtyard to enable the Lieutenant, where he stood, to make out that this man was armed with a long dagger. He thought, too, that the outline of the figure was not unfamiliar to him.

As the man approached nearer to him his first impression was confirmed, for he recognised in his adversary, the Neapolitan lover of the beautiful girl whom he (MacIver) had first met at Santa Maria. Now he had not the slightest doubt that this revengeful Italian had enticed him to this lonely house for the purpose of assassinating him.

With the spring of a wild beast the Neapolitan flew at the Lieutenant, his dagger raised for a fatal stab, and at the same time exclaiming passionately:

"You have robbed me of my love! You shall die!"

Ronald MacIver, however, was too quick for his opponent, and whilst easily parrying the attack, ran the would-be murderer through the right wrist with his sword.

The wound was severe, and with a howl of rage and pain the Italian dropped his dagger. The next moment he cried loudly for help, and in answer to his call, two men armed with swords rushed through the second of the doorways.

It was now MacIver's turn to shout for assistance, as he knew not how many assassins might be at hand. His voice rang out clear and lustily:

"Scott! Scott! to the rescue!"

The ruffians were now upon him, but he not only managed to parry their first attack, but to drive them back a pace or two; then, as by the dim light, he was making a fierce lunge at one of his foes, his foot slipped, and he fell to the floor.

However, before the rascals had time to take advantage of his position, there was a violent crash, and a tall figure, sword in hand, sprang across the room at a bound, and stood over the defenceless MacIver.

It was Bob Scott, whose broad shoulders had burst open the door, and he was not a moment too soon. The gallant Lieutenant of the British Legion was only just in time to receive on his own sword a savage cut intended for the head of his friend. MacIver quickly recovered his feet, and he and Scott between them speedily settled their two adversaries— the Neapolitan lover had already slipped away from the room.

"Now, Mac, let us be off," said Scott, making for the door by which he had entered.

"All right, my boy," replied the other, as he followed his friend.

But they found that although the lock had been forced by Lieutenant Scott, the door had been re-fastened, or was being held from without. Not knowing how many assassins might be on the landing, the friends consulted for a moment.

"The window," suggested MacIver. "Let us try that."

Scott nodded assent, and they moved cautiously across the floor, and managed to open the sash with but little noise. They then dropped into the court-yard and looked around them. At first they could see no sign of any one being about, but when they crossed the yard and reached the archway, they found to their dismay that there was a little crowd of Italians armed with knives prepared to cut off their retreat.

"We are in for it now, Harry," said Scott. "This is a regular ambush we have fallen into, and how are we to get out of it?"

"Make a dash for it, Bob."

"Come along, then!" exclaimed Lieutenant Scott. "We must either fight our way out, or stay here to be killed."

Grasping their swords tightly, the friends made a vigorous rush at the mob which crowded the narrow archway, and drove them into the street, the cowards in their first panic giving way before the couple of determined Scotchmen.

But, though the two Lieutenants had fought their way into the street, they were beset on every side. The Italians, recovering from their sudden terror, clustered around the Garibaldian officers like a swarm of hornets, too much afraid, however, to come within reach of the glittering steel of Scott and MacIver, who, back to back, swept a clear space with their swords.

Whether the gallant pair would have been able to keep their enemies at bay, and to have eventually escaped, it is hard to say. Fortunately at that opportune moment, several Garibaldians came through the street, and immediately went to the assistance of the two officers. With their help MacIver and Scott made their way out of the neighbourhood unhurt.

Some gendarmes also came up, and, taking the side of their fellow-citizens, tried to make some arrests among the Garibaldians. The latter, however, were too strong for them, and escaped.

Scott and MacIver managed to reach the "Café de l'Europe" in safety, neither of them the worse for their night's adventure, and in spite of the danger which they had escaped, laughing heartily at what had occurred. The pair afterwards with a keen appetite enjoyed supper together at this noted restaurant.

CHAPTER VI.

A SEQUEL TO THE ATTEMPTED ASSASSINATION—A PROJECTED ELOPEMENT

THE strange night adventure of the two Lieutenants, MacIver and Scott, was little known or spoken of at the time, unless it might be amongst their immediate friends, but it afforded a theme for various conversations between the principals in the affair, who both came to a pretty correct conclusion as to the intentions of MacIver's Italian rival. Scott and Ronald had long been great friends, but this incident made them even closer companions. Subsequently they were both to fight for the Confederate States, and poor Scott, as an officer of the 8th Alabama Regiment, to die gallantly at the battle of Gettysburg.

A few days after the base attempt to assassinate him, MacIver paid a visit to the young Signorina, the fair lady who, unwittingly, had been the cause of the cowardly attack made upon his life. When they had chatted for some short time on ordinary topics, the Lieutenant adroitly turned the conversation to a remark about the Signorina's Italian lover, and inquired how he was.

"Have you not heard," exclaimed the fair lady, whose name was Bianca, "that he has been seriously wounded in a duel?"

"No," replied MacIver; "may I ask with whom he fought?"

"That I cannot tell you," said the Signorina. "Although he has been questioned more than once, he very strangely refuses to reveal with whom the unfortunate encounter took place."

Lieutenant MacIver paused for a few moments ere he made any further remark, undecided as to whether he should tell the whole truth to the fair Neapolitan. At length he decided that it was only right that she should know all, and, as cautiously and as delicately as possible, he told what had actually occurred.

As the girl listened, her astonishment and horror

were displayed in her face, and for a time she was too much affected to speak. When, however, she had somewhat recovered from the first shock of being told the baseness of her countryman, who, besides, was her own cousin, she stamped her little foot in indignation. On hearing further how narrow had been her visitor's escape, she confessed that her opinion of her Italian lover had never been very high; although enjoying the favour and sanction of her parents, her own feeling had been one of mistrust towards him.

"I beg you, Signor," she continued, her beautiful eyes fixed earnestly upon the Lieutenant, "to conceal nothing from me. Tell me, I entreat, where is this house situated into which you were so basely inveigled, so that I may describe it to my father? I assure you this despicable attempt on your life will be thoroughly investigated and the perpetrators punished by him."

Ronald MacIver would have preferred that the matter should go no further; but the fair Italian insisted that, if only for her own peace and happiness, everything should be disclosed. In indignant, passionate terms she spoke of her countryman's cowardice, and declared that henceforth he would not only be repudiated by herself and her relations, but by all his friends.

True to her promise, Bianca at once told her parents, and the result of the investigations made by the father fully brought to light the foul and cowardly plot which had been concocted by the Italian lover against his British rival. Fortunately for MacIver—the intended victim—the scheme had failed in its successful carrying out, owing to his suspicions being aroused by Scott and the caution he had displayed on first entering the room into which he had been decoyed.

It appeared that the intended assassins had reckoned upon MacIver unsuspiciously stepping up to the couch of his supposed sick countryman immediately on entering the room, upon which the Signorina's Italian lover, who was concealed in the bed, was to have plunged his dagger into the Lieutenant's breast whilst his rival was off his guard. Had this proposed dastardly stroke not been fatal, the hired bravos who were waiting without were to have rushed in and despatched the young officer.

It was a very narrow escape for him, as the reader has seen, for had not it been for the advice of Lieutenant Scott, the probability was that his comrade would have walked carelessly into the trap prepared for him, and thereby have lost his life.

As it was, the proposed assassins paid dearly for their attempt to murder the Garibaldian officer. The principal in the affair had to have his arm amputated below the elbow, whilst one of the hired bravos died from the wounds he received, and the other was so seriously hurt that his life for a considerable time was despaired of by the surgeons.

As we have before mentioned, this intended assassination was but little commented on, although occurring in the Neapolitan capital. Unfortunately such brawls and adventures were by no means uncommon, and scarcely a day passed at this time without some Italian or Englishman meeting his death in a quarrel.

Now that the engagement between Bianca and her countryman was for ever at an end, MacIver became very earnest in his attentions to the fair Neapolitan. This, however, did not meet the approval of the young lady's parents, who, on seeing the increased intimacy between their daughter and the Garibaldian Lieutenant, and the favour with which his suit appeared to be received, peremptorily put an end to the acquaintance.

It was the intention of these good people that their daughter—who was not yet sixteen—should marry none but an Italian; and here, to their dismay, was she listening to love speeches from a foreigner. Such a state of things could not for a moment be tolerated, and both the father and the mother of the Signorina forbade her to continue her friendship with the young officer. With many tears the girl obeyed, and MacIver received his dismissal.

The gallant lover, however, although discontinuing his visits to the house, was too much enamoured of the fair Bianca to be so easily got rid of. Day after day he watched eagerly for the appearance of his lady love either out driving or walking alone, but on each occasion he was doomed to be disappointed.

At length, one morning, fortune favoured the lovers. As the Lieutenant was strolling along he caught sight of a carriage, in which the Signorina was riding, she being accompanied only by her maid and the coachman. Raising his hat to the lady, MacIver at the same time made a sign to the driver, who, recognising him as a former visitor to his master's house, immediately pulled up.

The Signorina spoke English fairly well, which, luckily for the lovers, neither the waiting-woman nor the coachman understood, and the suitor pleaded his cause so earnestly and persistently, that the young lady yielded to his solicitations to become his wife, and then and there the youthful couple plighted their troth.

In the open street in those few brief minutes, it was agreed that so soon as Lieutenant MacIver was free to leave the Italian service they were to elope and to be married at the nearest French port—of course, it not being possible to find any priest who would unite them on Italian soil. After the ceremony the Lieutenant and his bride were to proceed to England.

Such were the plans arranged by these youthful lovers for the future; and they parted with mutual vows of undying constancy. Their vows were sincere and heartfelt enough at the time. How they were fulfilled we shall ere long see.

CHAPTER VII.

A RASH PROMISE, AND A FOOLISH EXPEDITION—FALLS AMONGST ROGUES; BUT NOT DISCOURTEOUS ONES—A NIGHT AMONGST THE BRIGANDS

WE have now arrived at a period in our story when Lieutenant MacIver was artfully cajoled into an adventure that, subsequently, in his calmer moments, he looked back upon with regret. Although he was but a lad in years at the time, and no harm resulted from the escapade, he blamed himself subsequently for listening to the temptress, and for being dared into an undertaking which was not only foolish, but actually wrong.

One evening Captain de Rohan, naval aide-de-camp to General Garibaldi, asked MacIver to dinner at the "Hotel Victoria," where he was to meet, as the only other guest, the Countess de la Torre. Ronald accepted the invitation, and found that fascinating lady had already arrived when he reached the hotel.

There was very little conversation during the repast, but after dinner, and when they had sat some time over the dessert and wine, the host, Captain de Rohan, referred to the flag of the British Legion, and to its ultimate destination when the war was at an end. The Captain asserted that it was the intention of Colonel Peard, the Commandant, to keep it for himself, and stoutly maintained that the Colonel had no more right to the colour than any other individual who had fought with the Legion.

The Countess de la Torre at once took up the subject very warmly, and spoke in strong terms of this—as she pleased to style it—"misappropriation of a national emblem."

MacIver had heard some rumours before in reference to the flag, but as he had now no connection with the Legion, he made no comment, but sipped his wine and listened to what the Countess and the Captain had to say.

"The fact is, MacIver," said De Rohan, "Colonel Peard has no more right to the flag than either you or I. Its proper destination ought to be the British Museum, and there, I may inform you, it is my intention to send it if I can possibly get hold of it. The Countess de la Torre and I have talked the matter over on more than one occasion, and her ladyship agrees with me that the flag should be sent to England as a memento of our share in the war."

The Countess nodded assent.

"But the question is, Madame la Comtesse, how are we to get the flag?" continued Captain de Rohan, with a light laugh; "unless, indeed, some bold spirit, such as our gallant Henri d'Ecosse here, will procure it for us."

Ronald MacIver, as we know, was always ready for any daring adventure; however, on this occasion, he did not respond to the evident invitation, but merely smiled and shook his head in dissent.

"I would give much to see the flag sent to your British Museum," said the Countess, as she toyed with her fan; "but, alas! I fear me these are not the days of chivalry. Even Signor MacIver—'le brave Ecossais,' as they have named him—is afraid to risk the danger, although its reward be to win a lady's favour," and the beautiful siren laughed low and musically, and flashed her brilliant eyes upon the young Lieutenant.

"Afraid! Madame la Comtesse," exclaimed Mac-Iver, who was excited by the wine he had taken and perhaps by his courage being questioned by a woman. "Afraid! I will bring you the flag of the Legion here to-morrow!"

"Bravo! Enrico mio," said the Countess, flashing another of her brilliant smiles. "I find there are knights-errant yet left in this prosaic world of ours."

The Countess's compliment affected young Mac-

Iver but little. He would have been glad if his hasty exclamation could have been unsaid; but the rash promise had been given, and whether it was right or wrong, he was not the one to take back his word.

Now that the die was cast he lost no time in undertaking his ill-judged venture. On the day following the dinner at the "Hotel Victoria," he started for Salerno, which was nearly thirty miles from Naples, and where the British Legion then was.

On his arrival there, as he was approaching the town, he was stopped by a squad of men belonging to the Legion.

"Lieutenant MacIver," said the officer in command, "I have orders to conduct you three miles from Salerno. Further, if you are found within the town to-night, our orders are to place you under arrest and take you before the Commandant."

MacIver tried to laugh the matter off as a joke, but the Captain was not to be deceived, and was firm in the purpose which he had been instructed to carry out.

"We are well aware with what intention you came, sir," said the Captain; "but you won't get the flag at present, Lieutenant MacIver. It was a daring plan, and might perhaps have succeeded if your own friends had not betrayed you."

MacIver saw at once that all was discovered, and that there was nothing for it but to submit quietly. In fact, if the truth must be told, he was only too glad to be relieved of an adventure into which he had been entrapped at an unguarded moment. He had tried to keep his word but had failed, and was delighted to get out of a scrape which he had brought upon himself by his own folly.

He told the officer that he was ready to obey any orders he had to carry out, and on his submission was immediately marched off. They had not got many yards when they were met by an old acquaintance of MacIver's, it being none other than Captain Hoskins. This officer had not forgotten, nor forgiven, the thrashing which he had received on board the *Milazzo*, and now he retaliated in a very small and mean way by indulging in a boisterous laugh at the expense of his enemy.

Captain Hoskins, however, had not the satisfaction of seeing his old opponent annoyed, for MacIver quite ignored his presence, and requested the officer in command to carry out his duty as speedily as possible, as it was getting dark. This silent contempt we have little doubt vexed Captain Hoskins more than that gentleman's laughter chafed the Lieutenant.

After Hoskins had left them, MacIver was marched three miles from Salerno, where the officer and his squad of men left him; but not without a second warning that if he returned to the town he would be liable to be shot.

The Captain, however, was only carrying out his orders and performing his duty, and now that his unpleasant office was at an end, he bade his countryman a cordial "good-night" as they parted in the darkness.

Although he was again left to himself, the position of Lieutenant MacIver was not one to be envied.

The night was well advanced, and he was many miles from his destination. The country around was infested with brigands, and his only weapon was a short sword. However, he had no one to blame but himself for his awkward predicament, and like a true soldier he concluded to make the best of it.

Fortunately the district was not unfamiliar to him, and he stepped out briskly, on, as he anticipated, the long and weary night march before him. Humming a tune as he walked, he had not proceeded more than a mile when he imagined that he heard the sound of other footsteps besides his own.

He stopped instantly, and listened, but all was still; then he went on again, but still uncertain as to whether his ears had deceived him or not. Once more there was the same noise that he fancied he had heard before. This time he felt certain that he was not mistaken, and placed his hand on the hilt of his sword.

Had he now had any doubt on his mind as to the neighbourhood of other night wanderers besides himself, it must have been speedily set at rest. Presently he saw two men coming towards him, and as they approached near enough to make out their forms, he instantly recognised them, by their picturesque costume, as brigands.

"Keep your arms down by your side, or we shall fire!" shouted a voice in Italian; and MacIver saw that he was covered by their rifles.

Under the circumstances resistance was useless and to stir meant death. MacIver waited quietly, with his hands down by his side, as he had been ordered, until the brigands were within a few steps of him, the muzzles of their pieces still pointed at his body. Then he addressed the two robbers in a little speech which not only astonished them, but aroused their risible faculties.

"Gentlemen of the road," he said, "I beg first that you will lower your weapons. In the second place I am not a rich traveller. I have only seven napoleons; you are quite welcome to the half, and the remainder, if you do not object, I shall keep, as just at present I require the money very particularly for my own use."

This cool address caused the two brigands to burst out into an immoderate fit of laughter, and one of them exclaimed:

"As I live, it is Enrico di Scozzia!"

"Yes, gentlemen," said our cool friend, "Enrico di Scozzia, very much at your service. But I must confess that you have the advantage of me, as I do not remember to have ever had the privilege or pleasure of meeting either of you before."

At this sally the mirth of the brigands was renewed. Then they held a brief consultation, apparently as to what was to be done with the Garibaldian officer. MacIver expected that their next proceeding would be to relieve him of his purse and watch, but they showed no disposition to rob or in other way molest him.

Presently he was told that he must consent to be blindfolded and accompany them to their chief. To this MacIver politely assented, wisely deciding in his own mind that discretion was the better part of valour. If he resisted he might probably get a bullet through his head, and by accompanying the brigands he could not be in a much worse position than when he first met them.

They were evidently no novices at their trade, from the adroit manner in which they blindfolded their captive. Walking one on each side of him, they guided the Lieutenant for a considerable distance, and through what he felt must be a very lonely part of the country, as he could not hear any sound as of persons stirring.

After a time he could tell that the track that they were traversing was over rising ground, and that at each step the path became more steep, difficult, and intricate. Occasionally, too, a signal would be given or answered by his guides, and thrice they were challenged as by a man on guard. By all this caution MacIver concluded that he was being conducted into the retreat of the brigands amongst the mountains, nor was he wrong in his surmise.

At length they came to a halt, and after some short delay his eyes were uncovered, and he was ushered into the presence of the brigand chief, who, with several of his band, had evidently just sat down to their supper. The robber captain was a handsome, picturesque-looking rascal, and a number of his men were fine stalwart fellows; but the majority were a set of ill-conditioned villains that seemed capable of committing any crime.

There were also several women present; some looking old in age and crime, and others mere girls. All this Lieutenant MacIver realised during the few brief moments whilst his two captors whispered to their chief. Then the latter rose and politely welcomed the Garibaldian officer by the name which had been given to him by the Italians, Enrico di Scozzia, and desired him to be seated and to join them at supper.

MacIver was hungry, and with a keen appetite at once commenced an attack upon the viands placed before him, which were simple enough yet palatable. The fare provided was goat flesh and bread, with the accompaniment of milk or wine.

When the meal was at an end, the brigand captain offered a very excellent cigar to his involuntary guest, and after he had lighted one himself commenced a conversation as to the war and its results, as might have done some ordinary acquaintance in one of the *cafés* at Naples.

The rest of the brigands were more noisily engaged than their chief. Some were singing, some dancing with the women, and others gambling with cards or dice. Occasionally fresh members of the band would come in, or others quietly depart, and the whole of these looked formidable enough, being, so to speak, armed to the teeth. Once or twice quarrels arose over the cards, but these were as quickly suppressed as they were begun. A word or a look from the chief, who seemed to rule with an iron sway, instantly put an end to the disputes and ensured quietness.

An hour or two having passed away, the brigand chief courteously suggested to the Garibaldian officer that as the night was far advanced, a bed such as they had to offer would be provided for him, and that in the morning, under certain conditions he would be free to depart. After retiring to rest, MacIver saw no more of the chief, and although his couch was primitive enough he slept soundly in his strange quarters until after daylight.

He had fully expected that in the morning his valuables would be taken from him, but in this he was agreeably disappointed. An excellent breakfast was served to him, after which he was blindfolded, as on the night before, and a hand grasped his wrist and led him away from the cavern into the open air.

Before starting he was told that if he attempted to remove the bandage from his eyes he would be instantly shot, but otherwise no harm would happen to him. His steps were carefully guided, and by the steep descent he concluded that he was passing over the same route as on the previous evening.

Eventually, his guide and he reached the level plain, and after a few miles had been traversed he was told in a voice that sounded strangely youthful, that he could remove the bandage from his eyes. He needed no second bidding, and when he looked about him he discovered that he was close by the spot where he had met the two robbers on the previous night.

But, strangest of all, standing by his side was a very small boy, under whose custody and guidance he had been since leaving the stronghold of the brigands. The little fellow was staring up into MacIver's face with an expression half comical, half laughing, as though having charge of so tall a man was good fun, and something to be proud of.

"Ah! my youthful brigand," said MacIver, looking down upon the urchin, "and so it is in your terrible charge that I have been for the last hour or two?"

"Si, Signor," laughed the boy, revealing his glistening teeth, as undauntedly he returned the glances of the stalwart Garibaldian.

"Well, my little man, there is a napoleon for your trouble," said the Lieutenant, "and may you never come to a bad end."

Grasping the shining golden coin, the boy took to his heels, whilst MacIver resumed his interrupted journey at a more leisurely pace, looking back occasionally at the distant range of mountains, and wondering where lay the spot in which he had so strangely and romantically passed the night.

CHAPTER VIII.

MACIVER RECEIVES THE CROSS OF SAVOY—A LOVER'S STRATAGEM

LIEUTENANT MACIVER had proceeded but a short distance from the brigands' stronghold, after parting with his youthful guide, when he noticed a horseman galloping towards him. As the rider approached nearer, he saw to his annoyance that it was none other than Captain Hoskins.

Hoskins, as he rode up, accused MacIver of having been again to Salerno, and threatened to shoot him there and then. The Captain was mounted, and had his loaded revolver with him, whilst the other was on foot and armed only with a short sword; but MacIver was not to be intimidated either by Hoskins's bluster or his pistol, and told his old enemy to dismount and fight him with his sword.

One hasty expression begat another, and soon there were high words between the two officers. Captain Hoskins had lost all control over his temper, and it was not improbable that in his rage he might have carried out his threat, and fired at MacIver. Fortunately, however, in the heat of the dispute, two Garibaldians opportunely appeared in sight, and the Captain changed his mind.

Putting spurs to his horse, Hoskins galloped off in the direction of Salerno, and MacIver saw no more of him. It was a pity that Captain Hoskins was inclined to be so quarrelsome, for he proved himself to be a brave man in the field. During the American War he was severely wounded whilst engaged on a scouting expedition, and being taken prisoner by the Federal troops, he subsequently died of his wounds.

When Captain Hoskins had ridden away, Ronald MacIver joined his comrades, the two Garibaldians, and in their company reached Naples in safety. Nevertheless, he was thoroughly disgusted with his late adventure, or rather with his own rashness and folly in being entrapped into such an expedition.

At the first convenient moment after his return to the capital he sought out De Rohan and told him what had occurred at Salerno. Captain de Rohan showed by his indignant look how much he was annoyed at what had taken place. He was a man of position, and a right good fellow, and his friend knew that he would be one of the last upon earth to act a double part.

"MacIver," he exclaimed, when he had heard all, "it is the Comtesse de la Torre who is at the bottom of this. After leading both of us into this foolish affair she has betrayed us. Why, it is impossible to guess, but betrayed us she most certainly has."

MacIver agreed with his friend De Rohan as to the improbability of any other person except the Comtesse having given information to Colonel Peard. There had been none present at the dinner at the "Hotel Victoria" besides the Comtesse de la Torre, MacIver, and Captain de Rohan, and it was scarcely possible that there could have been listeners to the conversation which had taken place.

Lieutenant MacIver knew that Captain de Rohan was entirely removed from suspicion of treachery, and that he could only be indebted to his fair friend the Comtesse de la Torre, firstly, for leading him into an attempt which his reason assured him was entirely wrong and indefensible; and, secondly, for betraying the purport of an expedition which she had used all her wiles and blandishments to incite him to undertake.

As MacIver felt towards the Comtesse at that time, it was very fortunate for Madame that she was a woman. Had she been of the opposite sex she would have had a bitter foe in one who was apt neither to forget nor forgive a betrayal of friendship. As it was, however, the treachery of the Comtesse merely served to put him on his guard, and to teach him a lesson that he was likely long to remember. Although Lieutenant MacIver and the Comtesse de la Torre were to meet again, the reader may be assured that the fascinating intriguer did not lead him into any more scrapes.

The war in Italy might now be said to be at an

end. Naples had been freed from oppression, and the down-trodden Italian nation liberated; Giuseppe Garibaldi's mission was, for a time, finished, and his gallant soldiers were free to lay down their arms. Those men who had fought under the great chief, more for the love of freedom than for gain, were at length to be disbanded; to cast aside the rifle or the sword and resume the ordinary occupations of life, which the mass of them had given up at the call of the "Liberator."

As they had volunteered for service, now when the war was ended they quietly ceased to be soldiers. Their work was done—done nobly—and they were released from the obligations which they had undertaken for their Fatherland.

But before the army of the "Liberator" was disbanded, there were honours to be awarded for the brave deeds that had been done. Amongst those marked out for special notice was Lieutenant MacIver—"le brave Ecossais," as the French had chivalrously styled him; Major Pogam, of the Legion de Flotte—in which MacIver had served when he first joined Garibaldi and again during the latter part of the campaign—had named the young Highlander in his report in terms highly flattering to a soldier.

The Major recommended that Lieutenant Henry Ronald MacIver should be decorated for distinguished conduct in the field; for bravery displayed on several occasions when before the enemy; and for remarkable coolness when under fire; combined with some talent and aptitude in the art of war.

With such recommendations from the Lieutenant's commanding officer, and with his own experience of MacIver's services in the field, General Garibaldi placed the young Highlander's name on his list to receive the decoration of the Cross of Savoy and the medal. This honour was subsequently awarded to the youthful soldier, which decoration General MacIver is entitled to wear amongst the numerous medals, crosses, and orders which he has since won by his valour.

Being now free to return to his own country, or to wander whither he felt inclined, MacIver bade farewell to most of his companions-in-arms. His career as a soldier, if not at an end, was, at least for a time, in abeyance, and his thoughts naturally turned to the fair young Signora who had promised to be his wife.

He had had her assurance at their last interview that she would become his bride whenever opportunity should offer—that she was prepared to give up her own beautiful Italy for the man who had won her youthful affections.

As we have hinted before, however, to be married in Italy was quite impossible without the consent of the lady's relations. Their sanction to the union both MacIver and his *fiancée* felt assured they should never be able to obtain, as the Signora's parents, if not actually opposed to the Lieutenant personally, were utterly antagonistic to his country.

Under the circumstances no priest could have been found who would have dared to unite them, and the only chance for the youthful lovers was to escape to Marseilles, where there would be no difficulty in having the marriage ceremony performed. There were many obstacles, however, in the way, which must be surmounted before even this plan could be carried out.

In the first place, now that MacIver was at liberty to depart from Naples, how was he to communicate with his sweetheart? From the day on which he had met her driving out in her father's carriage, accompanied only by her maid, he had not been able to exchange a word with his promised wife. Once or twice since, he had seen her certainly, but that was all, for on each occasion she had been with some member of her family.

To call boldly at the house and ask for an interview on the plea that he was leaving for England had more than once occurred to him. This idea was the one most in accordance with his bold disposition and candid nature; but would the lady's friends allow him to see her alone? On further consideration he believed not, for he knew that they had distinctly forbidden the Signorina to hold any further intercourse with her English admirer.

Whilst yet undecided what to do, MacIver endeavoured during several days to obtain a few words with the youthful Signora, or to convey a note into her hands. In vain he watched for her appearance alone in her carriage, or formed stratagems to bring about a meeting. Nothing came of his plans. These disappointments, however, instead of disheartening him, only added zest to his determination to succeed.

At length fortune was to favour the lovers. One evening the Lieutenant had an invitation for a ball at a private mansion. He had intended to have sent an excuse several days previously, but having forgotten to do so, he felt himself in a measure bound to attend. It was thus quite by accident that he happened to be present.

He had not been long in the ball-room, and was paying his respects to the hostess, an Italian lady of title, when, chancing to turn his head, to his great joy, he caught sight of the fair object of his affections. There were a great number of guests present, the majority of whom were already dancing; but the Signorina was seated between her father and mother at the opposite end of the room to that where MacIver was standing.

Without turning his glance again in the direction of the young Signora and her parents, MacIver continued to converse with his noble hostess, but at the same time maturing in his own mind a plan which he imagined might be successfully carried out. At the first opportunity that offered, he withdrew to one of the ante-rooms, where he was likely to be unobserved, and wrote rapidly a few lines in his note book. This done, he tore out the leaf, and folded it again and again until it was not larger than a napoleon.

The words which he had written conveyed the full particulars as to the sailing of the next mail boat from Naples to Marseilles, and intimated that it was by that steamer he intended to depart. He further asked if the Signora was still prepared to accompany him and to unite her future with his. As there was no signature to this scrawl, and as it was also without address, there was little to dread if it should fall into the wrong hands. Of this, however, MacIver had no fear, trusting to his own adroitness to convey it, unperceived by others, into the fingers of the Signorina in the course of the evening.

On returning to the ball-room, to avoid suspicion, he forbore approaching the spot where his *fiancée's* parents were still seated; and as his hostess was conversing with several of her visitors, he joined the group. Dancing was again going on, and as he glanced around he saw that Bianca was amongst the gay crowd.

Presently, when the music ceased, the dancers commenced the promenade of the room, and the young lady, with her partner, an Italian nobleman, approached where the Lieutenant stood. The eyes of the lovers met for an instant, and the next moment, as the lady passed, MacIver's hand was stretched forward slightly, and her taper fingers closed upon the piece of folded paper. The movement had been unobserved by all, and the missive which was intended to decide the future of this youthful pair reached its destination.

More to avoid observation than from any desire just then to dance, the Lieutenant chose a partner upon whom his attentions soon seemed to be entirely centred. But, although none appeared to enter more fully into the pleasures of dancing, his thoughts were with his *fiancée*, and his eyes continually wandering in her direction.

An hour or more must have elapsed, when chance or intention again brought the lovers almost side by side. A waltz was just over, and MacIver was speaking to an acquaintance, the husband of his late partner. There was a continuous crowd of promenaders passing—suddenly a white glove dropped at his feet.

Instantly stooping to lift it from the floor, he looked up quickly, to detect, if possible, the owner.

Walking slowly away was Bianca, leaning on the arm of a Garibaldian officer, and doubtless the glove must be hers.

Although the action might be suggestive of some meaning, MacIver scarcely imagined at the time that the Signora could have had an opportunity of even perusing his note, and certainly not a chance of answering it; but as his fingers closed on the glove, his touch told him that there was something within it. A few hasty strides carried him to the side of the young Neapolitan and her partner. With a low bow the Lieutenant restored the lost trifle to its fair owner, the lady receiving and acknowledging it with one of her sweetest smiles.

With a second graceful inclination of her head Bianca passed on, whilst MacIver rejoined his friends; but holding tightly grasped within his palm a piece of paper which he had found within the dropped glove.

CHAPTER IX.

AN INTERCEPTED ELOPEMENT—HOME AGAIN

LIEUTENANT MACIVER was very anxious to know the contents of the paper which had been concealed within the glove of the Signora; but he could not read it in the ball-room, and he found some difficulty in getting away from his friends. As to leaving the house altogether, it was impossible at so early an hour. At length, however, he was able to allay his impatience.

As he carefully unfolded the precious piece of crumpled paper, and smoothed it out, he gave a start of dismay. To his chagrin he saw that it was his own note returned to him. A second glance, however, reassured him, for on turning the paper over he discovered that some words in Italian were scrawled in pencil on the other side. They had been so hurriedly written as to be rather difficult to decipher; but a lover's eyes are proverbially sharp, and the Lieutenant quickly made out these brief sentences, which caused his heart to beat with rapture.

"I am ever yours," ran the lines. "My maid and I will join you at the appointed time. I will write further to your hotel."

After reading these, to him, precious words, MacIver returned to the ball-room, but as soon as he could retire without showing discourtesy to his entertainers, he made his way home to the hotel at which he was staying. It was already three o'clock in the morning, and as the mail-boat sailed for Marseilles before noon on the following day, he had not much time to spare for carrying out the necessary preparations for his departure from the shores of Italy.

He took but a few hours' sleep, and not long after he had partaken of breakfast he received a note, as promised, from the Signora. It was brief, but it confirmed more fully than the few lines of the night before her determination to accompany him to Marseilles. Having at once packed his luggage he sent it on board the steamer, so that he might have the entire afternoon and evening before him for taking leave of his friends. He had experienced much hospitality in Naples, and formed a large circle of acquaintances, so that he had numerous calls to make in the few hours at his disposal. Some of the people, too, were out or away from the capital, and to these he had to make his leave-taking by note.

The morning on which the mail-boat was to leave for Marseilles was one of those days which are only to be found under a southern sky. The sun was shining in cloudless splendour on the far-famed bay of Naples, its limpid waters blue as the heavens above. Around stretched the lovely landscape, more beautiful than pen can picture, or the mind conceive. None but those whose eyes have been blessed by a sight of this masterpiece of Nature's handicraft can realise the scene that MacIver gazed upon as he stood on the deck of the steamer, looking his farewell on the fair Neapolitan capital.

As may readily be imagined, the ex-Garibaldian officer waited with an impatience which he could scarcely control for the appearance of his lady-love. The anxious moments seemed to go slowly by, but at length he was made happy by the sight of the young Italian, accompanied by her waiting-woman. She had been compelled, it seemed, to take her maid into her confidence, and the abigail had readily consented, not only to connive at her mistress's elopement, but to join in her flight.

It was not more than half-an-hour before the time appointed for the sailing of the steamer when the Signora and her attendant arrived on board. MacIver had engaged a cabin especially for the use of his *fiancée* during the passage, and to this the young lady and her maid at once retired.

Although, as the lovers fondly believed, all their

arrangements had been carried out so secretly as to leave but little fear of discovery until too late for pursuit, the Lieutenant thought it more prudent that his intended wife should not be seen on deck until after the vessel was well under way.

Minute after minute flew rapidly by. The boilers were blowing off steam, and the captain had taken his post on the bridge preparatory to the departure of the boat. Time after time MacIver had looked anxiously in the direction of the shore to see that they were not followed, and again he took a last glance.

Now to his surprise he saw that a party of the gendarmerie were coming towards the vessel, and making signs as though they wished to draw the attention of some person in authority on board the boat. They were approaching very rapidly, and as they came nearer, the lover, to his dismay, saw that they were accompanied by the father of the Signora.

The scene that followed baffles description. The gendarmerie boarded the ship, and the irate father walked up to the ex-Garibaldian, and in passionate language demanded his daughter. His would-be son-in-law had no words at his command to reply, unless he stooped to a falsehood, and he merely shrugged his shoulders and took an extra whiff at his cigarette, thereby only increasing the anger of the fiery Italian gentleman.

Seeing that he could get no satisfaction out of his daughter's lover, Bianca's father requested the gendarmerie to search the ship. There were a great number of passengers on board, but the poor girl was speedily discovered and forced from her cabin. Weeping bitterly, she was conveyed on deck, her maid following with an air so nonchalant that to her it might have been but an event of every day's occurrence in which she was engaged. Possibly the pursuit and capture of her mistress did not very much surprise the too pliant abigail.

As for the defeated one, he had to endure as best he might the indignant threats and reproaches of the enraged parent. Resistance, of course, was out of the question, and persuasion was equally unavailing. In vain he appealed to the Signora's father for permission to marry his daughter. He not only refused point-blank, but even denied MacIver the mournful pleasure of bidding farewell to the weeping girl, who was hurried off without being allowed to exchange a word with her lover.

Of course MacIver's first idea on seeing his intended bride taken from the ship, was to return himself to the shore; but whilst he was yet undecided, the captain gave the command to "go ahead," and the steamer's paddles began to revolve.

Thus, when he had time for calmer thought, his reason assured him that remaining in Naples would have been useless. He felt how little chance he would ever have had of seeing the Signora again. Now that all was discovered, doubtless she would be so carefully watched and so strictly guarded that a meeting would be next to impossible without the consent of her parents; and of that consent he was without hope.

How the discovery of the proposed elopement was made, he could never learn. The probability was that the young lady's waiting-woman had—if not actually faithless to her mistress—given some hint of what was about to occur.

The disappointed lover arrived safely at the port of Marseilles, a sadder if not a wiser man. On landing he immediately wrote to the Signora, and remained long enough in the South of France for a reply to reach him, but no answer came. As it was useless for him to wait longer he started for England, and after a short sojourn in London went on to Scotland, where he had many friends.

We must do him the credit to say that he grieved for a time over his love disappointment. He also wrote several letters to Bianca, none of which, in all probability, ever came into her fair hands, not any notice being taken of them. Neither did the Lieutenant ever meet again the fair daughter of the Sunny South, who for a time had entirely won his heart.

Whilst in town, before starting for the north, he met with a few old comrades who had fought with him under Garibaldi. Three of these—Brooks, Stevens, and Hayward—he was especially glad to see again.

In Scotland he remained for some time, leading the life of a quiet citizen; a great change after the excitement of a soldier's career. Events, however, were brewing in the world's history which soon were to call him as an actor in that sphere of fighting and adventure which he so much loved.

CHAPTER X.

THE OUTBREAK OF THE CIVIL WAR IN AMERICA—MACIVER ARRIVES IN WASHINGTON AND REFUSES TO TAKE SERVICE UNDER THE FEDERALS—IMPRISONED AT ALEXANDRIA (VIRGINIA) AS A SECESSIONIST

As early as the beginning of the year eighteen hundred and sixty, a strong feeling of discontent and of ill blood towards their brethren of the North had been shown by the people of the Southern States of America. These unhappy bickerings, which had more than once threatened to end in a serious quarrel, reached their crisis by the election of Abraham Lincoln to the presidential chair.

To understand what was to follow requires but a brief explanation. The dwellers in the South were planters merely and growers of raw material, which produce was confined almost exclusively to the three great staples of cotton, tobacco, and sugar. On the contrary, the people of the Northern States were already a great manufacturing nation, and to protect these manufactures they determined to impose very high import duties.

This new impost was known as the "Morrill Tariff," and whatever opinions may be held as to the wisdom of its enactment, it was certainly entirely one-sided, for although it might benefit the Northern, it was death to the Southern States. Hitherto the latter had relied upon exchange or barter with foreign countries, but under the new tariff her ports might be said to be virtually closed.

But if this may be presumed to be the primary cause of the dispute and the secession of the Southern States, there was afterwards to arise a far more important matter — the question of slavery or its abolition.

On the twentieth of December, eighteen hundred and sixty, South Carolina seceded from the Union, and declared itself a sovereign and independent State. Twenty days after—on January the ninth—Mississippi followed suit, and the same month—a few days later—Alabama, Florida, Georgia, and Louisiana joined them.

In February, Texas also seceded; in April, Virginia; and in May, Arkansas, Tennessee, and North Carolina. Maryland alone remained undecided or neutral.

The Secessionists at once formed themselves into a republic, and elected Mr. Jefferson Davis as President of what was called the Confederate States. This was in February, eighteen sixty-one. The Southern people fondly believed that they had inaugurated a new nation; but their brethren of the North refused to recognise them, and moreover proclaimed them as rebels to the Union.

Nothing daunted, the first acts of the Confederates were to seize the forts and arsenals of the United States—wherever practicable—in the South. After this, all chance of an amicable and peaceful arrangement was at an end. Hitherto many whose passions had not been inflamed by the dispute had hoped that the horrors of a civil war might be averted, but now that weapons had been drawn that hope was dead.

President Lincoln being determined to suppress the rebellion by force of arms, had strengthened the regular army, and called out the militia to the number of seventy-five thousand men. But two days before Lincoln issued his proclamation as to the reserve forces, the first blow had been struck by the Confederates. Fort Sumpter, which was defended by Major Anderson, of the United States Army, had been captured by the South.

The Confederate troops, which had won their first success in the coming struggle, were under General Beauregard, to whose standard men flocked from all sides. The first shot fired at Fort Sumpter might truly be said to be the commencement of the Civil War.

It is not necessary that we should refer further to what followed for the next ten months. The fighting began at Fort Sumpter and raged fiercely, with varied success, throughout the year, but up to that time the war was certainly in favour of the Confederates, both by land and sea.

From the first outbreak of the American Civil War young MacIver had been anxious to take up his sword on the side that claimed him by all the ties of association, and he might even say of birth, for if not born in Virginia, he first saw the light within sight of her shores. But however desirous he might be to join the South, he was unavoidably detained in England for a time, and did not sail for America until some months after the fighting had commenced.

Amongst other causes that delayed him was the great difficulty he experienced in reaching Virginia by water, but at length, not being able to meet with a passage on board a blockade runner, he determined to sail for New York, with the hope of being able to make his way down South by land.

He had a quick run across the Atlantic. On his arrival he found that the first battle of Bull's Run had been fought, and that the Federals were organising all the possible force that they could raise. His first step was to proceed to Washington, which he reached at the time when General McClellan was forming his Army of the Potomac.

Officers who had seen service were of course much needed and sought after, and from his past military career Lieutenant MacIver might at once, had he so chosen, have been appointed to an important rank on the Federal side. In fact, much inducement was held out to him to join General McClellan's force, but nothing would influence him to fight against dear old Virginia, the cradle of his mother's birth.

MacIver, however, was now treading on dangerous ground, for at this time Washington City was full of Federal spies, and from his refusal to take service on their side he at once became suspected of strong Southern proclivities. Wherever he went he found that he was constantly dogged and watched, and that all his movements were reported at headquarters.

At length, however, by some trouble and a little stratagem, he managed to leave Washington, and succeeded in reaching Alexandria, in Virginia, uninterrupted. But there he found that he had before him the greatest difficulties which as yet he had had to encounter, as it was next to impossible to get through the Federal lines.

He had hoped that once at Alexandria, the way would be easy enough, but the Northerners were not only in full possession of the country beyond Culpepper Court House, but every point was watched and guarded with the strictest vigilance. There was no chance, he was compelled to admit, of getting over into the Confederate lines for the present, and he was obliged to remain at Alexandria for a considerable time. In the end he was detained, not only against his will, but within prison walls.

In Alexandria, as at Washington, he unfortunately became suspected of having strong leanings in favour of the South. Probably this was chiefly his own fault, through want of discretion in not keeping his views to himself. However, he was one evening drawn into a very serious brawl with two Federal officers. No doubt the affair was premeditated, and it had been fully arranged that they should force the quarrel on him.

One of the officers called MacIver a Secessionist, affixing to the term other words too gross for record. This insult was immediately followed by a physical attack from both men. In self-defence he then drew his revolver, but before he had a chance to use the weapon he was seized from behind by several of the companions of the Federal officers, and the end of the affray was that he was lodged in the Alexandria prison.

There he was detained for two months, and could get no other explanation except that he was a suspected Secessionist. At length, seeing no chance of his release, and being heartily sick of his confinement, he determined to escape at whatever risk, even if the attempt should cost him his life.

Whilst waiting for a favourable opportunity, he arranged all his plans to ensure success. Unfortunately his money had been taken from him, and he knew that should he even succeed in evading his jailers, he could have little hope of procuring food during the time that must elapse before he could reach the Confederate lines. This difficulty, however, he provided against by saving pieces of bread from his prison fare for several days previous to carrying out his design. These precious morsels he concealed about his person.

At length his chance came, and one night, about a couple of hours before midnight, he managed not only to escape from the prison and to leave the town, but to make his way round the Federal lines undetected. The risk that he ran was very great, for at any moment he was in danger of being shot by one of the sentinels; but by a miracle, as it seemed to him at the time he avoided both scouts and outposts.

After a lonely night march full of excitement from the peril to which he was exposed, he arrived at daybreak within a short distance of Warrington. Being both tired and hungry, he—having first looked carefully around him — sat down to rest and to satisfy the cravings of his appetite. As to gratifying the longings of the latter, he had nothing but the pieces of dry bread which he had saved in prison.

But little disheartened, however, he commenced his luxurious breakfast of bread and water with that keen zest which hunger gives to the most humble fare. Having finished his primitive meal, the Lieutenant was inwardly congratulating himself upon his fortunate escape from the Federals, and further with the prospect before him of ere long being amongst friends, when he imagined he heard a jingling of steel.

As he turned round all his castle-building at once faded into thin air, for he saw that close upon him was a squadron of Federal cavalry. The troopers were rapidly approaching the spot where he sat; escape was impossible, and in a few minutes more in all probability he would be again a prisoner.

CHAPTER XI.

AMONGST THE FEDERALS—ANOTHER FORTUNATE ESCAPE—BORROWED PLUMAGE.

MacIver seeing that there was not the remotest chance of avoiding the Yankee troopers, instantly made up his mind to put a bold face on the matter. Rising leisurely from the ground he walked boldly forward to meet the cavalry squadron, until they approached near enough for him to speak to the officer in command.

Putting on the most innocent look he could assume, he inquired which direction he should take to gain the nearest headquarters of the Federals. Whilst the Commandant, without replying to his question, eyed him suspiciously for a few moments, MacIver was considering how best he could outwit him. To do this he was determined, if possible, as he had been so badly treated by the Federals whilst in prison that he considered any subterfuge which he might make use of would not only be fair, but justifiable.

"What do you want at headquarters?" at length demanded the cavalry captain.

"I wish to find my brother," replied MacIver, "and to join the cause."

This was deception first and second, for he had never had a brother, and decidedly had no wish to fight under Federal colours.

"Where is your pass? Let me see it," said the cavalry captain.

"I had one to pass the lines at Alexandria," answered the other, coolly, and apparently quite unconcerned as to any consequences that might occur, "but I am afraid I have lost it."

"Where do you come from?" queried the officer.

"Scotland," said MacIver; "I'm a Highlander."

"I can hear that you are a Britisher by your tongue," laughed the Captain, "but I guess I didn't ask you what country you hailed from, but whence you came last?"

"Oh," ejaculated the Lieutenant, with simplicity personified, "I see. I came down here South from Washington to look for my brother."

"Well," said the Captain, "I guess anyhow you ain't a rebel. I can see that you have been a soldier, and are a well set-up one, too. What do you say, Britisher, to joining my corps?"

Whether the ex-prisoner had ever heard the story of the Irish recruit who enlisted in the Eighty-seventh Regiment so that he might be near his brother, who was serving in the Eighty-eighth, we do not know, but his reply was worthy of that obtuse son of Erin.

"Well, Captain," he answered, "if my brother is in the cavalry I don't mind joining your troop; but, you see, I rather fancy he is in the infantry, and I want to be near to him."

"Anyhow, you must come with us now," concluded the Captain, laughing, and without further parley he told a sergeant to bring up a spare horse for the stranger. Our friend was then ordered to mount and to ride by the side of the Commandant.

The squadron proceeded for some few miles in the direction of Warrington, and then, much to MacIver's satisfaction, halted for breakfast. A capital breakfast it was, too, with good hot coffee, a luxury which he had not tasted for two long months. Considering the bad look-out at the beginning, he had cause to congratulate himself on falling into such pleasant lines.

An hour or so after breakfast the good-natured cavalry leader passed MacIver through the pickets up to Warrington, and believing his story, told him that he could go and look after his brother. After having made inquiries, he was to return to the Captain at his quarters, who really desired to enlist in his troop so promising a recruit as the young "Britisher" appeared to be.

Entering Warrington under such favourable auspices as were afforded by the friendly cavalry captain's protection, there was no suspicion attached to MacIver, and he had a *carte blanche* to wander about wherever he chose. This gave him the opportunity of not only acquainting himself with the position of the Federal forces, and of judging the distance of the pickets, but further calculating how best he might escape to the Confederate lines.

To once more make an attempt for freedom he had fully determined, and but waited for the cover of darkness to carry out his design. In the meantime he returned to the quarters of the squadron of cavalry which had surprised him in the morning. Later in the afternoon he met the Captain, who inquired if he had succeeded in hunting up his brother.

This was rather an awkward question to answer, so he contented himself with a simple negative. At the same time he hinted that as he was without money he thought he should be inclined to join his —the Captain's—troop, but had not quite made up his mind.

This half-promise was, of course, intended to put the friendly Federal officer off his guard, and no doubt was successful. MacIver was really sorry to deceive one who had been so kind to him; but after all the vile treatment he had received from the Northern Government, he felt that he was absolved from any code of honour in dealing with their followers.

The Captain readily granted until the next day for MacIver to decide as to enlisting in his troop. He promised, too, that if our friend should come to the conclusion to join him, that he would do all in his power to advance him, remarking that he could see that he was a gentleman, and had not served as a private soldier in his own country.

The Federal officer also ordered that the stranger should be entertained at the sergeants' mess, where he

G

was at once cordially received and welcomed. This was more than he had expected, and not exactly to his liking, as he was afraid it might interfere somewhat with his freedom of action. Such, however, did not prove to be the case, as after a time he found himself almost alone in the tent.

At length, when darkness came over, MacIver left the non-commissioned officers' quarters, and after strolling leisurely along for a short while, suddenly changed his route, and stepped out briskly in the direction of the high road leading towards Richmond. He had not proceeded far, however, when it occurred to him that it would be foolish to undertake the great risk before him unarmed, and that he was without any defensive weapon.

This idea caused him to at once retrace his steps to the sergeants' quarters. There, after a short delay, he managed to appropriate unobserved not only a couple of loaded revolvers, but some spare ammunition. Again he proceeded on his way, hidden by the darkness of the night, and made direct for a pine forest which he had noticed in the daylight, flanking Warrington on the left.

By his observations in the earlier part of the day, he had ascertained that the outlying vedettes of the Federals only extended to a bridge crossing one of the branches of the Rapidan River. Once beyond this bridge he imagined he had but little to fear, but the difficulty and danger was how to pass it. The darkness was in his favour, and there was just a chance, he thought, that the bridge might be left unguarded; or at least that a sentinel was not actually upon it.

Whilst these thoughts were occupying his mind, MacIver stole along the skirt of the pine forest almost as silently as might have done one of its denizens, for in all probability on his extreme caution depended his life. Several times he paused to listen, but on each occasion glided on again, reassured by the stillness that reigned around.

At length he was close to the river where it was crossed by the bridge, and he stole carefully out from the forest, but still keeping within the shadow of the lofty pine trees. At first he could only make out the dark outline of the bridge, but a second glance warned him that there was a mounted man on guard at the end nearest to him, and not twenty paces from where he himself stood.

Instinctively he drew back behind one of the pines. For a minute or two he was quite undecided as to what he should next do.

If the vedette caught sight of him, in all probability he would be instantly shot, and if he turned back and happened to be taken prisoner by the way, it meant certain death, so that to advance or return seemed equally dangerous.

The first thought that occurred to him, as he still kept his eyes fixed on the trooper, was that if he could manage to reach the bridge unseen, he might perhaps be able to creep along any projecting part of the structure concealed by the coping; but, again, if even such a ledge existed, he was compelled to admit that in the darkness the feat would be next to impossible.

Minute after minute went by, and there the vedette sat, striding his horse as motionless as a statue, but no doubt, as the watcher thought, with his ears on the alert, and listening for the slightest sound.

It was very tantalising to be so near freedom, and this solitary vedette the only obstacle to his escape. MacIver was so near to the Federal, that by advancing a step or two, he could have easily shot down the trooper with his revolver, but such a course was out of the question. Shooting a man in cold blood, and with a cowardly shot, was quite foreign to his mode of warfare, and even if he could have felt justified in performing such a deed, it would have been madness, as the report of his revolver must have at once brought down upon him one or two of the outlying scouts.

However, he was not inclined to wait longer with freedom before him. To return he decided was not to be thought of, and with his usual boldness he came to the desperate determination of making a sudden rush upon the vedette, trusting to his strength and good luck to overpower the trooper before the latter could give an alarm.

Advancing cautiously along step by step, with his body bent low, and so silently that he could not even hear the movement of his own footfalls, he crept undetected, until he was so close to the vedette, that two or three bounds would bring them face to face. At this critical moment the Federal trooper turned his face away. It was an unfortunate movement for him, for instantaneously there was a sudden rush, and the unanticipated enemy was upon him.

"Surrender, or you are a dead man!" exclaimed MacIver, his voice low but determined, and the barrel of his revolver pointed full between the eyes of the astonished and no doubt alarmed vedette.

"Keep your hands still, don't move them, or I fire!" continued he, imagining that he saw a movement on the part of the trooper towards his saddle-bow.

The warning, however, was unnecessary, for the unlucky vedette had been so overtaken by surprise, and was so overwhelmed by dismay at his mishap, that he offered not the slightest resistance, nor made any attempt to escape, as perhaps he might have succeeded in doing had he driven his spurs into his horse.

"Give me your carbine!" said MacIver.

Silently the Federal obeyed, for the revolver was still pointed ominously at his head. With a sudden swing of his left arm MacIver pitched the carbine into the river, and then ordered the trooper to dismount. The scout obeyed the command with alacrity, slipping nimbly from his charger, no doubt anxious to remove himself out of the way of that threatening barrel into which his eyes had been fixed.

"Now then, give me your sabre."

For the first time the scout seemed inclined to resist, but it was only for a moment, for his enemy's hand grasped his shoulder with a vice-like grip, and the cold steel of the terrible revolver was placed against his temple. Thoroughly cowed, he not only gave up his sabre, but took off his cloak when ordered.

Buckling on the former, and throwing the latter across his arm, McIver sprang on the back of the troop-horse, and galloped off, leaving the Federal standing on the bridge utterly dumbfounded.

CHAPTER XII.

CROSSING THE CONFEDERATE LINES—MEETING WITH COLONEL SCOTT—PROCEEDS TO RICHMOND

Lieutenant MacIver rode at full speed for a mile or more, and then he drew rein to listen if there was any sound of pursuit. All, however, was quiet, and after wrapping the trooper's cloak about him, he again pushed forward. Keeping on at a gallop, it was nearly dawn when at length he slackened the pace of his tired charger.

He was riding slowly along just as day was breaking, when he perceived a horseman in front of him, and presently made out that it was a vedette in the Confederate gray uniform. The sight was a welcome one, and he slightly quickened his pace; but suddenly it occurred to him that he might be fired upon by the scout in mistake.

As this thought struck him he pulled up, and hastily removed the cloak which he had worn throughout the night. It was the work of an instant, but he was none too soon, for the Southern trooper had his carbine pointed at MacIver's head. As it would not do to seem to hesitate, the latter took the bridle reins in his mouth, and throwing up his hands to show that he was not going to resist, rode forward and surrendered.

The Confederate soldier eyed his prisoner very suspiciously, and then told him to ride on in advance, and he would follow in the rear. At the same time the trooper warned the stranger that if he saw the slightest movement to escape, he should instantly shoot him. In this way the two proceeded for a little while, when the scout fired a shot. This was rather startling to the prisoner, after the late caution of his captor, but he soon found that it was only a signal, for scarcely had the report died away when he saw some half-dozen horsemen approaching.

These proved to be a Confederate sergeant and six troopers, who came up at a gallop. After exchanging a word or two with the vedette, the sergeant ordered the prisoner to surrender his arms. He was, however, saved any trouble by the troopers immediately and unceremoniously taking the weapons from him. When this had been done, the non-commissioned officer sharply interrogated the new arrival.

"You are on a Yankee horse, you have a Yankee cloak, and carry Yankee arms," he said. "Who are you? And what the devil are you doing here?"

"I am no Yankee, but a friend," replied MacIver, smiling. "I am a soldier with a Virginian heart, and am almost a Virginian by birth. If you wish to know why I am here, I have come to fight for the dear old State."

"Well, that may be so," said the sergeant; "but for the present I guess it is my duty to hold you a close prisoner. I must take you before Colonel Scott, the officer in command here, and he will judge upon your case."

"I am quite willing, sergeant," answered MacIver, who knew Colonel Scott by repute as an old and gallant officer.

The prisoner was at once taken before this venerable old gentleman, who at one time had held a commission in the United States Army. Many years, however, before the quarrel between the North and the South, Colonel Scott had retired from the service, and settled on his property in the South. At the outbreak of the war the old officer had again drawn his sword, but now on the side of the Confederates, and had formed the corps of Mounted Rangers then under his command.

Colonel Scott received the stranger who had been brought into his tent as a prisoner with the greatest courtesy and kindness. He first asked his name and profession, and what had brought him into the Confederate States; and when MacIver briefly explained his former career, and the rank which he had previously held, the old officer ordered the sergeant to retire, and requested the visitor to be seated.

Having heard further that the young soldier had come to offer his services to the South, Colonel Scott frankly said to him that his aid would be very acceptable, and that he could not have arrived at a more opportune time, as the Confederate troops were shortly about to make a move and commence active operations. He further added that he should be glad if he would join his own corps of Rangers. If so, it would afford him, the Colonel, great pleasure to recommend his visitor to Secretary Randolph for an immediate appointment as a lieutenant.

The Colonel's offer was quite in accordance with his visitor's plans, who replied at once that he should be only too glad to have the honour of belonging to so distinguished a corps. He would prefer, however, he said, going on first to Richmond for a few days, so as to report himself, as he had several influential friends in that city.

To this proposition the Commandant of the Rangers readily assented, and it was arranged that MacIver should leave for Richmond on the following day. Subsequently the two held a long conversation in reference to the latter's experiences since arriving in America; MacIver relating all his adventures after leaving Washington. The kind old Colonel then introduced his visitor to the officers, and left him for the time as the guest of his future comrades.

The following morning the ex-Garibaldian left the camp of the Rangers on his way to Richmond. The old Commandant supplied him with a fresh horse in exchange for the Federal charger, and furnished him with a pass in case he should need it. The Colonel also insisted upon his new friend taking a loan of money to pay his expenses on the road. Two days later, without meeting with any adventure worthy of record, he arrived safely in the city of Richmond, the capital of Virginia, and the seat of the Confederate Government.

On calling upon a relative of his mother's he was joyfully welcomed and most hospitably entertained. Funds, too, were placed at his disposal, so as to enable him to make a more presentable appearance. A thorough new rig out was not only very acceptable, but almost indispensable, for what with his imprisonment and the exposure to the weather which he had undergone since his escape from Alexandria, his clothes were in a somewhat worn condition. Money, however, soon set all this to rights.

In due course, the Lieutenant was presented to Mr. Secretary Randolph, who received the young soldier with that courtesy which seemed a part of his nature. After hearing from him his past history as regarded his military life, and having listened to a recital of his adventures since arriving in America, the Secretary told his visitor that he should be pleased to give him a commission in the Confederate cavalry.

Mr. Randolph at once fulfilled his promise, for on the day following his interview with the Secretary, MacIver was appointed an officer in the Confederate States Army, with the rank of First Lieutenant. In addition to this he was named as Cavalry Instructor, and ordered forthwith to commence his duties in Richmond.

He had given a sort of half promise to Colonel Scott that he would join that officer's corps of Mounted Rangers, but the appointment which Secretary Randolph had bestowed upon him left him no choice, as he was placed under allowance as Cavalry Instructor, and told off for duty that same day. He, however, wrote at once to the kind old Colonel, explaining what had transpired.

It was a busy, active life that he found himself so suddenly engaged in, but it was quite to his liking. Recruits were flocking in in large numbers daily, and new corps were being quickly organised. With those men who were enlisted for the cavalry, Lieutenant MacIver worked hard from morning till night; but his duties were considerably lightened by most of those volunteers being persons of intelligence who readily took up their drill. They easily conformed, too, to the discipline of a military service.

Although his whole heart and soul was in the work which had been allotted to him, he would have much preferred, could he have had the choice, to have been actively engaged at the front, instead of training recruits in the capital. He grumbled, perhaps, a little to himself, but found contentment in the thought that the time he wished for must soon arrive, and that ere long he would be told off for service with the army.

In the meantime the new Lieutenant did his best to make the recruits under his charge efficient. By this constant attention to his monotonous duties he soon won golden opinions from his superior officers, and in the end gained the respect and thanks of Secretary Randolph.

After acting for a few weeks as Cavalry Instructor, MacIver one evening, much to his gratification, received orders to hold himself in readiness to be the bearer of despatches from Secretary Randolph to General "Stonewall" Jackson, who commanded the Confederate troops in the Shenandoah Valley. The next morning he left Richmond, and reached his destination in safety, without meeting with any adventure on the road of particular note. The Lieutenant was received very heartily by his new commanding officer, General Jackson, to whom he had been ordered by Secretary Randolph to report himself for duty.

The gallant old General at once placed him on his staff, and a few days after his arrival he was ordered to organise a small body of scouts. These men were to be picked from the different cavalry regiments, and the corps, which was intended to operate with the brigade of General Trimble, was to be under MacIver's command.

The Lieutenant's present appointment involved the requirement of no little care and tact, as his duty was principally to reconnoitre and to report to General Trimble the position of the Federal troops. It was a service, too, of considerable danger, as Trimble's brigade was posted on the extreme left.

The scouts, however, that he had chosen were all tried soldiers—men picked for their efficiency—well mounted, and no novices to the particular work before them. What was of more consequence still, they soon began to have confidence in their youthful leader, and MacIver's corps speedily became celebrated for its dash and daring.

Many a lonely night march through a country literally swarming with enemies did the gallant little band make, and many a perilous, yet successful reconnaissance was carried out under their Lieutenant's command and supervision, much to the chagrin of the Federals and the satisfaction of the Confederates.

While commanding these scouts, he was brought into very intimate acquaintance with General Trimble, with whom he was closely connected for some time. He met, too, several men serving with General "Stonewall" Jackson's army who had been his comrades in arms during the Garibaldian campaign in Italy.

Notable amongst these were two officers who had been his intimate friends—General Wheat and Captain Atkins.

The former of these gentlemen, although he had held a general's commission under Walker in the Nicaraguan expedition, had waived his rank, and was ow contented to serve the cause of the South as a major. MacIver was much pleased to renew his friendship with Wheat, for whom he had a great liking. The General, too, showed how much he was gratified at meeting another old Garibaldian.

CHAPTER XIII.

JACKSON'S CAMPAIGN IN THE VALLEY OF VIRGINIA—AN IRISHMAN FOR THE FIRST TIME UNDER FIRE—THE BATTLE OF FORT ROYAL

WE must now revert to General "Stonewall" Jackson's position in the Shenandoah Valley. His force was very small, even with the addition of General Ewell's division, which had been sent to operate with him in that part of the Southern States.

The primary object of the combined force was to divert the army of General McDowell at Fredericksburg from uniting with that of McClellan, and in other respects to act purely on the defensive. Beyond this duty the authorities at Richmond had no expectation from "Stonewall" Jackson's small command, which they believed to be too weak to act on the aggressive.

But, however inadequate might seem the little army which Jackson had to work with, in effecting any but the design for which he had been sent to the Shenandoah, he was not the man to be contented with merely holding McClellan and McDowell in check, and speedily came to the decision to force fighting on the enemy. In fact, the bold idea had originated with this adventurous Southern Commander to essay the extraordinary task of driving the Federals from the valley, then under the three commands of Banks, Fremont, and Shields.

To better understand the work before Jackson, and to realise the result, we must premise that the disposition of the enemy's forces west of the Blue Ridge was designed to co-operate with McDowell at Fredericksburg. These included the troops of Generals Banks and Shields in the Shenandoah Valley, and those of Fremont, Milroy, and Blenker in Western Virginia.

After once the idea of driving the Federals from the valley had taken possession of his mind, "Stonewall" Jackson lost no time in commencing operations. As soon as he had been reinforced by General Ewell's division, which crossed the Blue Ridge at McGackay'sville, he proceeded in person to the position of General Edward Johnson, who, in command of a little Southern force, was posted in a narrow valley at a village called McDowell.

When the Southern Commander joined his Lieutenant (Johnson) he found the latter drawn up in a strong position, with the heavy brigades of the Federal Generals, Milroy and Blenker, in line of battle before him. "Stonewall" Jackson at once ordered an attack upon the enemy, and so fierce was the onslaught of the Southerners, that after a brief engagement the Federals were driven back with considerable loss.

This success of Jackson so frightened Milroy and Blenker, that they called upon Fremont, who, with a strong force, was a few miles behind them, to hurry up to their assistance. Knowing that Fremont would now move up to the front, Jackson determined to trust to stratagem, and if possible to deceive the enemy.

Jackson at once fell back, moving down the Valley Pike at a rapid rate, as though his retrogression were an actual retreat. Proceeding to Newmarket he was there joined by General Ewell's force, which had been awaiting him at a place called "Swift Run Gap." After a brief rest at Newmarket, Jackson marched across the Shenandoah Mountains, his whole united force then amounting to about fourteen thousand men.

Meanwhile Generals Banks and Shields, thinking that Jackson was busily engaged in a distant quarter, and not likely to trouble them in the Shenandoah Valley again, were making a movement towards Fredericksburg. Thus, unsuspiciously and unprepared, on the twenty-second of May, the two Federal Generals were marching leisurely along, unconscious of danger and little thinking that "Stonewall" Jackson, with his fourteen thousand men, was then meditating an attack on their rear at Fort Royal.

Jackson and Ewell fell upon the Federals like an avalanche. So unexpected was the attack that the Federal rear-guard, consisting of the 1st Maryland Regiment, was, it might be said, annihilated. Every man in it—except fifteen—was killed, wounded, or captured. Judging by the result, something very like a panic must have seized the Northerners.

Soon they were in full retreat towards Strasburg, pursued by the Southerners. The latter took nine hundred Federal prisoners, and destroyed a vast quantity of their enemy's stores. The retreat might almost be called a flight, but it was to be shortly followed by one more disastrous.

The only effort made to retrieve the day was by the Northern cavalry, but after one desperate charge they were routed by the Confederate horsemen under that gallant leader, Turner Ashby. In this short but brilliant hand-to-hand fight, MacIver took part, and, although in the thick of the *mêlée*, escaped unhurt.

Hotly pursued, General Banks made a rapid retreat until he nearly reached Winchester, where for a brief space he rallied his men, and faced the enemy. But according to the most reliable accounts the Federal General stood but a few minutes before Winchester, and broke and fled at the sound of a distant fire of artillery.

A general panic seemed now to have seized both Banks and his men, for they turned tail and made a disgraceful flight for the town of Winchester, which they entered on the twenty-fourth of May in a frantic retreat. Many of the fugitives were on the run, and they were not only received with shouts of derision, but shots were fired at them from the windows of houses.

Never, surely, was there such a shameful flight as this of General Banks. His only desire seemed to be to place the Potomac between himself and danger. He abandoned in Winchester all his commissary and ordnance stores, and left behind him four thousand prisoners, and one million of dollars in his treasury chests.

This panic on the part of the Federal soldiers

recalls to us the comical alarm of a Confederate recruit — an Irishman — in the Shenandoah Valley, when for the first time under fire.

The Southern troops were in line of battle with the enemy before them, and MacIver, who had just conveyed an order from General Jackson to the commandant of a brigade posted on the extreme right, was galloping back as fast as his horse could carry him. Suddenly he came upon a couple of Confederate soldiers, who were seated on the grass some distance away from the troops.

"What the devil are you two men doing here?" asked MacIver, as he reined up his charger.

"Sure, and your honour, and we've fallen out jist to rest ourselves," answered one of the men, with an unmistakable Irish brogue.

"Rest yourselves, indeed," exclaimed MacIver, angrily. "Get back to your ranks at once, or I shall report you. To what regiment do you belong?"

"Sure and it's to his honour's General Trimble's brigade," replied the spokesman. Then with a coaxing voice he continued, "Sure, and, Captain darling, you wouldn't be after getting two poor innocent boys into trouble?"

Whilst these brief questions had been put and answered, the enemy's skirmishers had opened fire, and the zip, zip of the rifle bullets were whistling past where the two soldiers had been stopped by the Lieutenant.

At the peculiar sound made by the leaden messengers, which can only be realised by those who have been under fire, one of the men—both of whom had risen from the grass when the aide-de-camp addressed

H

them—suddenly put up his right hand, and motioned as though he would brush something off his ear. A moment or two afterwards he made a dash at his left ear with the other hand.

"What the deuce does it all mane, Dan?" he said, as another and another bullet went "zip! zip!" near to him. "Be jabers, I hear bees buzzing round and round, and I can't see them."

"Arrah! get out with your bays, Pat," replied his comrade. "They're not bays at all at all, they're bullets."

"Bullets! bullets!" exclaimed Pat. "Holy murther!" and down he dropped on the grass, burying his face in the ground. "Sure I'm dead now and I know it. Oh! Dan, Dan, I wish we were back in the ould country agin."

The whole scene was so absurd that MacIver had as much as he could do to prevent himself from laughing outright. Drawing his revolver, he threatened to shoot both the recreant recruits if they did not immediately rejoin their corps.

"Get out of this," said the Lieutenant, "and do your duty like men by joining your command at once. Your countrymen are noted for their bravery all over the world, and I'm sorry to find an Irishman chicken-hearted."

"Sure, Captain jewel," said Pat, who had somewhat recovered from his panic, although the zip, zip of the bullets were becoming warmer, "I'd better be shot by the enemy than your honour's revolver," and at the double the two made a hasty return to General Trimble's brigade.

Oddly enough this same Irishman who had been

so alarmed at the first sound of a bullet, turned out a very brave soldier, and did gallant service for the South until the close of the war. There were a large number of his countrymen in the Confederate service, who fought with great distinction for that cause.

During the battle of Fort Royal Lieutenant MacIver met as an enemy a former comrade. A body of Confederate troopers, to which he was attached, engaged on a scouting expedition, fell in with a squadron of Federal cavalry—the 1st New Jersey—commanded by an Englishman named Percy Wyndham. Wyndham had been an old Garibaldian officer, and had previously served under the Austrian flag. He was well known to MacIver, Wheat, and Scott, and several other officers now fighting for the South.

As the New Jersey cavalry was nearly double the strength of that to which MacIver was attached, the Confederate horsemen fell back slowly, exchanging shots with the enemy as they retired. Wyndham, probably fancying that he was being drawn into an ambush, divided his squadron, and sent the right wing three or four miles away to deploy into line, so as to avoid a surprise, and to give timely warning in case of a flank movement being attempted by the Confederate cavalry.

The commander of the latter, however, judging the distance to be favourable for an attack on the enemy, deployed his troops, and after driving back the Federals, posted his own men in line under cover of a wood.

Whether Percy Wyndham imagined that the Confederates had retired when they disappeared amongst the trees, or whether he relied upon his superior strength, was not known, but at all events he advanced his men. This movement proved to be an unfortunate one for him, for at the moment he arrived within a convenient distance, the Southern commander gave the word to charge, and dashed down upon the Federals.

So fierce was this onslaught that Wyndham's men were routed, about twenty of them being left dead upon the field, and some fifteen wounded. There were but few Confederate casualties, but MacIver was one of the sufferers, being slightly wounded.

As he was returning at a gallop, after the first charge, he caught sight of a squad of eight men, led by an officer, who were attempting to escape at the back of a plantation. MacIver, at the head of four or five troopers, charged down upon the Federals, who at once wheeled round and opened fire with their revolvers.

One of the bullets struck MacIver in the side, grazing a rib, and causing what at the time was a very painful wound. He lost a considerable quantity of blood, but, after being in the surgeon's hands, he did not suffer much subsequent inconvenience, being able to get into the saddle again in a couple of days.

CHAPTER XIV

THE BATTLES OF CROSS KEYS AND FORT REPUBLIC—THE DEATH OF TURNER ASHBY

AFTER the routing of General Banks' army—a result which caused great rejoicing throughout the Southern

States, and gave the Federals not a little chagrin and disappointment — the main body of the Confederate army in the Valley of Virginia was moved forward in the direction of Fort Republic.

General Jackson was in command in person, and by the sixth of June had reached his proposed halting place. Fort Republic, subsequently to become famous as the scene of the battle of that name, was but a little village situated on an angle formed by the North and South Rivers, tributaries of the south fork of the Shenandoah.

General Jackson encamped his troops in a strong position on the high ground near to the village, and to the north of the river. General Ewell's division was posted some four miles further away, near to the road leading from Harrisonburg to Fort Republic.

When "Stonewall" Jackson reached the Shenandoah, the Federal General—Fremont—had already arrived with his army in the vicinity of Harrisonburg. Fremont's command consisted of seven brigades of infantry, besides a strong body of cavalry, and the necessary artillery.

General Shields, also, with a considerable number of Federal troops, was moving up the east side of the south fork of the Shenandoah River, and was then some fifteen or twenty miles from Fort Republic.

Without doubt the object of the two Federal Generals had been to form a junction, and to act in concert, had not Jackson arrived in time to prevent them. His scouts had informed him as to the relative positions of the Northern Commanders, and Jackson's military genius at once grasped the situation.

When he reached Fort Republic he was at about an equal distance from each of the Federal Generals, and he lost not a moment in sending forth a strong body of men to destroy the bridge at Conrad's Stone. This bridge spanned the south fork of the Shenandoah, and was the only means of communication between Fremont and Shields, and its destruction served to thwart the plans of the Northern Commanders, and probably had much to do with the results that followed.

Lieutenant MacIver was on scouting duty during the destruction of the bridge; but the Federals, not suspecting Jackson's intention, did not put in an appearance.

When too late, Fremont found out that a junction with his colleague was now impossible, and he came to the determination—relying on his strength—to attack the Confederate army unaided, and without further delay moved down upon Ewell's position.

General Ewell, however, was prepared for his opponent, and threw forward a strong body of skirmishers, with their supports, to hold Fremont in check, or at all events to harass his advance. During the greater part of the action which was to follow, the Confederate Commander had but three brigades of infantry, and at no time throughout the battle had he cavalry, excepting a partisan squadron, which was out on vedette duty. Ewell's total strength was under five thousand men.

It was about ten o'clock on the morning of the seventh of June that General Fremont began to feel along his front, preparatory to posting his artillery. Shortly afterwards, with two brigades of infantry, he made an attack upon General Trimble's brigade on the right. Brigadier Trimble, however, not only stood his ground, but repulsed the Federals. Following up his advantage, Trimble in turn became the attacking party, advancing at the charge, and driving the Federal brigades back at the point of the bayonet for a mile or more.

This position on Fremont's flank, which the gallant Trimble had won, he continued to hold, remaining ready at any moment to make a final attack on the enemy. The artillery fire, however, had been heavy through the day, and several unavailing attempts had been made by the Federal cavalry to force Trimble's ground.

So far the fight had been fiercely contested, but Ewell felt that the advantage was in his favour, although the force opposed to him was in numbers so superior. At a late hour in the afternoon the Confederate General advanced both his wings, and drove in the Federal skirmishers. Following up this advantage, Ewell forced the enemy's position—Trimble charging just at the nick of time—and when night set in, the Confederate General was in possession of all the ground previously held by the Federals. This battle, which we have briefly described, is known as that of Cross Keys. It was another signal success for the South, although purchased by a loss on the Confederate side of forty-two killed and two hundred and eighty-seven wounded. The loss to the North was officially estimated at two thousand men, but it was supposed to be really in excess of that number.

Meanwhile, General Jackson was preparing for an

attack upon General Shields on the other side of the river, hoping to inflict a last and final blow On the morning after the battle of Cross Keys, Ewell's forces were recalled by their chief to join him at Fort Republic. As day broke they had commenced their march.

When "Stonewall" Jackson came within sight of the enemy, he found that Shields had judiciously selected his position on a rising ground near Lewis House, where with his artillery he could not only command the road from Fort Republic, but could sweep the plain for a considerable distance in his front.

The battle commenced by the Confederate General Winder being ordered to move forward his brigade. Instantly the enemy opened upon him with a heavy fire of shell. The Confederate batteries replied with a well-sustained fire, but it proved unequal to that of the Federals. General Winder had been reinforced by a Louisiana regiment, but he was under such a hail of shot and shell that he found there was nothing for it but to fall back or charge the Northern batteries; and like the bold man that he was, he chose the latter alternative, and gave the order to advance. With a ringing cheer his men pushed forward, and with great courage proceeded a considerable distance, but they encountered such a terrible fire of musketry and artillery as to cause not only great loss but much disorder in the ranks. At length Winder found his command so disorganised that he was compelled to fall back, although it was greatly against his will. His ranks, however, were broken, and to have advanced further would have been actual madness.

THE DEATH OF TURNER ASHBY

Emboldened by the successful repulse of Winder, the Federals now advanced across the open plain, and with such a well-sustained fire from their musketry as to drive back the Confederate supports. The Confederate artillery, too, being deprived of their supports, had to limber up their guns in great haste and to retire. For the time things looked bad for Jackson, and it seemed as if luck had turned against him, and that the battle was lost.

It was a crisis that seemed to hang on the balance, but it was turned in favour of General Jackson by the appearance on the field of his second in command, General Ewell. The latter came up at this opportune moment and drove back the enemy. Two Confederate regiments of Ewell's—the Forty-fourth and Fifty-eighth Virginia—dashed with a cheer upon the Federals, taking them in flank and driving them back in great confusion and disorder. It might be said to be the first check that Shields had experienced that day.

The Confederate cavalry, with which was MacIver, also charged down upon the discomfited Northern infantry, and cut their way through and through, doing much execution in the ranks of their enemies.

It was about this time that the cause of the South sustained a great loss in the death of the brave partisan cavalry officer named Turner Ashby. This remarkable man had distinguished himself greatly in the service—especially in the Valley of Virginia—and was as much dreaded by the Federals as he was admired by his comrades. He was shot dead when the Fifty-fourth Virginia Regiment became engaged with the Pennsylvania Bucktails. Colonel Johnson at the same moment came up with the Maryland Regiment, and by a brilliant charge took the enemy in flank, and forced him back with terrible loss.

Poor Turner Ashby was on the right of the Fifty-eighth Virginia, the men of which were suffering from the fire of some Federal marksmen, who were under cover of a wood close by. He had just given the order to dislodge the concealed enemy by a charge of bayonets, when he was shot dead. The bullet which killed him was, it was said, fired from behind a fence, not many yards distant, aimed at him by a man who afterwards boasted of the deed. However that might be, the Confederate States had lost one of its brightest ornaments and bravest partisans.

Whilst General Ewell was doing such good work on his part of the field, another Confederate officer, General Taylor, was as actively engaged on the Federal left and rear, where, from the fierceness of the attack, he not only succeeded in diverting the enemy's attention from his front, but in concentrating the chief Federal force upon himself. To Taylor's gallantry and devotion was due in a great measure the success of that memorable day. Largely outnumbered in force, and attacked by the Federals, not only in front and flank, but with their heavy guns in position within point-blank range, the dauntless Taylor determined to carry the enemy's battery. To the astonishment of the Federals, his voice rang out:

"Charge!"

His men rushed forward at a run, and in another minute or two the Federal battery of six guns was his. But the Northerners were not going to lose their guns without another struggle, and charged in their turn. After a desperate hand-to-hand fight, the Federals retook their battery and drove out the Southerners. Taylor, however, only waited to breathe and reform his men, when he charged the guns for the second time, and again took the battery. Mad with rage and chagrin, the Federals once more rushed forward and recaptured their guns.

But Taylor was as obstinate as he was brave, and for the third time his men leaped into the battery and drove the equally gallant Federals out. Three times was this battery lost and won in the desperate and almost superhuman efforts on both sides to take and recapture it. At length the brave Confederates were overpowered by numbers, and, attacked both in front and flank, Taylor was compelled to evacuate the battery, and to fall back on the skirt of the woods.

The terribly hot work, however, in which he, unaided, had been engaged, had not escaped the notice of General Winder, who, having settled his own antagonists and rallied his men, marched to the support of his comrade in arms.

When Winder arrived within range, the Federals were moving upon Taylor's left flank, apparently with the intention of surrounding him in the wood, but Winder at once opened fire upon the enemy, checking his advance.

The final struggle was now to come. Taylor, finding himself reinforced by Winder, in turn, pushed forward, the Confederate artillery at the same time opening a steady and well-directed fire from their guns upon the enemy. The Federals stood their ground for a brief space, hesitated, and then fell back. They had had enough of fighting for that day, and in a few minutes after Winder came up Shields' army was in full retreat. Another crushing defeat had been inflicted on the North by "Stonewall" Jackson. The battle of Fort Republic had been lost and won, and the Confederate forces were again victorious.

CHAPTER XV

CAPTURE OF PERCY WYNDHAM—JACKSON'S OPINION OF TURNER ASHBY—THE MARCH ON RICHMOND—THE BATTLE OF GAINES'S MILLS, AND THE DEATH OF WHEAT

LIKE many others, Lieutenant MacIver had a long day in the saddle at the fiercely-contested battle of Fort Republic. The Confederate cavalry were soon in full pursuit of the retreating Federals, and took some four hundred and fifty prisoners, and what remained of Shields' artillery.

Whilst General Shields was in full retreat, the army of Fremont, which had been beaten the day before at the battle of Cross Keys, appeared on the opposite bank of the south fork of the Shenandoah, and opened fire from his guns upon Jackson's men. Fremont's artillery practice, however, had little effect upon his victorious foe. Finding that he could not do much hurt, Fremont withdrew his force the next day, and returned down the Valley of Virginia.

During the battle of Fort Republic, Percy Wyndham was taken prisoner, with the whole of his regiment, the 1st New Jersey Cavalry. As Colonel Wyndham, as a prisoner, was passing the command of General Wheat, the latter officer recognised his old Garibaldian comrade, and called out:

"Ah! Wyndham, my boy, I am sorry to see you engaged in such a bad cause. I never thought you would have fought against us."

"Neither did I, Wheat," replied Wyndham. "And I confess that I am sorry, too. I should have preferred to be with you but for circumstances placing me where I am."

Percy Wyndham was shortly afterwards exchanged, and little more was heard of him during the war. Subsequently, when peace was proclaimed, he returned to England, where he met a wealthy Indian lady, whom he married. He accompanied his wife to the East, and met his death in a balloon whilst engaged on some scientific experiments.

The battle of Fort Republic was the close of "Stonewall" Jackson's campaign in the Virginian Valley. He was hailed as the most successful of Confederate Generals. In a little more than a fortnight he had defeated three strong Federal armies, and had swept the Valley of Virginia of the presence of Northern soldiers. But besides the prestige which he had won for himself, and the loss he had inflicted on the enemy, he had rendered an incalculable benefit to his own cause. By the check which he had given to the Northern Commanders, he had entirely thwarted their purpose to surround Richmond by large converging armies.

There was one thing that seemed to mar Jackson's satisfaction at his signal victory at Fort Republic, and that was the loss of Turner Ashby. The chief appeared to feel his death acutely. Jackson was a very reserved man, and the way in which he wrote and spoke of the deceased officer surprised many. The following words from the General's pen referring to the dead man are on record :

"As a partisan officer I never knew his superior. His daring was proverbial; his power of endurance almost incredible; his tone of character heroic, and his sagacity almost intuitive in divining the purposes and movements of the enemy"

On the twelfth of June—four days after the battle of Fort Republic—Jackson encamped with his army near to a place known as Weyer's Cave. A few days later he received orders to move forward towards Richmond, and he at once commenced his march for the capital with part of his army, leaving Ewell behind him. A great contest for the possession of Richmond was expected by the Confederate Government. General McClellan with a large army was threatening it, and it was felt that Jackson's presence could not be longer dispensed with. He alone was a tower of strength, and the very echo of his name seemed to ensure safety.

MacIver did not then accompany General Jackson's command to Richmond, although fate willed that he was to follow quickly. The Lieutenant remained with General Ewell's division, but attached to Trimble's brigade. General Ewell had orders to follow his chief—who was pushing on to Richmond by forced marches—as rapidly as possible with his division, and lost no time in obeying the command.

A few days after "Stonewall" Jackson's departure

Lieutenant MacIver was sent on after him by Captain Brown, Assistant-Adjutant-General to Ewell. He was the bearer of despatches to his chief from the latter General, and reached Richmond safely, although he had one or two narrow escapes from falling into the enemy's hands. On the same evening that he arrived at the encampment, close to Gaines's Mills, with his despatches, he slept in the tent of the General—"Stonewall" Jackson—lying down across the entrance. This was on the twenty-sixth of June, the night before the battle of Gaines's Mills.

The morning following his arrival, "Stonewall" Jackson gave MacIver a letter of introduction to the celebrated Confederate cavalry leader, Major-General Stuart. The note recommended him to the notice of the latter commander as a gallant and highly intelligent young officer, whose interest was to a certain extent with the South. It concluded by requesting Stuart to place the Lieutenant in any position which might be of benefit to the cause in general.

When MacIver reached Major-General Stuart's headquarters, the battle of Gaines's Mills had already commenced, and the handsome cavalry leader, in the gay costume which he so much affected, was about to mount his charger. Although there might seem, under the circumstances, but scant time for ceremony, General Stuart received his visitor with that courtesy which he extended to all officers, whatever their rank.

"All that I can do for you at present, Mr. MacIver," said Stuart, after he had read Jackson's letter, "is to place you temporarily on my staff. If I mistake not I shall find you plenty of work before the day is out."

MacIver briefly thanked the General, and that was all that passed on this his first interview with the gallant Stuart, who, from his dashing exploits, had been named the Rupert of the South.

The battle was soon at its height, and as Stuart had promised, his new Aide had as much galloping to and fro as his horse could well get through. Oddly enough, almost the first person whom he recognised that he knew was his old friend Bob Scott, who had been his second in the Neapolitan duel and his close companion while with Garibaldi in Italy. Scott was now serving as a lieutenant in the Eighth Alabama—Wilcox's brigade—and, as MacIver subsequently heard, had won for himself the reputation of being the best marksman in the Confederate Army of Virginia. Bob and Ronald had no time for anything but a smile and a nod just then; but even that was a pleasure to both, and reminded them of the old days.

There was another dear friend of MacIver's present at the battle of Gaines's Mills, and upon whose kindly face he was to look his last that day. This was General Wheat, the hero of many a field, who was now fighting his last fight. Poor Wheat, under a heavy fire, was leading on his regiment, the Louisiana Tigers, and had just given the order to "charge," when a rifle bullet struck him in the forehead, and he fell back into the arms of one of his men, dying in a few moments. The last words that he uttered were:

"BURY ME ON THE FIELD."

At the time when his friend General Wheat was advancing with his regiment, MacIver was carrying an order to a distant part of the field. He was on his way back to rejoin his chief, and was close to the Louisiana Tigers when Wheat was hit. So near at hand, in fact, was MacIver, that he had to reign up his horse to let the "Tigers" pass before him in their charge, and was within a few feet of Wheat when he fell back mortally wounded. As he looked down upon the dying man he fancied there was a smile of recognition.

It was perhaps well for the feelings of MacIver that duty at once called him away from the dead man's side. He had a sincere regard for Wheat as a soldier and a gentleman, and in calmer moments would have been much shocked by his sudden death. The battle-field, however, is the last place for the indulgence of sentiment, and he was obliged to ride off almost as soon as he realised that his friend was killed. But, although MacIver could not remain, there were other tender hands hard by—rough soldiers though they were—to render the last offices to their late commander, and to carry the dead General to the rear. Meanwhile the battle was being fiercely contested on both sides. Federals and Confederates struggled stubbornly for mastery, and many a brave man besides poor Wheat bit the dust that midsummer day.

The battle had raged furiously for two hours before Jackson reached the field, but when he did appear his men swept on with a force there was no resisting. During the heat of the fight, the canopy of smoke was so thick that the sun was quite

I

obscured; while the clouds of dust raised by the advancing and retreating squadrons of cavalry was almost blinding.

Before the day was out the enemy's troops were driven back on every side, their batteries stormed, and their breastworks and entrenchments taken. Fourteen pieces of artillery were captured, and although fresh Federal troops were continually arriving, and repeated attempts were made to rally the Northerners, it was all in vain. In every direction the Federal troops were forced back with slaughter, and when night put an end to the pursuit it fell upon a great Confederate victory. Dead and wounded marked each spot where a stand had been made by the enemy, and the field over which he had retreated was strewn with the slain.

Stuart's cavalry made repeated and brilliant dashes. The gallant General frequently led the charges in person, inflicting severe punishment on the enemy. MacIver took part in most of these desperate encounters, and saw as much real fighting on that one day as few men would like to look on again.

CHAPTER XVI.

THE SEVEN DAYS' FIGHTING ROUND RICHMOND — THE FIGHTING AT SAVAGE STATION, FRAZER FARM, AND MALVERN HILL—THE BATTLES OF CEDAR RUN AND MANASSAS—MACIVER WOUNDED AND TAKEN PRISONER

THE Confederate victory at the battle of Gaines's Mills had forced General McClellan from his original stronghold on the north side of the Chickahominy, and it was somewhat prematurely presumed by the Southern officers that the enemy, surrounded as he was by their troops, would be unable to extricate himself from his awkward position by any other means than by that of capitulation. General Lee and his lieutenants no doubt had good grounds at the time for this supposition, but their expectations were entirely upset by the want of a little caution. Owing to the imperfect watch kept by the Confederate vedettes on General McClellan's movements, the Federal Commander succeeded in massing his entire force, and in making a masterly and successful retreat. Nevertheless, he was compelled in his haste to destroy a vast supply of stores, and to leave behind him at his late position a large quantity of clothing, and most of his camp equipage. So cleverly, however, had all McClellan's arrangements been carried out, that it was not until daybreak that it was revealed to the Confederates that their enemy had stolen a march upon them.

As soon as the retreat of the Federal army was discovered, General Lee at once ordered Generals Huger and Magruder in pursuit. The latter officer was to follow the Williamsburg Road, with the idea that he would be able to attack McClellan in his rear, whilst Huger, whose route was the Charles City Road, was instructed to take the Federals in flank. At the same time "Stonewall" Jackson was ordered to cross with his command at Grapevine Bridge, and move down the south side of the River Chickahominy. Operating with Jackson was a body of General Stuart's cavalry, to which for the time being Lieutenant MacIver was attached.

General Magruder was so successful in carrying out his instructions, that he came up with and routed the rear guard of the enemy at Savage Station, but, unfortunately, "Stonewall" Jackson had been delayed in his pursuit, owing to a misapprehension as to the movements of the Federal army. When he found out his mistake, General Jackson at once commenced a forced march, hoping to come up with the enemy before an engagement took place; but whilst he was hurrying forward with all haste, an action was being fought at Frazer Farm. Here McClellan was again defeated with great slaughter, although he was superior in numbers to the Confederates, and had posted his troops in a very strong position.

"Stonewall" Jackson, however, on the first of July, reached the battle-field of the previous day. He had succeeded in the difficult task of crossing the White Oak Swamp with his men, and arrived in time to capture a part of the Federal artillery and a number of prisoners.

General Jackson was ordered to continue the pursuit of the retreating enemy, and came up with McClellan at Malvern Hill, where the Federal Commander had again turned at bay. Here his position, with the river at his back, seemed almost impregnable. He not only occupied a high range in a formation of great natural strength, where his powerful artillery was protected by earthworks and strong masses of infantry, but had the assistance of the Federal gunboats on the river, which could easily rake the lines of the Confederates with their heavy guns. Moreover, to carry the position the Southern troops must advance through swamps and over broken ground.

Nothing dismayed, the dauntless Jackson made his preparations for fighting a pitched battle. He formed his line with General Whiting's division on his left, and General D. H. Hills' on his right, a brigade of Ewell's occupying the interval. Never, perhaps, was a more courageous attack, nor a more desperate defence. In all the sanguinary engagements which took place between the North and the South, not one, perhaps, was so fiercely contested as this terrible battle of Malvern Hill. Charge after charge did the Confederate troops make to carry the enemy's guns; each time to be repulsed with deadly slaughter on both sides, and again to be renewed until the field was literally red with human gore.

Although greatly outnumbered, the tide of success had been once more with the Confederates, yet when night set in the battle had not been actually won. Part of General Ewell's and Jackson's own division was held in reserve, as were the commands of Longstreet and D. H. Hills; the two latter Generals taking no part in the engagement.

McClellan retreated during the night, the great army with which he had threatened Richmond being almost annihilated. In one week the Confederates had routed their enemy in battle after battle, had taken more than ten thousand prisoners, including several officers of high rank, and captured or destroyed stores valued at millions of money. They had acquired, too, thirty-five thousand stand of arms and fifty-two pieces of artillery. It was a proud hour for General Lee and his lieutenants, and there was great rejoicing amongst the Southern people at their success against an army much superior in number and equipment.

The series of defeats which General McClellan had sustained led to his immediate removal from the command of the Federal army by President Lincoln's Government, and to the appointment in his place of General Pope. A more unfortunate selection of a successor to McClellan could not have possibly been made. Pope was the greatest braggart that ever wore a sword, and totally incompetent to command an army in the field. If boasting would have won, there would soon have been an end to the war after the organisation of another Federal army by Pope. His address to his men was full of egotistical bluster and of vain boasting as to how he would thrash the Confederates whenever they could muster courage to meet him. He was to be brought face to face with them sooner, perhaps, than he liked or had anticipated.

General Jackson arrived, on the ninth of July, within eight miles of Culpepper Fort House, and found that the new Federal army, under Pope—with Banks for his lieutenant—was posted near Cedar Run, a short distance north-west of Slaughter's Mountain. This proximity of the opposing armies speedily brought about a battle.

It was now that young MacIver, who had been engaged in most of the fighting since the battle of Gaines's Mills, had a narrow escape from death. He had moved with the cavalry round to Gardenville and Cedar Mountain, and arrived in time to take a part in the battle of Cedar Run. The enemy was advancing in great force, and was feeling his way with a strong body of skirmishers. Young Captain Pelham, who commanded Stuart's Horse Artillery, was sent forward to hold the skirmishers in check, and at once opened fire with his guns. MacIver, who was with the battery, was sitting on horseback near to Pelham, when a shell burst close by, a piece of which struck him on the head. Although stunned for a few moments, the wound proved to be very slight, but an inch more, the surgeon said, must have killed him. He, however, gave little thought to his hurt, for the fighting was soon at its height.

After the Federal skirmishers had been driven back the battle opened with a heavy fire of artillery on both sides, which continued for about two hours. It was during this time that the gallant Confederate, General Winder, was killed. He was directing the movement of his own two batteries when he was struck.

The result of the battle of Cedar Run was scarcely at any time in doubt. Although again largely outnumbered, fortune once more smiled on the victorious Jackson. Pope and Banks were defeated with great loss, and driven back over the Rappahannock to Fredericksburg. It was a flight rather than a retreat, yet the braggart Pope, although he had seen his men flying for their lives from a field where their comrades had been slaughtered by hundreds and hundreds, boasted that he had "licked" the Southerners.

After the Federals were driven back, MacIver was stationed at Hanover Court House for about three weeks. Here he again met Lieutenant Scott and several of his old friends. It was about the last that he was to see of poor Bob Scott, who died gallantly at the battle of Gettysburg.

About the middle of August Major-General Stuart moved on towards Verdiensville. With him were

Major Fitz-Lee, Captain Mosby, and Lieutenants Gibson, MacIver, and Dabney. The last-named officer was from Lynchburg, and was a great friend of MacIver's.

Shortly after the Confederate victory at Cedar Run it became apparent to General Lee that Pope's army was being largely augmented, and that preparations were being made on an extensive scale for some important movement. Lee, forewarned in time, quietly awaited the coming events.

On the twenty-ninth of August the armies of the North and South met once more on the plains of Manassas. The battle commenced at once, and was fiercely contested on both sides during the day, but when night put an end to the fighting success was slightly in favour of the Confederates.

During this first day's engagement at Manassas, Lieutenant MacIver was wounded in the wrist and taken prisoner by the enemy. He had been ordered on scouting duty in the morning by General Stuart, but towards evening charged with the cavalry under Fitz-Lee.

So furious was the onslaught of the Confederate troopers, that they penetrated and passed through a large body of the enemy's cavalry. On returning, however, a portion of Fitz-Lee's command was outflanked and cut off. MacIver was with the latter, and having been disabled by a pistol bullet passing through the wrist of his sword-arm, he was taken prisoner with several others.

On noticing that his right arm was hanging useless at his side, his captors took him on the heights with the other prisoners, where his wound was dressed by one of the surgeons. This gentleman turned out to be an Irishman who had entered the Federal service, and to his skill, and for the great attention which he gave to MacIver's wound, the latter was much indebted.

His arm having been made as comfortable as possible, he was immediately marched off. As the prisoners passed through the ranks, the Federal soldiers abused and scoffed at them, and, inhuman as it may appear, these Confederate prisoners, by order of General Pope, were taken to positions on the field most exposed to their own—the Southern—fire, and kept there for more than an hour, until the Federals were driven back themselves. After this the prisoners were marched to Fairfax Court House.

Meanwhile, as we have before mentioned, General Lee was having the best of it, until darkness put an end to the engagement. When on the following morning, the thirtieth of August, the action was resumed, both sides commenced with a heavy fire of artillery, which was kept up for many hours. In fact, the greater part of the second day's battle was fought with the batteries of heavy guns.

But at length General Lee ordered his line to advance, and when regiment after regiment charged with the bayonet, the battle was won. Nothing could withstand the onslaught of these serried ranks of glistening steel. With brilliant effect the Confederate infantry swept on, and then a panic seized the Federals, and they turned and fled. Never in the war was a more brilliant victory on the one side, or a more disastrous defeat on the other. The Federals, in their flight, were shot down or trampled to death by their pursuers. As the panic-stricken masses of fugitives were driven across Bull's Run many were literally dragged or crushed under the water by the frenzied men pressing and trampling upon each other.

Besides the fearful slaughter of Federal soldiers, the North lost during the series of engagements on the Manassas Plains twenty thousand stand of arms, thirty pieces of artillery, and an immense amount of stores. As to the wounded, killed, and prisoners, they were estimated at fully twenty-five thousand men.

CHAPTER XVII.

LIEUTENANT MACIVER TAKEN TO ALEXANDRIA—MEETS AND IS RECOGNISED BY HIS FORMER JAILER—LEE'S OPERATIONS IN THE ENEMY'S TERRITORY

FROM Fairfax Court House the Confederate captives were transferred to Alexandria as prisoners of war. They experienced no further ill-treatment after the first day of their capture. No doubt General Pope would have liked to have vented his spite and ill temper upon them if he had had the opportunity. To show the character of the man, and his savage nature, we may mention that early in July, Pope, in conjunction with General Steinwehr, issued an order directing that all civilians found guilty of violating their oath of allegiance by siding with the Confederates, should be shot.

Pope, however, never carried his infamous instructions into effect, for immediately on its being made known, President Jefferson Davis directed that Generals Pope and Steinwehr, and all commissioned officers under their command, should cease to be considered soldiers, or entitled to the benefit of cartel if taken prisoners. If any such were captured they were to be held over, so that in the event of any unarmed citizen of the Confederacy being murdered, with or without trial, under the pretence of being spies or hostages, or on any other pretext, an equal number of the Federal prisoners should be shot by command of the Confederate General-in-Chief.

President Davis added that this order did not extend to Federal private soldiers, nor to any other divisions of the Federal Army except those of Pope and Steinwehr.

On arriving at Alexandria—where, the reader will probably remember, he was confined shortly after his arrival in America, on suspicion of having Southern proclivities, and from which prison he managed to escape—MacIver was somewhat dismayed to find himself face to face with his old jailer. Although his appearance was no doubt much changed by the uniform of a Confederate cavalry officer, which he now wore, he saw that the man recognised him as his former prisoner the instant that they met. Greatly to his satisfaction, however, neither at their first interview nor subsequently did the man betray his past knowledge of him.

Probably the jailer, although in the Federal pay, had Southern sympathies, for he kept a still tongue in his head, and also allowed MacIver to go into the prison-yard and to bathe his wound, which was then very painful. Of course, under the arrangement which existed for the exchange of prisoners of war, the Lieutenant was eligible for the cartel, and knew that he would not be kept long in confinement. He waited anxiously for his release, which, although not long delayed, and counted but by days, seemed to him an age.

We must leave MacIver for a time in his uncomfortable quarters, and return to the victorious General Lee, who, after the signal defeat of Pope at Manassas, carried his operations into the enemy's territory. Pursuing the flying Federals, he followed closely upon them until at last General Pope's army—or what was left of it—reached Centreville and the strongly-defended lines of Washington, before which the Confederate General was compelled to halt.

Finding their capital actually threatened by the victorious Southerners, the Federal Government hastily recalled General McClellan, who had landed with his beaten army at Acquia Creek. Pope was removed from his command, and it was proposed that McClellan should supersede him.

General Lee now at once hurried up the river, and crossed the Potomac into Maryland, in the hope that the inhabitants of this neutral State would rise *en masse* and join him. But the spirited address which he issued to the people of Maryland was coldly received, and he found that his journey had been useless.

In the meanwhile General McClellan, who had been appointed to the command of the Federal forces in and around Washington, was calling in men and reorganising his army for a fresh campaign, it being intended that he should crush the daring Confederate General by mere might of numbers. At the same time General "Stonewall" Jackson was meditating an attack upon the Federal garrison at Harper's Ferry, which was held by twelve thousand men, besides being a place of great strength. Jackson had set his mind upon having this Northern stronghold, and was not one to be turned from his course by difficulties, however great and apparently unsurmountable.

We will now return to Lieutenant MacIver, who, on a day or two following his arrival at Alexandria, was with several other prisoners of war put on board a steamer, and taken down the Potomac and up the James River, and exchanged.

He then went on to Richmond for a week, when his wound continuing to improve, and he no longer being debarred from entering into active service—the ten days' cartel at once being at an end—he proceeded to Harrisonburg to report himself to General Stuart.

But although anxious to return to duty, he was quite unable to wield the sabre, his sword-arm being in a sling and almost useless.

On arriving at Harrisonburg he found the Confederates under Lee falling back on Sharpsburg, General McClellan, with a great army, being on the march from Washington with intention of giving battle to the Southern leader. General Stuart received MacIver very kindly, and congratulated him upon his release. At the same time he told him to go on to Winchester until his wound was quite healed, and he was fit to resume duty.

The Lieutenant, however, entreated the General

to allow him to remain, as a battle was expected to be fought next day, remarking that although not able to wield the sabre, he was strong enough for work in the saddle. So, after some further demur, Stuart consented.

On the thirteenth of September, three days before MacIver's arrival at Harrisonburg, General Jackson had succeeded in investing Harper's Ferry. His attack upon the garrison began at dawn. He opened with a heavy fire from his main battery, and also simultaneously from the others which he had placed on Maryland and Loudon Heights.

Jackson's fire was so well sustained, and his gunners made such good practice, that in about two hours the garrison surrendered. It was a rich prize the Confederate General had won by his valour. Besides the twelve thousand prisoners, he took an immense amount of military stores, thirteen thousand stand of small arms, and seventy-three pieces of artillery.

On the seventeenth, four days after Jackson's capture of Harper's Ferry, General McClellan came up with General Lee, and the latter gave his old opponent battle at a place on the Potomac called Antietam, near to Sharpsburg. McClellan had no less than ninety thousand men, whilst Lee's command did not exceed forty thousand. As the sun rose the batteries on each side opened fire, and soon the two armies were hotly engaged.

This battle had nearly proved MacIver's last, as he was so dangerously wounded that for a time the doctors had little or no hope for him. He had conveyed an order from General Stuart to Captain

Pelham for the latter to open fire from his guns from a certain position. Pelham, who had just received the message from the Aide, was moving his battery into action, when a heavy force of Federal cavalry appeared on his left flank.

The gallant young artillery officer, who was supported by a squadron of Confederate cavalry, wheeled rapidly round, unlimbered his guns, and opened fire on the Federal troopers. By the time this manœuvre was carried out, the enemy's cavalry were so close to Pelham's battery that they opened a revolver fire upon the gunners. At this moment MacIver, who, although he could not use a sabre, had drawn his revolver with his left hand in self-defence, was hit by a pistol shot. The bullet knocked out four of his upper front teeth, passing through the mouth, ripping the roof of the tongue, and finding its exit at the back of the neck, close to the jugular vein. For a few seconds the wounded man kept his seat in the saddle. Then he fell back into the outstretched arms of one of the troopers, the blood gushing from his mouth. Unfortunately the man missed his grasp, and MacIver rolled on to the ground, further hurting his injured wrist.

The remainder of the battle of Sharpsburg was stubbornly fought on both sides. It ended in a repulse of the enemy by the Confederates, although both sides claimed the victory. The Confederate soldiers were greatly exhausted by the terrible struggle for mastery. The loss of the Northerners must have been very large.

Lee, on his side, had two thousand killed and six thousand wounded. Included amongst the killed were two Southern general officers—Stark and Branch. Lee now crossed the Potomac and returned into Virginia. General McClellan, from the loss he had sustained in the battle, and after the capture of Harper's Ferry by Jackson, did not think it prudent to follow, although his army was so superior in numbers, and he claimed for himself a victory over his enemy. For some time he remained inactive, until at length he began to advance towards Richmond, following the eastern slope of the Blue Ridge Mountains.

Lieutenant MacIver, after his desperate wound, was carried from the field of battle in a senseless condition, and taken to a plantation not far from the spot where had been fought the late action. The wounded man was left under the charge of a gentleman, a planter, the ladies of whose family kindly undertook to nurse him. His wound, however, was considered so dangerous that the surgeons had but little hope of his recovery, but they lost no time in commencing operations. It was necessary that a silver tube should be placed in the throat to enable him to take the necessary sustenance, and this had to be procured from the nearest city. The agony which he suffered for some time was very hard to bear up against, but at length he progressed towards recovery, and the pain left him. Yet so weak and weary was he that he seemed to hang between life and death. In fact he was ill for six weeks, and it was nearly a month later before he was convalescent.

CHAPTER XVIII.

CAMP LIFE AT WINCHESTER—THE END OF THE SIXTY-TWO CAMPAIGN—A NIGHT ADVENTURE ON THE MISSISSIPPI —THE CONFEDERATE BATTERIES AND THE FEDERAL GUNBOATS

AFTER recovering in a measure from his late severe wound, Lieutenant MacIver went to Winchester, Virginia, where, and in the vicinity, the Confederate army were encamped under General Lee. This was towards the end of the month of October, and after being so long absent from his comrades, MacIver was very glad to again meet many old friends and acquaintances. Amongst others whom he found at Winchester was the young artillery officer, Pelham, who had been promoted to the rank of Major for his gallantry before the enemy.

To this day General MacIver remembers with affectionate regard one kindly act of young Pelham towards him, when they were stationed together at Winchester. The Confederate officers and soldiers were sadly deficient in under-clothing, and although the Southern ladies devoted all their spare time to the knitting of stockings, making shirts, and providing other necessaries for the army, the men who were fighting the battles of their country were often put to what in after days seemed ludicrous shifts for a change of garments. One morning Major Pelham came to MacIver, and said:

"Mac, my boy, my sister has sent me two pairs of stockings from Alabama, and you must have a pair of them. Here they are," and he held out

K

before the Lieutenant's half-longing eyes what, under the hardships of a soldier's life, were a priceless treasure.

Much, however, as he required the stockings, MacIver did not like to take them from his friend, knowing that the Major wanted them badly enough himself; but Pelham, like the gallant soldier and good fellow that he was, insisted, and would take no denial from his comrade. It was such little acts as these that cemented more strongly the friendships formed during the war.

It was at this time that Lieutenant MacIver made the acquaintance of the Honourable F. Lawley, the special war correspondent of the *Times*, who was a guest at General Stuart's headquarters. This gentleman highly distinguished himself whilst in Virginia, winning the admiration of Stuart, his staff, and the whole of the Confederate commanders, for the quiet and courageous manner in which he carried out his duties—frequently under heavy fire—as "special" for the great English journal.

Bob Scott, also, was at Winchester, and one or two other ex-Garibaldians, besides several officers who had been MacIver's comrades in the cavalry or on the staff. When he was well enough to indulge in such meetings, many pleasant, jovial evenings did he spend in camp amongst these kindred spirits. Songs, anecdotes, stories, and old reminiscences enlivened the hours, and helped materially to pass away the time of inaction. Here, by the way, he again met poor Frank Vizetelly, a most amusing, gentlemanly fellow, and two or three English newspaper correspondents whom he had before known.

After the last great battle between Lee and McClellan in September, there was little or no fighting until the close of the year. In the meanwhile General Halleck had been appointed Commander-in-chief of the army of the North, and in November, by the authority of President Lincoln, he superseded General McClellan, and appointed General Burnside to succeed him. The latter officer decided to advance on Richmond with his army, and in the second week in December he crossed the Rappahannock near Fredericksburg, and took up his position between that town and the strongly-fortified lines of the Confederates. Two days afterwards, on the thirteenth of December, Burnside made a desperate attack upon the Southern forces, but being unable, after a severe and gallant struggle, to carry the position of the enemy, was compelled to fall back with enormous loss. As winter had set in, and he realised that the Confederates were too strong for him, General Burnside had no resource but to retreat. On Christmas night there was a tremendous fall of rain, and taking advantage of the darkness and the storm, the Federal General succeeded in crossing the Rappahannock by his pontoon bridges, undisturbed by the Confederates. The retirement of Burnside on Washington ended the campaign of the year sixty-two.

After remaining for about a month at Winchester, Lieutenant MacIver went to Richmond, where he stayed for a short time. He then received orders to proceed to Shrieveport, on the borders of Louisiana and Texas, to join the Trans-Mississippi Department, under General Kirby Smith. There he continued until the advance of General Banks early in the year, who was driven back with great slaughter beyond the Red River by General Dick Taylor.

As MacIver had never been really well since his wound at Sharpsburg, and the unhealthy climate of the Louisiana swamps was beginning to affect him, General Kirby Smith kindly decided to send him on to Richmond as the bearer of despatches to the Minister of War. It was a long and dangerous journey which was before him, yet he received General Smith's orders to hold himself in readiness to depart with inward satisfaction.

The first peril he had to encounter was crossing the Mississippi, a task of no little difficulty and danger then, as night and day the Federal gunboats were constantly flying up and down the great river on the look-out for the Confederates. The feat, however, had to be accomplished, and when MacIver made the attempt, a dark night favoured him and his companion—for he was not alone.

It was some hours after daylight had gone when he and his comrade—Captain Pike, a son of the celebrated General Pike, the great Missouri Indian fighter—rode up to a lonely hut on the banks of the Mississippi. Through threats and the promise of a substantial reward, the negro occupant had agreed to supply them with a small punt, and had promised to row the two Confederate officers across the broad river, now rolling dark and majestic under the canopy of night.

By the advice of the negro, however, the attempt was not to be made until midnight, and for a couple of hours or more the two officers had to while away the time with a smoke, or as best they could. As, wrapped in their horsemen's cloaks, Pike and MacIver stalked to and fro like two tall spectres in the darkness, more than once the light from the fires of a passing Federal gunboat threw a bright glare on the sombre waters of the mighty stream.

At length the time came when the attempt to cross should be made, and, guided by the negro, the comrades as quietly as possible led their horses down to the bank of the river, to the spot where the punt was moored, a little higher up the stream from the point where the hut stood. The boat was a frail cockle-shell of a thing, hardly fit to carry more than two people. A deathly silence reigned around, broken only by the lap of the waters, as Pike and MacIver took their saddles from their horses and gave them to the negro to place in the bottom of the punt.

It was arranged that Captain Pike should keep a look-out from the bow of the boat, MacIver sitting in the stern to hold the bridle reins of the chargers, which were to swim across behind the punt. There was some difficulty at first in forcing the horses into the river, but after one or two failures the poor animals took the water. The negro boatman pulled in a course slightly down stream with the current, and the chargers once off their feet gave very little trouble.

They must have reached about midway across, when MacIver, who, with a bridle rein in each hand, was intent on his duty of looking after the horses, was startled by a warning "Hist" from Captain Pike. At the same moment the negro ceased rowing, and MacIver, turning his head, asked:

"What is it?"

"Hush!" replied Pike in a whisper; "be silent.

It is one of those confounded Yankee gunboats coming down the stream."

MacIver, as he crouched down in the stern sheets of the boat, listened, and then clearly enough he heard the sound of the approaching steamer. Presently, too, his eyes, which had become accustomed to the darkness of the night, made out the black hull of the gunboat apparently not more than a hundred and fifty yards away. A light flashed for an instant, and then was gone, and to his horror it seemed as if the steamer in her course must run down their little punt.

Almost before MacIver could realise all the danger of their position, the gunboat shot past with lightning speed, and so close to them that the back wash from her paddle wheels nearly upset the crank little punt, and caused the horses to struggle in the water with fright. Fortunately for the Confederate officers their boat was so low that they were passed undetected by the Federal watch, and like a black phantom of the night the steamer vanished in the darkness.

Half dead with terror, the negro was now pulling lustily towards the opposite bank, and MacIver speedily forgot their recent narrow escape in his anxiety for the horses. At length Pike had the satisfaction of making out the river bank looming dark above the water, and in a minute or two more they were safely landed. The horses, which seemed very little the worse for their long swim, were quickly resaddled, and the comrades mounting, rode rapidly away, leaving the friendly negro, with his well earned reward, to make his lonely journey to the Louisiana side of the river.

Their direct road, now that they were in the State of Mississippi, was towards the town of Jackson, which the comrades reached safely, although not without one or two adventures. Then they made their way down to Meridian. There they left their horses and took the train to Mobile in Alabama. At Mobile MacIver met some people whom he knew and was introduced to several others. However, he had not much time to remain, and proceeded direct by railway to Richmond, Virginia.

On reaching the capital, Lieutenant MacIver went at once to the War Office, where he delivered his despatches to Mr. Randolph, the Secretary. Subsequently the Minister granted him leave of absence for a month, in order that by rest he might recruit his health. It was on this visit to Richmond that he first heard, with great sorrow, of the death of his dear old friend, Bob Scott. He had risen to the rank of captain in his regiment—the 8th Alabama —and was shot in the leg at the battle of Gettysburg, whilst gallantly leading on his company in a charge on one of the batteries of the enemy.

The Federals were too strong for the 8th Alabama, which, after a desperate struggle to carry the battery, had to fall back, leaving some of the wounded on the field. Amongst them was Captain Scott, who was taken prisoner, and subsequently had his leg amputated. Either through some mistake or neglect on the part of the Federal surgeon, poor Scott had to undergo a second operation, the limb being taken off higher up, and under this he succumbed. He died the death of a gallant soldier, and his only regret was that he must leave behind him a young wife.

Only a few months before the battle of Gettysburg, Captain Scott had married, at Fredericksburg, a Miss Maggie MacDougal, a young lady of Scottish descent, although born in Virginia.

Besides poor Scott, there was another soldier in the 8th Alabama, Henry Herman, the now distinguished dramatic author, who was well known to MacIver during the war. This gentleman sacrificed a large fortune by joining the army of the South. He served both in the infantry and cavalry, and rising to the rank of lieutenant-colonel on detached service, fought with great gallantry, and was seriously wounded. Although an Alsatian by birth, no one could have shown greater devotion to the Confederate cause. After sacrificing all his wealth, Colonel Herman came to this country, and by his genius has now established a reputation as one of the most successful dramatists of the day.

When MacIver's leave was up, he received orders from the Secretary for War to return to the Mississippi, and to report himself for duty to General Adams, the cavalry leader. With Adams the Lieutenant was continually on the wing, moving from place to place. The General, shortly after his new officer had joined his command, appointed him Cavalry Drill-Instructor and Provost Marshal. The former office suited MacIver very well, but the latter was anything but to his taste. There were a number of Federal spies about, and but short work was made of these miserable adjuncts of war, if they chanced to fall into the hands of the Confederates. In his duty of Provost Marshal, these executions were very disagreeable to him, as at length he candidly told his Commandant. The General said that he regretted to lose so active and efficient an officer for that duty, but as it was distasteful to him he would recommend MacIver for promotion, and as soon as his captaincy was confirmed, he would appoint him to the command of a squadron.

During the time that Lieutenant MacIver was with General Adams, he took part in numerous cavalry dashes which were continually being made by the Confederate troopers upon the enemy. A favourite method of harassing the Federals used to be to take a battery of twelve or eighteen pounders down to the bank of the Mississippi at about midnight, and to suddenly open fire on any passing Federal gunboat or transport.

Of course the Federal seamen returned a shot as quickly as possible, but they were generally too late, for they had nothing to guide them in the darkness but the flash from the Confederate battery, and by the time that the Federals had brought their guns to bear upon the spot, their enemies had limbered up and galloped away, higher up, or lower down stream, as the case might be, to again open fire on the gunboat when she came within range.

As this occurred nightly, not much rest was obtained by the officers and soldiers of the army of General Adams. Besides this, there were many night attacks made on the camp by the Federal soldiery, and as General Adams was a man not to be outdone in politeness by his foes, these visits were, of course, duly acknowledged and returned, sometimes with results far from favourable, but more often they were attended with success.

CHAPTER XIX.

AN UNFORTUNATE ACCIDENT—CAPTAIN MACIVER RECEIVES ORDERS TO PROCEED TO EUROPE WITH DESPATCHES—RUNNING THE BLOCKADE—ARRIVAL IN ENGLAND

MacIver received his captaincy in due course, but, unfortunately, very shortly afterwards he met with an accident which, if not severe, was very painful and unpleasant, and again, much to his disgust, incapacitated him from duty. He was standing in the camp, one day, close to some cases of ammunition which had been taken out of a waggon, when suddenly a shell from the enemy dropped on one of the cases and exploded the contents.

The shots literally tore off one of his riding boots, and inflicted numerous flesh wounds below the knees. He was also burnt by the powder, and his hurts, though superficial, left large scars. Captain MacIver was not the only victim, for unfortunately two men were killed, and several wounded by the explosion. After he was able to get about again, he was invalided to Mobile for several months.

Whilst staying in that city the Captain received a letter from the War Office, requesting him to proceed to Richmond immediately, for the purpose of waiting upon Mr. Randolph, the Secretary. MacIver was at a loss to know why his presence was required in the capital in such haste, but he lost no time in obeying his instructions, and left Mobile without a moment's unnecessary delay.

On reaching the Government offices in Richmond, and reporting himself at the War Department, he was at once ushered into the presence of Mr. Randolph. The Minister looked up as he entered.

"Ah, Captain MacIver," he said, "I am glad to see you. As I was aware that you knew Europe well—and that your health not being at all good, that a change would benefit you—I have mentioned your name to my colleague, Mr. Benjamin, the Foreign Secretary. He has asked for an intelligent officer to proceed to England, and from what I had seen and heard of you, I recommended you for the mission."

MacIver briefly thanked the War Minister for his kindness, and Mr. Randolph touching the bell, a non-commissioned officer entered, who was told to conduct Captain MacIver to the Foreign Secretary's room. Mr. Benjamin, who had probably expected his visitor, informed MacIver in a few words that he required him to proceed to Europe, as the bearer of despatches to be conveyed to Mr. Mackay, the Confederate agent in London, and that his papers would be ready on the morrow.

This was MacIver's first interview with Mr. Benjamin, the Confederate Foreign Minister, who during the unhappy struggle between the Northern and Southern States of America so ably and conscientiously performed the arduous duties allotted to him, winning the respect of all parties, and even the commendations of his enemies. After the war was at an end, Mr. Benjamin came over to this country, and by his great talents soon became equally eminent at the English bar, gaining in the end a very large practice and a Queen's Counsel silk.

Unfortunately, some time back, Mr. Benjamin

met with an accident whilst in Paris, and he has since so suffered in health that he is compelled now to retire from the profession of the law. Could he have remained, doubtless he would have risen to be an ornament to the Bench, and probably might have obtained the very highest honours. By a curious coincidence, before sitting down to write these lines respecting this gentleman, we read that on the last day of this month of June a complimentary dinner is to be given in the Inner Temple Hall, by the members of the British Bar, to their brother of the gown, Mr. Benjamin, on his retirement from amongst them.*

On the morning following his interview with Mr Benjamin, Captain MacIver again called at the Foreign Secretary's Office, and had handed to him the despatches which he was to convey to Mr. Mackay. Somewhat to his surprise, too, but much to his satisfaction, he, on the same day before leaving Richmond, received from Mr. Randolph his commission as a Major of Cavalry.

After leaving the capital, Captain, or rather Major MacIver, as we must now call him, proceeded to Wilmington, in North Carolina, where he hoped to find a vessel about to run the blockade for Europe. In this, however, he was disappointed, but he found a steamer waiting for a favourable opportunity to evade the Federal cruisers, the destination of which was Bermuda.

The Major decided to take his chance in this vessel, and was detained a few days at Wilmington,

* Mr. Benjamin died not long after the above was written, deeply regretted by his numerous friends in England and America.

RUNNING THE BLOCKADE

until one dark night the captain of the blockade runner determined to put to sea. It was known that there were a couple of Federal ironclads outside the port, besides three or four fast Federal cruisers, and the master of the little steamer, whose long black hull lay very low in the water, stole cautiously along the coast.

With all steam up, but running at half speed, the blockade runner gradually left the lights of Wilmington behind her, the captain hugging the land as closely as he dared. Not a word was spoken on board above a whisper, and not the faintest glimmer of a light shown. But despite the silence that reigned amongst her people, the regular beat of the vessel's engines sounded ominously loud to Major MacIver, who stood aft near to the man at the wheel. There was a calm sea and but little breeze, and the motion of the vessel was scarcely perceptible as the steamer glided through the water, leaving a white line of foam in her wake.

The night, although dark, was clear, and hitherto there had not been a sign of a vessel but their own. Major MacIver, who was now leaning over the steamer's quarter, was beginning to think that after all they were displaying an amount of unnecessary caution, when suddenly there was a bright flash seaward, followed by a loud report, and the rush of some heavy body overhead.

Almost ere the sound of the first report had died away, there was a second flash and the deep boom of another heavy gun. The shots came from one of the Federal ironclads, but their range was too high, and they passed harmlessly over the blockade runner, which was now rushing through the water at full speed. Shot after shot followed in rapid succession, but each alike innocuously, and the saucy little steamer was fast running away from her huge enemy.

The ironclad ceased firing, but a few moments afterwards a rocket shot up in the sky, quickly followed by answering signals further out seaward. The captain of the Confederate steamer then changed his course, giving the land a good offing and taking advantage of the breeze, which had freshened, to get some sail on his ship. The little vessel now seemed to fairly fly through the sea, burying her nose in the water, and dashing the spray over her bows. But fast as she was, the captain knew that she was being chased by Federal cruisers as fleet, and probably in better trim, and that unless he could elude them in the darkness, it would be as much as he could do to hold his own, and should anything give way, there was no chance of escape when day broke.

Major MacIver was too much excited to turn into his berth, and all night long he paced the deck with the master of the steamer.

He had tied a piece of lead round his despatches, and when the firing was going on stood close to the ship's side, so that in case he was shot his papers might drop from his hand into the sea. At length a faint gray tinge in the east heralded the dawn of another day, and soon a stronger light spread over the face of the waters.

"Sail ho!" shouted a man with startling suddenness.

"Where away?" quickly asked the captain.

"A couple of points on the starboard quarter, sir," answered the seaman.

The master turned his glass in the direction indicated, where about three miles away a large vessel, under steam, was plainly enough visible to all eyes.

"Sail on the weather beam, sir," cried another voice.

"Keep her away a point or two," said the captain, having scanned the horizon for a minute or so with his telescope. "There's a couple more of the Yankee cruisers low down astern, but they are too far off to do us any mischief."

The Federal cruisers had evidently made out the blockade runner at the same time, for they too altered their course, and the nearer of the two fired a shot to try his range, which, however, spent itself a good half mile from the Confederate steamer. It was now a fair trial of speed, but although a stern chase is proverbially a long one, it soon became apparent to all on board the little vessel that the Federals were overhauling them, and that unless their steamer was lightened they must be captured. Speedily, by the captain's orders, the hatches were unbattened and all hands at work getting up the cotton. Bale after bale went over the vessel's side in quick succession, the master with his eyes fixed anxiously on the Federal steamers, and the mate with the log trying the speed of the ship. Presently the latter said:

"I think she'll do now, sir. We are beginning to show the Yankees our heels."

It was true. Lightened of some of her cargo, tho

swift blockade runner was in proper trim, and was gradually gaining on her pursuers, who continued to fire shot after shot. Ere many hours the Federal cruisers were hull down astern, and all danger past.

Major MacIver arrived safely at Bermuda, and from thence took an English steamer for Liverpool, which port he reached in due course. It was in the afternoon when the boat entered the Mersey, and he was in time to catch a train for London, getting up to town late at night. He, however, at once took a cab to Mr. Mackay's address, but found that the Confederate agent had gone to Paris.

That he might lose no time in delivering his despatches the Major sat up all night, starting for the Continent by the first train *viâ* Dover. On arriving in Paris he proceeded to Mr. Mackay's hotel, and was received by that gentleman's secretary, Captain Walsh, who at once conducted him to the Confederate agent's room. Major MacIver delivered his sealed despatches into Mr. Mackay's hands, the contents of which to this day he never knew, but, judging from the expression of the countenance of the Confederate agent, they must have been of great importance.

CHAPTER XX.

A NICE LITTLE PLOT INTERRUPTED—THE END OF THE AMERICAN WAR—MACIVER STARTS FOR MEXICO—ANOTHER FATAL DUEL

During his stay in Paris Major MacIver became the guest of Mr. Mackay, the Confederate agent for

Europe. A bedroom was provided for him in the same hotel, and on the night of his arrival in the French capital Mr. Mackay invited one or two Southern gentlemen besides Captain Walsh, the secretary, to meet him at supper.

This was neither the first nor second visit of Major MacIver to Paris, so that he was quite at home in that gay French city, and during the week he remained there, before returning to England, entered with great zest into all the amusements and enjoyments at his disposal. After the recent hardships of the campaign, Paris appeared all the more alluring.

When Mr. Mackay started for London, MacIver accompanied him, his instructions being to await the agent's pleasure as to the return of despatches to Virginia. As for a time there was nothing important to convey, the Major went on a visit to Scotland, Mr. Mackay being kept duly advised as to his whereabouts. Thus some time elapsed before he received an intimation from Mr. Mackay that he must return to America, as he had now important despatches ready for the Confederate Foreign Secretary of State.

As the readiest way to reach Virginia, Major MacIver took the steamer to Havannah, hoping on his arrival there that he should have no difficulty in finding a vessel about to run the blockade into one of the Southern ports. In this, however, he was mistaken, and had to remain in Cuba for a considerable time before he had an opportunity of leaving the island.

At length, after having been nearly tired out with

waiting, he heard of a little Spanish schooner which was about to sail for Matamoras, a port on the Rio Grande del Norte, in Mexico; from thence he anticipated no great trouble in making his way across Texas, and so down to Mobile.

Fortunately, as it afterwards turned out, two other officers—Colonel Smith and Captain Granger—had taken passage in the schooner, and Major MacIver made their acquaintance some days before sailing. Having obtained his passport for Matamoras, he went on board the schooner with his two new friends, each hoping for a speedy run across the Gulf.

However, shortly after sailing the little vessel met with calms, and the voyage was lengthened for over a fortnight. Meanwhile, when they were about half-way across, Major MacIver became seriously ill, and no doubt the symptoms were very like yellow fever, if it was not an actual attack of that dreaded disease, which that year had been very prevalent in the Havannah.

One morning, early, he was sitting on the quarter-deck of the schooner, feeling particularly unwell, sick, and miserable. He could not help noticing, too, that the Spanish seamen eyed him in a mysterious sort of way, looking at him suspiciously whenever they passed. The master and his mate at the same moment were holding a whispered conversation aloof from the rest of the crew, but glancing at the sick man from time to time. Suddenly, to his surprise, MacIver heard the Spanish captain say "Vomitica."

This much-feared word—which he could not doubt was applied to himself—was bad enough to hear, but he little knew that the Spanish master and his mate having no doubt that their passenger was suffering from yellow fever, were then and there hatching a plot to throw him overboard, so as to prevent the further spread of the infection.

Luckily for the Major's chance of life, the other two Confederate officers, Colonel Smith and Captain Granger, were on deck, and the Colonel, who fortunately understood Spanish well, overheard the nefarious scheme to murder their fellow-passenger. Neither of these gentlemen until then had suspected that Major MacIver was so ill; but they now at once conveyed him to his berth, and having the proper medicines at hand, and understanding their use, administered a strong dose to the patient.

Colonel Smith, after giving the first necessary attention to the sick man, left him in charge of Captain Granger, while he (the Colonel) walked quietly on to the poop, where the master and his mate were still holding deep converse. Addressing the two cowardly rascals in Spanish, Smith told them that he had overheard their plot to murder his fellow-passenger, and pulling out his revolver said he and Captain Granger had each of them two similar weapons loaded, and that if either the master or his mate, or any of the crew, dared to approach near Major MacIver's cabin, they would instantly be shot like the murderers they were.

"A tras canallas" (retire, wretches), thundered the Colonel in a fierce voice, "or I swear I will kill like a dog the first of you who dares to look me in the face."

The Spanish master and mate slunk off, and probably told the rest of the crew what had passed, for Colonel Smith and Captain Granger noticed that the seamen, after the discovery of this little plot to throw a living man into the sea, were much more respectful in their behaviour.

Whether it was the prompt administration of the medicine, or whether MacIver was really not suffering from the yellow fever, we cannot say; but certainly he grew rapidly better, and by the time they entered the Rio Grande, he was nearly convalescent.

The fiery-tempered Major was terribly enraged when he heard at Matamoras of the novel idea entertained by the Spanish master and his mate for getting rid of patients suffering from the yellow fever, and how nearly he had escaped being thrown overboard. He vowed vengeance against the captain, and swore he would shoot him the moment he put his foot on shore. The Spanish master, however, hearing this, and no doubt believing in the sincerity of his passenger's threat, did not give him an opportunity of carrying it into effect, for he put to sea again with his schooner without waiting to discharge cargo.

At Matamoras the Major parted from his friends, Colonel Smith and Captain Granger, with feelings of mutual regret at separating. He had to push on as quickly as possible with his despatches; and having purchased a capital mount, set out on his long ride through Texas, making towards Shrieveport, which at length he reached safely and without interruption.

From thence, without delay, he proceeded to Richmond, and delivered his despatches to Mr. Benjamin. This was in March, 1865, when the war was nearly at an end. The glorious success which had at first shone on the South had changed, and on the ninth of April in that same year, sixty-five, General Lee surrendered with the whole of his force to General Grant. Thus it was fated that the last order that Major MacIver was to receive came from Mr. Benjamin, the Confederate Foreign Secretary of State.

There had been great changes during his absence in Europe. Many of his old friends had been killed in battle or had died from wounds received in the terrible struggle, which had lasted no less than four years. Notable amongst those who had gone to their rest was the dashing young artillery officer, Pelham. No braver heart ever beat within man's breast than in that of the gallant lad—for he was little more either in years or looks—who played a part so nobly in all the battles fought on Virginian soil.

"Pelham the gallant" people loved to call him, and well did he deserve the proud title that had been given to him. His death was that of a soldier, speedy and glorious. He was in the act of cheering on a squadron of cavalry, which was charging past his battery, when he was shot dead. None of his friends regretted the gallant Pelham's death more deeply than MacIver, who had a sincere regard for the young artilleryman, and who still speaks of his dead comrade with mingled feelings of admiration and regret.

His old commander, too, General "Stonewall" Jackson, and a host of others whom he had known, were gone, and, now that the war was over, our friend had little to induce him to remain in the States. He had lost nearly all that he was worth, for the property on his plantations had been destroyed during the war, and what money he had was spent or wasted.

It was at this time that MacIver determined to devote himself to the profession of a soldier of fortune, and to offer the service of his sword wherever fighting was to be had. His first step was to sell his estates, which realised but little, considering their former value. There was only the bare land, and as all property was at a very low ebb at the end of the war, this went cheaply enough to the first bidder. It, however, supplied him with ample funds for a considerable time to come.

Major MacIver, in company with Captain Gillespie, of Virginia, and seven or eight others, had concluded to join the Mexican Imperial army, and started for Vicksburg with the intention of making their way through Texas, and crossing the Rio Grande at the spot most convenient for attaching themselves to the Emperor Maximilian's forces.

This may appear to the reader an extraordinarily roundabout route to take; but the whole country had been so exhausted of supplies, that it was questionable if by any of the more direct roads food for themselves and provender for their horses would be obtainable.

Now that the war was at an end, duels between Federal and Confederate officers became of frequent occurrence, scarcely a day passing in which a report of some such an affair did not appear in one or the other of the newspapers. Unfortunately, Major MacIver became one of the principals in two duels which took place close to Vicksburg. His first had a fatal termination, and resulted in the death of his antagonist, Major Tomlin, of Vermont, late of the United States Artillery Volunteers.

The dispute, of course, arose over something connected with the war which had just ended, and this led to a duel the next morning with swords, two friends of each party being present at the deadly encounter. Captain Gillespie acted as MacIver's second, and the fight came off in a wood in the neighbourhood of Vicksburg. The quarrel being a political one there was no chance of an amicable settlement, and after the usual preliminaries swords were crossed. For some little while both escaped scatheless, but presently MacIver cut his antagonist across the face with his sword, Major Tomlin replying with a fierce lunge, which the other parried. An instant afterwards MacIver ran Tomlin through the body, who fell, exclaiming:

"Gentlemen, I am killed!"

And in a few seconds Major Tomlin had expired. Then one of MacIver's Confederate companions called out:

"Come, Major, let us mount and go; these gentlemen will look after their friend."

A negro boy brought up the horses, but, before getting into the saddle, MacIver said to the late Major Tomlin's companions:

"Gentlemen, my friends are in haste to depart; is there anything I can do for you? I hope you consider that this matter has been settled honourably."

There being no reply just then the Confederates rode off. This fatal quarrel was ended as nearly as possible as we have described, and we are but reproducing a portion of a paragraph which appeared at the time in one of the American papers sent by a Vicksburg correspondent, who was an eye-witness of the duel.

CHAPTER XXI.

ANOTHER DUEL—ANECDOTES OF MACIVER—A FIGHT WITH THE INDIANS.

THE quarrel which unhappily had led to the death of Major Tomlin was not to terminate there. Two friends of the deceased officer who had been present at the fatal duel challenged Major MacIver and Captain Gillespie, to another meeting for the following day.

This time the weapons chosen were pistols, and the double encounter took place not far from where Major Tomlin was slain. We are not anxious to dwell further upon these two hostile meetings, and will merely mention, that in the second, as in the first, fortune was against the Northern officers.

This last was Major MacIver's third duel, and each time he had escaped scatheless. No doubt, in a great measure, this good fortune was due to a remarkable coolness and nerve when in danger or difficulty. It has been remarked by those who knew him well that whilst irritated and put out by the merest trifles—losing his temper at frivolous matters which most people would pass by with a smile—he would face a great peril or annoyance, with a calmness that was remarkable.

Colonel Montgomery, who is now in London, tells often with great glee a story of young MacIver's *sang-froid* when fired upon by a Captain Forrest at a quarrel over cards. This gentleman, Colonel Montgomery, was formerly an officer in our own artillery, and subsequently served in the Confederate army as Chief of the Staff to General Pemberton.

The quarrel to which he refers took place at the Battle House, Mobile. Several officers—including MacIver and Forrest, the latter of whom was a brother of General Forrest—were playing at cards at a game called "Poker." MacIver had been very unlucky for a time, but fortune changing, he won a considerable sum, which he allowed to remain on the table. As he was about to draw the money towards him for the purpose of placing it in his purse, Captain Forrest for some reason, either through a mistake or for annoyance, said :

"What are you going to do with that money? it is mine."

"I beg your pardon," replied MacIver, "you mistake, it is mine, and I am going to take possession of it."

As he drew the gold towards him, however, Forrest put out his hand to intercept it. MacIver pushed the Captain's hand on one side, and took up the money. Instantly, before any one could interfere, Forrest drew his revolver, and fired across the table at MacIver. The shot was intended for his head, but being aimed a little high the bullet just grazed the top of the scalp, afterwards burying itself in the ceiling of the room. The blood poured freely over both the forehead and face of MacIver, but he, leaning across the table, seized Forrest's hands, and after a brief struggle wrenched the revolver from his grasp. During this contest for the possession of the weapon it again went off, however, and the bullet, strangely enough, passed through the tobacco-pouch in the right-hand pocket of MacIver's trousers. This was at the time when the trousers used to be worn very wide—pegtops they were called—and the pockets were somewhat capacious.

MacIver now turned the muzzle of the revolver upon Forrest and pulled the trigger, but it missed fire (caps were then in use for revolvers), and as he examined the pistol he saw that these had dropped from the nipples, no doubt during the struggle.

"Well, my boy," said MacIver as he wiped the blood from his face, and turned to Forrest, "you have had your little game, and now I want mine. Give me a couple of caps and let me return your compliment."

History, however, does not record that Captain Forrest found the caps so obligingly asked for. How the affair ended we do not know. Colonel Montgomery entered just as Forrest fired his first shot, and accompanying him was General Polk, and no doubt these two prevented further hostilities. By the way, the career of this last-mentioned officer was somewhat romantic, and may be new to most of our readers. Having as a young man graduated at West Point Academy, he in due course joined the United States Army. After a time, however, he retired from the military service and entered the Church. Being popular as a preacher, and a good churchman, he at length became a bishop, and held that office at the outbreak of the war between the North and the South. Polk then at once took up arms on the Confederate side, and was appointed a General in the service.

MacIver, Captain Gillespie, and their nine companions left Vicksburg on their way to Mexico, in high spirits. Two or three of the party were late Confederate officers, as well as the Major and the Captain. They were men not only used to fighting, but to taking life as they found it, and being well armed and well mounted, anticipated no danger nor difficulty before them in their long march which they could not surmount. First taking a boat down to Galveston, their intended route then was in nearly a straight line through Central Texas towards El Paso.

As they advanced further on their journey, they had frequently to turn aside or to make long detours to avoid the hostile Indians, and on more than one occasion had a brush with their savage foes. A sharp look-out and the dread which the Red Men had of the American rifles and revolvers generally, however, kept the prowling Indians at a safe distance.

One of Major MacIver's companions was no stranger to backwood and prairie life, and being an old hunter, this person's experience proved very valuable to his party. He had also been in the United States Army as a scout, and had seen and participated in many a fight with Indians along the border-land, where such a thing as quarter was unknown, either to white or Indian; and where the most fearful atrocities were committed on both sides —for neither woman nor child received the least mercy—the whites often outdoing the Indians in cruelty. Owing to his experience, too, as a hunter, this man Leslie kept them well supplied with venison and other game on the march.

One night they encamped on the edge of the

forest, picketing their horses on the prairie, where the feed was plentiful, and close at hand. After supper they sat over the wood fire smoking and whiling away the time with stories of adventure. One by one they dropped off to sleep, each man with his rifle or revolver ready to his hand. Soon silence reigned within the little camp, broken only by the deep breathing of the sleepers, or the prolonged cry of some beast of prey. The night was very lovely, and although there was no moon, the brilliancy of the star-lit heavens made the surrounding objects visible for some distance, except where the great trees of the forest cast their sombre shade.

MacIver had no idea how long he had been asleep, although it seemed by the gleaming embers of the fire that it could not have been more than an hour or two, when he was awoke by his arm being lightly pressed, and a voice whispering in his ear:

"Don't move, Major, but turn your eyes towards that prickly pear-bush, just where the shadow from the trees meets the grass, and tell me what you make out."

The speaker was the ex-backwoodsman Leslie, who, with his rifle ready to fire, was lying at full length by MacIver's side. The latter, who was now wide enough awake, peered into the night, but he could make out nothing unusual, and confessed as much to his fellow traveller. The bush which the man had mentioned, was some fifty yards away, and its shape was plainly enough visible by the starlight.

"Hist!" ejaculated Leslie, and he brought his rifle into the line of sight.

The next moment there was a bright flash of light

and a sharp, ringing report. As the crack of the rifle sounded on the night air, from the spot which the backwoodsman had pointed out, a dark body bounded from the ground in its death agony, and an Indian fell back dead. Most of Major MacIver's comrades, awakened by the report of the rifle, had risen to their feet, and whilst they stood thus a horrible yell filled the air, and a shower of bullets whistled about them.

"Down, men," shouted MacIver, "and give them a volley from your rifles."

But it scarcely needed the Major's words. Every man had dropped flat upon the earth by the natural instinct of self-preservation. The Indians were upon them by hundreds, but were driven back by the rifle shots and the bullets from the revolvers. Leaving several dead and wounded behind them, they disappeared as silently as they had approached.

One of the white men had been hit, but his hurt was not serious, and he scarcely knew in the excitement of the moment that he was wounded. It was found to be a little past midnight, and by the advice of the ex-hunter it was determined to make a move. The horses were unpicketed, and the eleven white men were speedily in the saddle, and galloping rapidly across the prairies. All night long they rode without halting, hoping to thus escape the Indians, pulling up at length for their morning meal and to rest the horses under the shelter of a "corral."

They had scarcely, however, finished their breakfast, when it was reported that there was a large body of mounted Indians approaching, and although yet some miles away they were evidently on their track. MacIver made them out as they swept over the crest of a bluff, and calculated that there could not be less than three hundred men. To think of escaping by flight was entirely out of the question. There was nothing for it now but to wait their advance, and should they attack, to fight them as best they might under the shelter of the "corral."

Well armed as the white men were, it was, perhaps, possible to keep the Indians at bay as long as the ammunition should last. Possibly, too, they might inflict such loss upon their savage foes as to cause them to withdraw for a time, when MacIver and his friends might hope to escape either after night again set in, or at the first chance that presented itself.

The Indians swept on in gallant array, waving aloft their long spears, or shaking their rifles in defiance. Splendidly mounted, they skimmed over the ground, riding in a circle, and gradually coming nearer to their anticipated victims. The Red Men, however, were evidently not aware of the long range of some of the rifles carried by the "pale faces," for a Confederate officer picking off one of the chiefs who rode a little apart from his fellows, the Indians, in surprise and in some dismay, as it appeared, retired to a safer distance for consultation.

It was only for a few moments, however, for the entire body of the savages advanced with great boldness, still galloping in a circle, but at each circuit drawing nearer and nearer. Firing as they rode, they poured a hail of bullets and arrows amongst the little party of white men, but without inflicting much injury in their first attack.

Under the shelter of the "corral," MacIver and his friends were enabled to deal death amongst the Indians without much exposing their own persons. The Major had been appointed by general acclamation to the command, and impressed upon his men the urgent necessity of not wasting a shot, and making every bullet tell. For a time so well sustained was the fire of the eleven determined men, that, outnumbered as they were by thirty to one, they not only kept their foes at bay, but seemed likely to compel them to give up the fight. So many saddles had been emptied amongst the Indians, in fact, that after about an hour's engagement they withdrew to a spot where they were safe from the range of the white men's rifles, and where they again appeared to hold a council of war.

CHAPTER XXII.

A DESPERATE DEFENCE—AN ATTEMPTED ESCAPE, AND CAPTURE BY THE INDIANS—LIFE AMONG THE RED MEN

So far the loss amongst the white men had not been great. One of the Confederate officers had been killed by an Indian bullet, and three others of the party wounded, but not so seriously as to place them out of the fight, so that there were still ten men left in the "corral" determined to fight for their lives to the last. Neither Major MacIver nor Captain Gillespie had been touched, and five others had escaped scatheless. Amongst these latter was the ex-hunter, Leslie, who was a big, powerful fellow, and from his knowledge of Indian fighting quite a host in himself.

After about an hour's consultation and breathing time the Indians again advanced upon the "corral," but this time much more cautiously than on their first attack. Their head chief was very conspicuous, not only by his noble presence, but by his daring, and several of the white men tried to pick him off, but without success.

Again and again did the Indian braves advance to the attack, each time to be driven back with loss by the handful of white men. But on every fresh assault the number of the gallant little band of defenders was being gradually lessened, until, as the day wore on, it was indeed few of those that were left with life.

Throughout that long day the brave band of white men fought with the desperate resistance that has made the Anglo-Saxon race so famous. Each man, holding his life in his hand, sold it as dearly as might be, never yielding whilst he had power to strike a blow One by one the survivors saw their comrades breathing their life away, until when darkness set in, but three out of the eleven were left alive. These were MacIver, Captain Gillespie, and Leslie, the backwoodsman. All three were wounded but not one was *hors de combat*, and yet three men as they were, they had driven the Indians back in a final attack made just before nightfall.

The latter had suffered severely, the scene of the desperate encounter being strewn with the dead and wounded savages. Surrounded as they yet were by the Indians, escape to most men would have seemed next to hopeless; but as soon as it was quite dark, the Major and his two remaining companions determined to make the attempt.

Choosing the three staunchest and fleetest horses, MacIver, Gillespie, and the hunter rode silently forth from the "corral," each of them scarcely daring to breathe, lest he should be heard by the watchful savages. Proceeding at a walking pace for some distance, and hearing no sign of their escape being discovered, they put their horses at a gallop, trusting to their speed to evade pursuit, should the Indians find out before daylight that they had evacuated the "corral."

With the backwoodsman leading, and Major MacIver and Captain Gillespie following in Indian file, the three rode all night as fast as their horses could carry them. Twice or thrice they had paused for a few moments to listen for any signs of pursuit, but only to hurry on again at a greater speed to make up for the brief seconds of delay. Once during the night they crossed a small stream, and their guide—for the hunter knew the country through which they were travelling well—took the precaution to walk the horses down the brook for a good half-mile before again striking into the open.

The three fugitives waited anxiously for the first streak of dawn, and as soon as it was light enough to make out surrounding objects, Major MacIver swept the horizon with his field-glass. They had halted on a slight eminence, from whence a good view could be obtained, and to the delight of himself and companions the Major could not discern any sign of Indians in the neighbourhood.

The three now concluded that they might breathe

M

their poor horses with comparative safety, and they proceeded for some miles at a more leisurely pace. Still, all danger of pursuit they knew was not at an end, as the Indians, panting for revenge, might follow up their trail for days; and they pushed on with all haste until noon. They then decided to halt for a short while. Their wounds were becoming stiff and very painful; they were worn out with fatigue, and had not tasted food since the previous morning. Pulling up at a spot where they had the advantage of water, and from whence they could command a view of the open prairie, they picketed their horses in the midst of a luxurious pasture.

Neither MacIver nor Gillespie had given a thought to food, and had left their wallets behind them in the "corral," but their guide had fortunately—taught by his experience of a trapper's life—provided enough for the three. After they had satisfied their hunger they bathed their wounds in the cool stream, and found almost immediate relief from that stiffness and discomfort which accompanies an unattended hurt.

Their first meal nearly exhausted their guide's wallet, and what they were to do for more food was a difficult question to solve. There was plenty of game about, but they durst not fire a shot, as their lives possibly might be sacrificed by such an imprudence. However, they required nothing for the present, and after a rest of a couple of hours they again rode on. If all went well, in one day more they might hope to cross the Mexican frontier, and as hour after hour went by and still no sign of Indians, they almost forgot their wounds and the late desperate struggle for life in the hope of the future before them.

It was getting well on in the afternoon when the three companions struck the edge of a large forest, along the border of which they skirted for three or four miles. Their view of the country was now much circumscribed, and the ex-hunter travelled with all the caution and watchfulness of an Indian scout. It wanted but a couple of hours of sunset, and Captain Gillespie laughingly remarked:

"Well, I reckon we have thrown those thieving Indians off the scent this journey."

Scarcely had he spoken when the backwoodsman halted and held up his hand as a sign for caution. At first the two officers could hear nothing unusual, but presently both thought that the sound of galloping horses reached them, as from a distance. Quickly dismounting, their guide led his horse within the shadow of the forest, Major MacIver and Captain Gillespie following his example.

As, concealed from view, they now listened, each moment the sound they had heard seemed to approach nearer, and it was no question that it was the rushing and thudding of unseen hoofs. Presently in the direction which they had come, but farther away on the open, as it might be in a route parallel with the path they had traversed, rose a cloud of dust, from which, as in a picture, emerged a long line of horsemen, their spears and shields glistening under the fast-sinking sun.

MacIver, with the eye of a cavalry man, saw at once that there were at least two hundred of them, and in his own mind had no doubt that they were their late foes in hot pursuit. His two companions agreed with him; but the question now was, would the Indians pass by without detecting them? This hope was soon cast to the winds, for the Red Men were seen to extend their line like a body of skirmishers, although in this instance their object was to search for or take up the trail of the white men they were pursuing.

A prolonged savage yell from the Indians warned MacIver and his two companions that their trail was discovered, and that they would in a few minutes have their foes upon them. A consultation was at once held as to what should be done; escape was now out of the question, and their capture or perhaps death was merely a matter of time.

MacIver and Gillespie were for resisting to the last, but the more wary hunter advised that they should all three walk quietly out of the forest, mount their horses, and ride forward to meet the Indians. As to any immediate danger threatening their lives, he said they had little to fear, and before the time came for the savages to carry out their vengeance, they might manage to effect their escape.

The two officers felt that the advice was prudent, and they at once proceeded to carry out their companion's scheme. At the sight of the three white men the Indians again gave a great shout, but whether of elation or of annoyance they could not tell.

At a signal given by the chief, about a dozen braves rode up to the white men, and finding that they offered no resistance, their arms were tightly bound with thongs of buffalo hide, but little care being given as to any pain that might be caused to a wounded limb.

With their horses' heads towards the setting sun, the Indians now rode rapidly on with their prisoners, continuing the march well on into the night, when they halted until daylight. The prisoners were lifted from their horses, but their arms were still kept tightly fastened, until the morning meal, when for a short while they were unbound.

For a day more they were in the saddle, and early on the second morning after their capture they approached the Indian village. They had rested for many hours on the preceding night, and their horses being fresh, the younger braves indulged in various equestrian feats as they neared their home. Most of the wigwams were permanent structures, but other dwellings were formed by tents of buffalo hide bleached to a snowy whiteness. It seemed to the prisoners that all the inhabitants of the place must have turned out to meet them. Hideous old squaws, comely Indian maidens, youths armed with knives and tomahawks, and little children that could scarcely toddle, lined the road.

The prisoners were taken to a wigwam nearly in the centre of the village, and here their arms were unbound; but a strict watch was kept over them, a dozen Indian braves being on guard night and day. So far they were not badly treated, and their wounds being dressed with some Indian simples, began rapidly to heal. Yet, that a terrible fate was before them, unless escape should offer, not one of the three doubted. In their desperate defence of their lives at the "corral" a great number of the Indians had been shot, and now there must be other victims sacrificed to appease the souls of these departed warriors.

CHAPTER XXIII.

THE MAJOR MADE INTO AN INDIAN CHIEF—A SUCCESSFUL ATTEMPT TO ESCAPE—CROSSES THE MEXICAN FRONTIER AND FALLS INTO THE HANDS OF THE REPUBLICANS—ROBBING A ROBBER

ONE morning the Major was agreeably surprised by being marched into the wigwam of the Sachem. Besides the chief and his squaws, a half-breed was present to interpret to the pale face what the Red Man had to say to him.

"My white brother is a great chief among his people," commenced the Indian. "His heart is big like that of the Buffalo and he knows not fear. He shall stay in the village of his red brother, and be a chief over his braves. He shall hunt with his young men, and the Indian maidens shall bring him soft skins for his mocassins."

To this complimentary invitation to become a member of the Sachem's tribe Major MacIver returned a fitting reply. Anything was better than being prisoner, and henceforth, for over four months, the two ex-Confederate officers and their companion remained with the Indians, hunting and shooting with them, and sharing their wild, adventurous life.

However, the white men were only waiting for a favourable chance of escaping, and at length the opportunity came. The Indians were encamped not far from the Mexican frontier, near Fort Mackenzie, and one dark stormy night Major MacIver, Captain Gillespie, and the backwoodsman took three of the fastest mustangs they could find, and got clear away.

Crossing the Rio Grande after some difficulty, but in safety, MacIver and his friends were making their way onwards through the State of Tamaulipa when they fell into the hands of a body of the Republican troops, who were little, if any, better than freebooters. The Republican party was under the command of a daring chief, Sirbando Carvales, who ruled with a rod of iron his half-brigand soldiers. At this time Don Mariano Escobado was General-in-Chief of the Army of the North, the Imperial forces being commanded by a Mexican Royalist, who had recently been created a duke—General Mejia.

It was in this State of Tamaulipa that MacIver and his two friends were captured by these freebooters, and they were at once conducted to the presence of the dreaded Carvales. The Republican Chief, however, received the two ex-Confederate officers politely enough, inquiring as to their rank and business, and the cause of their being on Mexican territory.

To have confessed their intention of joining the Emperor Maximilian's army would have entailed speedy death. MacIver knew that within an hour he and his friend would have been taken out by the order of Carvales, and shot. He therefore told the chief that they were American officers who were desirous of travelling in South America, which they wished to reach as soon as possible, having been detained by the Indians, and having consequently lost much time which they had intended to devote to pleasure. Subsequently Carvales sent them on to the General.

Don Mariano Escobado, hearing that they had

been Confederate officers, asked them why, now the war was over, they did not join the Republican party of Mexico, in which they would see plenty of fighting. He could offer them commands and good pay. The two friends, however, whilst apparently in good faith thanking Escobado for his offer, persisted in their intention to make their way down to the coast, where at some of the ports they might find a vessel for South America.

The General finding them determined, at once set the friends at liberty, and gave them a pass from his own hand, which would ensure their safety from Ceralvo to Commargo. The backwoodsman, Leslie, having a love affair with a Mexican girl, remained at Ceralvo.

Subsequently, as MacIver and Gillespie were riding through a chapparal of prickly pear-wood they were suddenly intercepted by three freebooters, no doubt members of Carvales' band, but engaged in a little brigandage on their own account. They were three rough-looking fellows in short Spanish jackets, and coarse cowhide leggings reaching half-way up their thighs, their villainous-looking faces surmounted by broad-brimmed sombreros, and in the sashes round their waists they carried long-barrelled pistols and murderous-looking knives. Taken all together, you could not have well found worse specimens of humanity in any country.

Without any parley they fired a couple of shots at the two travellers, one of the bullets hitting the Major's horse, killing it on the spot. As the poor beast rolled over in its death agony, MacIver, who was unable to extricate himself in time, had his leg jammed between the dead animal and the ground. However, if he could not get up, he could draw his revolver, and he immediately fired a shot in return, killing his man. Captain Gillespie had also fired two shots in quick succession, each proving fatal to one of the robbers. So quickly had all this occurred that in a few seconds Major MacIver's horse had been shot under him and the three would-be robbers killed. Captain Gillespie was a powerful man, but it was with no little difficulty that he succeeded in lifting the dead horse sufficiently to extricate the Major from his forced imprisonment. At length, however, the task was accomplished, and he was free, and little the worse for his fall.

MacIver and Gillespie thought it wise to see if the freebooters had any papers about them; but although they found none, they discovered something, just then, of more use. Having but little funds of their own, they were astonished and delighted to find each of the belts round the robbers' waists well filled with American and Mexican gold. Altogether there was about two thousand dollars.

At first the friends had intended taking the horses and arms of the Mexican robbers, but it occurred to them that it would be attended with considerable danger, as should they meet any of the Republican party they would recognise the horses as having belonged to their comrades. Major MacIver would have liked at least one of the horses to have replaced his own, but even this, with the saddle and bridle changed, would have been too dangerous, and he decided to trudge on on foot by the side of his comrade until he could buy another mount. A short distance below where they had been attacked by the robbers, they crossed the Rio Grande, where MacIver, now that he had plenty of money, found no difficulty in procuring a fresh horse.

From thence they moved down to Brownsville, in Texas, and afterwards crossed over to Matamoras. Here poor Captain Gillespie was taken very ill. MacIver remained with him for some time, until his friend was a little better, when he had him removed into Texas. This was the last that the Major ever saw of Captain Gillespie, for, by one of those strange chances of life, they have never since met.

CHAPTER XXIV

MACIVER JOINS THE MEXICAN ROYALIST ARMY—RECEIVES THE ORDER OF GUADALOUPE—THE END OF THE WAR, AND THE DEATH OF THE EMPEROR MAXIMILIAN — COLONEL MACIVER ENDURES GREAT PRIVATIONS, AND ESCAPES AT LAST

MAJOR MACIVER now proceeded to carry out the intention which had brought him to Mexico, which, as the reader knows, was to join the army of the unfortunate Emperor Maximilian, then fighting against the Republican party. The Major was presented to the Royalist Commander, General Mejia, whose force was stationed in Matamoras and the neighbourhood, by a Confederate officer, and the General, when he heard of his previous service and career, not only readily accepted his offer to join the Royalists, but appointed him to his staff, with the rank of lieutenant-colonel.

For some time subsequent to entering the Imperial service, Colonel MacIver, as we must now call him, had little to record but desultory fighting against the Republican forces, although in these small affairs there was frequently some very hot work and sharp fighting. At length Mejia advanced with his command as far as Monterey, and then a general engagement took place, the enemy, after a fierce contest, being driven back with heavy loss. (This battle is known as the *second* battle of Monterey, and must not be confounded with the engagement of the same name which was fought twenty years before by General Scott of the American Army against the Mexicans.)

Shortly after the battle at Monterey, Colonel MacIver distinguished himself in a charge against a battalion of Republican infantry, and was wounded. In the heat of the fight, whilst making a cut with a sabre, a soldier bayoneted him in the cheek. In this affair, as in most others up to this time, General Mejia was victorious.

For his valour in the last engagement and for his other services, Colonel MacIver was decorated with the Order of Guadaloupe, and he was also raised to the dignity of a Count of the Mexican Empire, although from the speedy overthrow and judicial murder of the unfortunate Maximilian, he never received his patent for the latter high-sounding, but somewhat worthless honour.

In the brief but persistent and fierce struggle between the Emperor Ferdinand Maximilian and his rebellious subjects, the most of the fighting was under the Sovereign himself, but in this Colonel

MacIver did not participate. But he fought on loyally until the last scene of the historical drama made infamous by the murder of a noble and heroic Christian Prince.

When the whole of the French troops quitted the shores of Mexico to return to their own land, the end soon came. Deserted by his allies, and left to carry on the war with native soldiers as best he might, Maximilian after heroic efforts had to succumb. Puebla was the first to fall in the beginning of April, and then commenced the siege of Mexico by the triumphant Republicans.

The garrison of Queretaro was already reduced to terrible straits, when at the same time that they besieged the capital, they surrounded this last stronghold of the Emperor. The place soon became quite untenable, and Maximilian had come to the desperate resolve to cut his way through the enemy's lines or to die in the attempt. But the opportunity was never given to him, for on the night of the fifteenth of May, the Republicans, under General Escobado, forced their way into the garrison, and after a brave but short resistance, the Mexican Emperor surrendered, and was taken prisoner with all his staff and principal officers. Whether this unfortunate fall of Queretaro was owing to the treachery of Lopez, the Royalist General, or not, it is now scarcely worth while to question.

What followed the capture of the Emperor is known and remembered by most living men. On the nineteenth of June, Ferdinand Maximilian von Hapsburg, with two of his generals, Miramon and Mejia, were cruelly shot to death at Queretaro, by order of

General Juarez and a council of war. The Emperor met his fate with heroic firmness, as did his two companions, and Mexico, by that cowardly, despicable act, was eternally disgraced.

We must now return to Colonel MacIver, whose life, like that of thousands of others, was not worth an hour's purchase. The whole country swarmed with spies and Republican soldiers, and his only hope of escape was to make his way down to some place on the coast where he might possibly chance to get out of the Mexican territory.

The late Emperor's officers were being hunted to death like wild animals—especially those of a foreign nationality—and to avoid capture by the human bloodhounds required the undergoing of great privation by the fugitives. Hiding by day in the woods and travelling by night afforded the only probable means of escape, and even with these precautions, and enduring actual starvation, but too many fell victims to their enemies.

In this way did Colonel MacIver endeavour to reach the coast, almost hungered to death, and with his clothes in rags. His handsome green tunic and red trousers had been so torn by the prickly pear of the chapparal, that they scarcely hung together, and his body was scratched and wounded from a similar cause. Fortunately, his high military boots saved his feet and legs, or his sufferings would have been greater.

He was not without money, but it was useless to him, for although he was almost ravenous from the want of food, he dared not venture to approach any dwelling where he might have purchased the necessaries of life. Hitherto, since the time he became a fugitive, he had had to subsist on the fruit of the prickly pear, or any edible roots that he could find, with one or two rare exceptions when he had been able to kill a bird or some small animal, and cook it by a wood fire in the chapparal.

On one occasion he was so hardly pressed by a party of Republican soldiers who had followed in his track that he had to remain concealed in a chapparal for four whole days and nights, knowing it to be certain death to venture forth. He was, however, now drawing near to the coast, and on the day after this adventure, having travelled all night, he lay down where there was little likelihood of his being seen, to snatch a few hours' rest.

He had scarcely thrown himself on the ground, when, from his hiding-place, he observed a Mexican Republican soldier approaching towards the spot where he (MacIver) lay. The man was alone, and as he came nearer the Colonel saw that he had a haversack by his side, which appeared to be pretty well filled. Had it not been for this, and the comfortable clothes which he wore, the half-famished officer might have allowed the other, enemy as he was, to pass by. But MacIver had suffered too much to permit so favourable an opportunity to escape him, and as the soldier came leisurely along, and arrived within a few yards of the late Royalist officer, MacIver sprang upon him. The astonished Mexican was in the grasp of a powerful and desperate man, and before he could realise his position, he was lying at full length, with the hand of his attacker grasping his throat.

In a few seconds more he found himself disarmed, and heard a stern voice commanding him in Spanish to rise. No doubt the soldier thought his time was come, for a pistol was pointed at his head, and he must have been most agreeably surprised when he found that no greater injury was to be inflicted upon him than that of giving up the food in his haversack, and exchanging clothes with the fierce-looking Imperialist officer.

Colonel MacIver made a complete exchange of garments with the Mexican excepting his boots; and, besides the ample store of food which the soldier carried, he had a small flask of native wine, which was almost as acceptable as the eatables. At parting the Colonel held out such fearful threats to the now thoroughly cowed Mexican as to what would happen to him if he attempted to follow, that he probably was too much frightened to spread an immediate alarm, or else was so pleased at his escape that he went quietly home. At all events, Colonel MacIver saw nothing more of him, and now that he was attired in the uniform of one of Juarez's soldiers, the risk that he ran was not nearly so great. He, however, used as much caution as possible in showing himself in the daylight until he reached the coast.

The dress that he wore, although so very acceptable after the rags to which his own uniform had been reduced, and that, moreover, had been so useful in facilitating his journey, was scarcely the one to start life with in another land, and he determined, if possible, to procure a change.

After some further difficulty he got what he required at the hut of an old Mexican, who for good pay provided him with a full suit of clothing and other necessaries. This was at Tampico, which town he had entered at night, and after sleeping at a humble lodging, MacIver went on board a steamer sailing for Para, at the mouth of the River Amazon, and made good his escape, but unfortunately not without having lost several documents of great value to him.

CHAPTER XXV

JOINS THE BRAZILIAN AND ARGENTINE ARMIES—COMMISSIONED TO FORM A FOREIGN LEGION—TWO ATTEMPTS ON MACIVER'S LIFE DEFEATED

COLONEL MACIVER reached the River Amazon safely, and from thence took a steamer to Rio de Janeiro, at which port he arrived at the end of July. At the Brazilian capital he met a number of ex-Confederate officers, and through them was made known to several influential people in Rio de Janeiro. Amongst others he was introduced to General Caldwell, who had been in the Brazilian Army for many years.

The General was an Englishman, with, by the way, only one arm, and he took a great interest in MacIver, presenting him to the Emperor, Don Pedro, and subsequently to the Minister of War. Colonel MacIver had several interviews with the last-named gentleman, and having expressed a wish to go to the front at the seat of war in Paraguay the Minister gave him a pass with free transport, and a letter of introduction to the Marquis of

Caciaus, Commander-in-Chief of the Brazilian Army in Carupaity.

Afterwards the Brazilian War Minister told General Caldwell how glad he was to have a young and active officer who was a Scotchman to send to the front, and that he had heard very highly of him from one or two of the ex-Confederate officers in the capital. MacIver, it seems, had the reputation of being a good military engineer officer, as well as a cavalry leader, having studied thoroughly the art of war in its various branches.

The Colonel stayed for about a month in Rio de Janeiro, and when he left, besides being provided with all things necessary for his journey, he carried with him many letters and cards of introduction from old friends who had made Brazil their home after the close of the American War. Amongst these letters, most of them dated Rio de Janeiro, 30th August, 1867, was one from C. B. Cencer, late Lieutenant-Colonel in the Confederate States Army, to Lieutenant W. A. Kirkland, commanding the United States man-of-war *Wasp* at Monte Video. Another note of the same date, and from the same gentleman, introduced Colonel MacIver to Colonel Loveless, late of the Confederate States Army. He had also a card to Lieutenant Kirkland from Captain M'Crohan, commanding a Spanish ship of war at Rio.

On arriving at Monte Video, MacIver remained there for about a week before taking the steamer for Buenos Ayres. Here he was detained some time waiting for a boat going up to the front, but passed the time pleasantly enough, as he again met some

American friends. Before starting from Buenos Ayres he was favoured with a letter of introduction from Mr. S. Jeteman to General don Bartolomée Mitre, the chief in command of the allied armies of Brazil and the Argentine Republic, then fighting against Paraguay.

At length the steamer by which he was to sail was ready, and he left Buenos Ayres for Carupaity, in the State of Paraguay, and situated on the river of that name, just above its junction with the Parana. The distance was between two and three hundred miles, and the journey up the Parana was very long and tedious. They were detained at Corrientes for a short while, and the next morning reached Carupaity.

From the latter place Colonel MacIver turned back to Itapiru, a few miles away, a short distance from which, at Tuqucuè, was the headquarters of the allies. There he was kindly received by General Mitre, who afterwards introduced him to the Marquis of Caciaus. Whilst at headquarters, he took part in one or two small affairs with the enemy, which was all the fighting he was fated to see in the service of the allies.

A consultation was held, shortly after MacIver arrived, between the two generals — Marquis of Caciaus and Don Bartolomée Mitre—and it was decided that he should be sent back to Buenos Ayres for the purpose of organising a Foreign Legion, of which he should take command. MacIver's credentials, a letter to His Excellency Señor don Marcos Pas, Vice-President of the Argentine Republic, bears the date of the 18th October, 1867, and is signed by General Bartoloméé Mitre. It requests that the bearer shall be appointed to the rank of Lieutenant-Colonel, and that he be commissioned to form a Foreign Legion of infantry.

MacIver hastened back to Buenos Ayres as quickly as possible, and almost immediately after his return there received from Don Marcos Pas his commission of Lieutenant-Colonel and the authority to raise a Foreign Legion for the service of the Republic. His first step was to insert in the *Standard* newspaper, a Buenos Ayres journal, an advertisement of which the following is a copy:

" Volunteers Wanted.—Lieutenant-Colonel MacIver, late of the American and Mexican Armies, is commissioned by the Government to organise and take command of a Foreign Legion. Foreigners wishing to take service can communicate with the commanding officer at the Legion headquarters, Plaza Barracks, Plaza del Retiro, who will inform them as to the bounty, pay, &c. Officers of experience and ability wanted."

This advertisement brought many applicants, and amongst them were several ex-British and other officers, who were anxious to obtain a commission in the Legion. So rapid indeed was the organisation, that, although the notice in the *Standard* did not appear until the third week in November, Colonel MacIver had raised over seven hundred men before the middle of December ; and after that date recruits were continually coming to the Plaza Barracks.

In the meantime, while the enlisting for the Legion was going on, the Colonel renewed his acquaintance amongst the families in Buenos Ayres to whom he had previously been introduced, and amongst his comrades of the late Confederate Service. One friend whom he frequently met was an Englishman, Captain G. W H. Hepburn, who had formerly been an officer in the Royal Engineers.

It was about the time when the Legion had nearly reached its full strength—the middle of December—that Colonel MacIver met with an adventure in which he had a narrow escape for his life. He was walking in the Calle Suppatche at midnight, followed by his orderly, Corporal Knox. The streets were quite dark, with the exception of slight glimmers from the bazaar windows, and almost deserted by passengers. MacIver, who was strolling leisurely along, was wearing at the time a cap, and as he turned the corner of a street, a long knife came with sudden force, cutting down the front of the peak and dropping at his feet with a sharp ring. As the knife fell, missing its mark, there was a fierce ejaculation of disappointment:

"Carracho!"

Instantly, MacIver realised that an attempt had been made to murder him by throwing the knife, a favourite mode of secret assassination, and turning sharply round he thought he caught sight of the shadow of a man. At the same moment, Corporal Knox, who was close behind, shouted out:

"There goes the assassin, Colonel!"

MacIver gave chase, and finding that he was gaining on the would-be murderer, called upon him to "halt." The man, however, not taking any notice, but continuing his flight at the top of his speed, his pursuer drew a small Derringer and shot the assassin between the shoulders, who fell mortally wounded.

A crowd quickly assembled, and soon, too, came a couple of city watchmen, carrying their night lanterns. As the head of the assassin was raised, he was recognised by the watchmen as one of those murderous convict Italian bravos who had been imported, or sent by their Government to South America before their time of punishment in their own country had expired.

These fellows had the reputation of being ready to commit any crime for a few passos. The dying man was too far gone to give any account of the affair, but it was concluded that he had been employed by others to assassinate the Colonel. The latter's orderly, Corporal Knox, was certain that he had seen two or three figures running away; and MacIver, too, had fancied that there were more shadows than that of the man who had thrown the knife. He was also pretty certain that the Spanish exclamation "Carracho," did not come from the mouth of the Italian.

The Colonel's Brigade-Major was an officer named Lagos, of the regular army, who had been specially detailed off for duty with the Legion by the Minister of War, and placed immediately under MacIver's orders. He was a very useful and competent officer, speaking English and French well, and MacIver soon came to value him as a friend as well as a comrade. On returning to his quarters, he of course told Lagos of the attempt to murder him. The Major shook his head, and said:

"Ah! my Colonel, I am afraid there is a great deal of jealousy in this, and I should advise you to be on your guard for the future. I have a large sword-cane that I will present to you, which you can take with you, when, as to-night, you go out without your sword."

After a little pressure MacIver accepted the gift, and subsequently had to use it and test its value in another affair. A few days later he had an invitation to a ball, and took with him this sword-cane and two pocket Derringers. The assembly was a very brilliant one, and he enjoyed himself immensely. He was introduced to some charming ladies of Spanish descent, whom he had not before met, and joined in the dances until midnight. It was then, when he had just resigned his late partner to another cavalier, that an elderly lady pressed his arm gently, and, with a look of sympathy and alarm combined, led him quietly away to a more secluded part of the room.

"Senor Commandant," she said, "I would request you to be on your guard, for you are in great danger. There are people—persons even in this room—who seek your life."

"Ah! madame," said MacIver, "I do not fear."

"Yes, that is it," replied the lady, "and it makes the danger the greater. If you cared more for your own safety, and were less abroad at night, there would not be such favourable opportunities for your enemies."

The Colonel thanked the dame courteously for her kindly warning, but really at the time thought little more about the matter. He had certainly had one or two love affairs, but they were merely flirtations, and he had given no real cause of offence to any one that they should seek his life.

It was between one and two o'clock in the morning

when the party broke up, and bidding farewell to his entertainers and some of his late partners, he proceeded on his way home on foot, reaching the Plaza del Retiro without thought of danger, or as far as he remembered seeing any one about. He was now within three or four hundred yards of the barracks, but had to cross the Plaza, which was in deep shadow from the tall and thickly-planted trees. There was no light of any kind, and the night was so dark that he could barely make out the gravel path along which he was walking. Just as he got into the avenue leading up to his quarters, he fancied he heard a step besides his own, or something like the crunching of gravel behind him. All at once the thought of danger and of the lady's warning occurred to him, and he swung round in time to see a man with a long knife rushing upon him.

Instantly his rapier was drawn from its cane, and parrying the intended stroke, he ran his assailant through the body. At the same time two other figures came into view. MacIver shouted "Guarda! Guarda! Guarda! Vienga acqui!" with all his might. Then drawing one of his Derringers from his pocket he fired right into the face of the man nearest to him. The third, on hearing the Colonel's loud shout for help and the report of the pistol, took to flight. MacIver followed across the Plaza, and again firing, shot the fellow through the side.

The Colonel's shout and the pistol shots had been heard at the barracks, and the guard turned out with Sergeant-Major Povy Oswald, and two or three officers, including Major Lagos. They brought lights with them and soon reached the spot. When their

Colonel told them how matters stood, the soldiers were so enraged that they bayoneted the bodies on the ground.

This was not only an unnecessary retaliation, but prevented MacIver from finding anything out, as to the real author of the attack, as the men might have confessed. The three dead men were left in a heap in the Plaza until daylight. A report of the affair was then written out, and the bodies taken from the city and thrown in a ditch. This Plaza del Retiro had always been a noted place for assassinations. Even before the war many innocent persons had been inveigled there and murdered.

CHAPTER XXVI.

MACIVER FIGHTS TWO MORE DUELS—A MUTINY IN THE FOREIGN LEGION—THE OUTBREAK OF THE CHOLERA IN BUENOS AYRES, AND ITS CONSEQUENCES

THE Sergeant-Major Povy Oswald mentioned in the last chapter was a very smart and trustworthy non-commissioned officer, and proved exceedingly useful to Colonel MacIver on numerous occasions amongst the unruly spirits he had in the Legion, which, being formed from so many nationalities, was very difficult to manage. Subsequently he had the pleasure of recommending Oswald, who came of a good family, for a commission, and the satisfaction of seeing him raised to the rank of a lieutenant.

In December MacIver had a serious dispute with an officer—a major—respecting a lady, which led to not only a duel with this gentleman, but to a second encounter. The Major had thrown out several insinuations respecting this lady in connection with the Colonel of the Foreign Legion.

As MacIver esteemed this lady very highly, at whose hands he had received many acts of kindness, and who belonged to a good old Spanish family, he sent his Brigade-Major to demand a written apology from her traducer. The officer, however, refused what was asked of him by Major Lagos on behalf of his Colonel, insisting that what he had said was quite true, and that he would not retract one word.

There was now nothing for it but a hostile meeting, which it was arranged should come off in the suburbs, pistols being the weapons to be used. The duel took place, the result being that the offending officer was shot through the shoulder, and MacIver had his neck grazed with his opponent's bullet. After the affair was at an end the Major acknowledged his error, and said that he believed he was wrong and had stated what was not true.

This would have been a satisfactory termination to the quarrel, but unfortunately the young lady's brother—a mere youth—hearing that his sister's name had been spoken of in connection with Colonel MacIver, called him out too. It was in vain that the latter tried to explain, for the passionate young Spaniard would not listen to reason.

At length, when he had tried every means to pacify the lad, he told him point-blank that he refused to fight with him, as he (MacIver) was guiltless of any wrong, and he did not wish to have the other's blood on his conscience. The fiery youth of nineteen, however, insisted, and declared that if Colonel MacIver would not go out with him he would brand him throughout Buenos Ayres as a poltroon.

MacIver could not stand this, and he accepted the challenge, determining at the same time, in his own mind, to teach the youth a useful lesson, if only for the sake of his sister. Before going out with him the Colonel told his own second, Captain Cavallos, that under no circumstances should he fire upon his challenger.

MacIver had had long practice as a pistol shot, and there were few things that he could not hit at a reasonable distance. On this occasion, as the reader knows, he had no purpose of injuring his young opponent, and unless he himself was hit, the intention was to punish the youth in another way.

On the signal being given to fire MacIver did not attempt to raise his pistol, but the lad's bullet ripped the side of the Colonel's jacket, cutting away a button. Scarcely raising his voice above his ordinary tone, the latter said :

"My young Caballero, for the sake of your sister, whom I esteem as a lady, I give you your life; but with this proof."

And raising his arm and taking deliberate aim at a mark on which he had fixed his eyes, he pulled the trigger and lodged the bullet in it.

No one appreciated Colonel MacIver's tact and courage in carrying out these two duels more fully than the young lady whose fair fame he had so gallantly defended, although the meetings gained him the good will and respect of many persons whom he had not previously known. In a few days, when the news of the affair began to spread, the Colonel of the Foreign Legion was quite a noted personage in Buenos Ayres, and he became overwhelmed with invitations from the best families in the city.

About a week after the second duel, however, Colonel MacIver had other business of more importance to engage his attention. An order came from the Minister of War for him to have his Legion ready to start to the front on the following day, and all haste was made to prepare for their departure. The morning came, and orders had already been given to the Brigade-Major to form the battalion in line, when Lagos came to the Commandant with the unwelcome news, that there was a mutiny amongst the men, who refused to march.

MacIver instantly sprang into the saddle and galloped down to the parade ground. He had enlisted men of all nationalities, and he knew that amongst them were a lot of bloodthirsty rascals that would stop at nothing unless governed by an iron hand and will. The men had fallen in, but had intimated to the Brigade-Major in pretty strong terms that they would not march.

The Colonel rode quietly down the line, and inspected his battalion as if nothing had happened, chatting to his officers, and taking matters very coolly. Suddenly he gave the word of command:

"Battalion, fours left, by your right, forward! Quick march!"

But to his annoyance not a man stirred. Again his voice rang out:

"If there is any man here who has a complaint to make, let him step forward, and give the reason."

For several seconds there was a dead silence in the ranks, and not a soldier moved. But at length two Italians and two Greasers (half-breeds) moved out from the line, and said that they all wished to have their pay before they left Buenos Ayres. These men had also several frivolous complaints to make, and the Colonel heard them to the end.

Then he again spoke.

"I have nothing to do with that," he said. "You have received your pay up to the time you have been here, and any arrears which may accumulate on the way will be given to you on reaching the front. I am only a soldier like yourselves, and have received my orders to march from the Minister of War, and, as your commanding officer, I expect obedience, and call upon you to follow me."

When the Colonel had finished speaking, Sergeant Redman, an excellent soldier, and an Irishman by birth, stepped from the ranks, and pointing to one of the Italians and one of the Greasers, said:

"These two men, Colonel, are the ringleaders, and the principal cause of this dissatisfaction. They have led off the other men and caused all the bother."

"Ah! is that so?" said the Colonel. "Then you will place these men under arrest."

As soon as the order was given, MacIver saw that there was an ominous, threatening commotion in the ranks, and it was a chance whether the men did not break out into open mutiny at once. If he wished for discipline to carry the day and his own authority to be respected, there was no time to lose, and strong measures were necessary, so he called out sternly:

"Sergeant Redman, march out a squad of men that you can depend upon, and take those two mutineers into the Plaza, and let them be instantly shot."

As he gave these instructions to Sergeant Redman, Colonel MacIver drew his revolver, and in a commanding voice ordered the other officers to do the same. Then he repeated that if there was any one with a complaint to make he was to step forward. There was no response.

"Battalion, fours left, by your right, forward! Quick march!" again rang out, and the Foreign Legion as one man stepped briskly forward. Before, however, the rear company had defiled from the barracks the rattle of musketry told that the execution had been carried out. It was a hard lesson to teach, but they were an unruly lot to command, and needed a harsh hand to curb them.

Colonel MacIver's battalion, however, had only just reached the outskirts of Buenos Ayres when an officer came galloping up to say that as the transports were found not to be ready for conveying the men up the river, the Legion must return to the barracks for a few days. That countermanding of the order to proceed to the front was the cause of great disaster to the Legion, as two days after the great plague of cholera broke out in the city, and in a short time swept away thirty thousand of the inhabitants. It was a fearful time—more terrible than the visitation of war itself. Out of upwards of seven hundred men in the Foreign Legion, more than half were soon dead and buried.

MacIver kept up almost to the last in this terrible trial, visiting the sick soldiers night and day, and doing all that he could to cheer them up. Amongst others his orderly, Corporal Knox, caught the disease. When he went to see him the poor lad shook his head in a desponding way, and said:

"Ah! Colonel, I am going to die."

"Nonsense, Knox," replied MacIver. "Cheer up, my man. You will live to get over this."

"No, Colonel," answered the lad; "I know I am going to die; and I want you to promise me that if ever you return to England you will see my father and mother in Liverpool and tell them how I died."

Poor Knox's words, alas! proved to be true, for in a few hours he was dead.

Colonel MacIver lived to convey the son's dying words to his parents in Liverpool, but not until he himself had passed through a fierce ordeal that brought him to the gates of death.

CHAPTER XXVII.

AT DEATH'S DOOR—THE END OF THE FOREIGN LEGION—LEAVES THE ARGENTINE SERVICE AND RECEIVES A COMMISSION FROM THE CRETAN PROVISIONAL GOVERNMENT

SHORTLY after Corporal Knox's death, his commandant was attacked by the cholera. MacIver rose from his couch feeling a little giddy, just as his servant came into the room to attend his master.

"Sir," said the man, "I think you are not well this morning."

"Oh yes, I am," he replied, although a cold shiver had seized him. "I am quite well; nothing is the matter with me."

The servant, however, was not to be deceived, and after he had finished the Colonel's toilet he sent for the doctor, but did not mention what he had done to his master. In the meantime the Brigade-Major, Lagos, came, and as he entered, said :

"My Colonel, here are despatches from the Minister of War. But," in an altered voice, "you are ill."

"Not at all," said MacIver as he tore open the despatches; "let me have my horse at once."

"My dear Colonel," said Major Lagos, "you are really not well enough to go out to-day."

"Oh yes, I am," insisted MacIver. Then, turning to his servant, he asked, "Where is my sword? Why do you not give me my sword? See that my horse is brought round. I am quite well and I am going to the Minister of War."

All this time he was staggering like a drunken man. Major Lagos tried to persuade him to return to his bed, but MacIver persisted in going down to the barrack square, where his horse was awaiting him. He put his hand on the saddle in the attempt to mount, but he had not strength enough to pull himself up. He managed, however, to place his foot in the stirrup-iron, and at a second bidding his new orderly lifted him on to the horse. Then he rode off, but had not proceeded far when he met a person whom he knew, who said, "Why, what is the matter with you, Colonel?"

"I don't know," replied MacIver, "but I am afraid I am going to be ill."

"Good heavens!" exclaimed the gentleman, "you have got the cholera," and he ran off in dismay.

Meanwhile Povy Oswald had followed in pursuit of his commanding officer, and was just in time to overtake MacIver as he was about to fall from his charger. He took him into a drug store near, where they administered a strong dose of chlorodyne. A cab passed, but when the driver knew what was required of him he attempted to drive off. Oswald, however, drew his revolver and threatened to shoot the man if he did not remain and take the Colonel to the barracks.

When they got MacIver to his quarters a little French doctor came from the town, and at once declared that nothing would save the patient but copious bleeding. At this time the disease was beginning to mount to MacIver's head, and he was getting delirious.

"Cut my neck, sir, cut my neck," he said. "I command you to obey orders, and cut my neck."

The doctor at once took out his lancet and bled him in the right arm, from which he took a large quantity of blood, many ounces of which were quite black, and the Colonel remembered no more until at length he awoke, when the plague had left him. His body felt so light and buoyant, that he seemed almost as if he could float in the air, but when he attempted to stir he found that he was perfectly helpless and as weak as a child, and could neither move hand nor foot. In this state the cholera had left him, and so he remained for many weeks.

What was left of the Foreign Legion was sent on to the front under another officer, and had to leave their Colonel behind them in Buenos Ayres. The men and officers had become accustomed to MacIver, and many were attached to him from his kindness during the cholera. Whether they took badly to a new commandant or whether it was the fault of the latter it is difficult to say, but they certainly did not get on well together.

Before long MacIver's Foreign Legion was drafted into other battalions. Through this he resigned his commission and sailed for Liverpool. He was only too glad to get out of the service of the Argentine Republic honourably, for his sympathy had been with the other side. After a passage of six weeks he arrived safely in England, and also quite well again in health.

On reaching Glasgow, where he went direct from Liverpool, he met a few old acquaintances. Amongst these was Bennett Burleigh, who had held a lieutenant's commission in the Confederate States Navy. He had done some gallant service round York Town, in Virginia, during the war, blowing up one of the Federal gunboats, and effecting other good work for the South, and was spoken of by all who knew him as a dashing officer.

When MacIver met him in Glasgow, the Cretan insurrection was going on, and Burleigh mentioned that he was thinking of getting up an expedition to help the islanders. After some consultation it was arranged that Colonel MacIver should proceed to Crete for the purpose of obtaining a commission to organise a body of troops for service. He started for

Greece, and after some difficulty managed to run the blockade from Piræus to Crete.

He found the Cretans only too glad to accept his offer of assistance, and received a commission from the Provisional Government, of which the following is a translation:

"By permission and approval of General Assembly of the Cretans, we give full power to Colonel Henry Ronald MacIver to make war on land and sea against the enemies of Crete, and particularly against the Sultan of Turkey, and the Turkish forces, and to burn, destroy, or capture any vessel bearing the Turkish flag, and permission to choose and command his officers and men. Colonel MacIver will bear in all his operations and attacks against the enemy the 'White flag of Crete,' with a red cross in the middle and the word Crete on it. And we beg all Political, Military, and Naval Powers to consider the said Colonel MacIver and all his officers and men under him as citizens of Crete and fighting in her defence.

"The present Commission has been issued at Aryssais, Amarion.

"Signed and sealed this day, 14th July, 1868.

"The Provisional Government. Aposilas G. Pylliantris, Joseph A. R. Brurdouratris, A. M. Torangivis, Basilis Spavidatris, S. G. Drsurtrokakis, A. G. Trohlis, A. Panagolakis.

"The Secretary of the Provisional Government of Crete,
"NICOLAIS BERNARDOS."

After Colonel MacIver had received his commission, he had to remain in Crete for nearly a couple of months, waiting for a blockade runner coming in. He went down to the sea coast, and in the interval amused himself by shouldering a rifle and joining the Cretan ranks, with which he saw a little fighting. At length he managed to successfully run the blockade through the Turkish men-of war, and to reach Smyrna, although chased and fired upon by a cruiser. From thence he took the French steamer to Marseilles, and so overland by Paris according to instructions.

At Glasgow he found Burleigh and a large number of others ready to join him. Unfortunately, however, when they were about to commence operations, the Turkish Ambassador got wind of the affair through the Glasgow detectives, and prevented them from getting the ship they required to carry out the expedition.

Finding there was now no chance in England, MacIver returned to the Mediterranean with two or three Scotchmen, being determined to try and organise a daring band at Piræus, for the purpose of seizing a Turkish gunboat, and thus materially assisting the Cretans in more ways than one. At Marseilles, too, Colonel MacIver met with an ex-lieutenant of the Royal Navy named Scroggs, and two or three other adventurous spirits, who were ready to join in their plan.

Having received passports from the Greek Consul at Marseilles, they proceeded to Piræus, close to Athens. But on reaching Greece they found, as ill luck would have it for the carrying out of MacIver's commission, although possibly very fortunately for themselves, that the Cretan insurrection had been quelled by the Turkish Government, and that those of the Greek volunteers who had escaped death or capture were returning to their own country.

All the plans and scheming of the Colonel and his friends for the liberation of Crete from the Turkish rule, had been thrown away, and the unhappy islanders were in a worse position than before they rose against the Sultan. Neither was MacIver or his comrades anything but losers by their interference in the affairs of Crete. Subsequently, however, the Cretan Committee in Athens kindly paid the expenses of those the Colonel had brought with him back to their homes. MacIver having nothing better to do, remained for a few months in Athens.

CHAPTER XXVIII.

COLONEL MACIVER'S SOJOURN AT ATHENS — JOINS THE GREEK SERVICE, AND SERVES UNDER CORRONEUS — BRIGAND HUNTING ON THE FRONTIER OF THESSALY — RETURNS TO AMERICA

During the three months that our friend MacIver sojourned in the Greek capital for pleasure, he was continually the guest of Colonel Corroneus, who had been the Commander-in-chief of the Cretan forces against the Turks. The Colonel, who was between sixty and seventy, was a Spartan by birth, as he was by nature, and was considered to be the most daring and dashing officer in the Greek service.

He was looked upon by all the Greeks as the noble

representative of the Spartan soldier, whilst MacIver speaks of him as the most true and honest Greek that it was ever his fate to meet. He seems to have been a great favourite with Colonel Corroneus, the old gentleman evincing quite a paternal regard for him, and subsequently he appears to have highly esteemed him, not only as a friend but as a soldier.

Another officer with whom MacIver was very intimate whilst in Athens, was Major Milligen, a son of Doctor Milligen, of Constantinople. The Major had formerly been in the Turkish Army, but had left it in disgust and offered his services to Greece. Great friends of his, too, were Messieurs Trinquetta, Minister of Marine, A. N. Rodostamos, Marshal of the Court, and Professor Gennadius.

During his stay in Athens, Colonel MacIver was presented to the young King, the brother of our much-loved Princess of Wales. His Majesty received MacIver very graciously, and was good enough to say that he highly appreciated his motives in offering his services and sword for Cretan independence.

The King, who spoke English very well, told him that he was sorry that he could not, owing to political reasons, recognise his services in another way, but hoped to do so on some future occasion. All this was very gratifying to MacIver, and more than repaid him for the disappointments he had experienced over the Cretan affair.

Amongst those whose acquaintance MacIver made during the Cretan insurrection was Mr. Hillery Skinner, the "Special" of the *Daily News*. This gentleman was decorated by King George's Government for services rendered to Greece.

When nearly three months had gone by, Colonel Corroneus was ordered to take command of a force against the brigands at Kisissia, on the frontier of Albania and Thessaly, who were very troublesome; but before departing from Athens, Corroneus asked and obtained permission from the King to take MacIver with him. In accordance with this arrangement, our friend's new Commandant gave him orders to proceed across the isthmus to Corinth, and thence to take steamer to Missolonghi.

Following out these instructions, Colonel MacIver lost no time in making his way on to Corinth, and, oddly enough, the morning after his arrival there, he met a well-known Scottish baronet. Much to his surprise his servant came up to his room to say that there were an English lady and gentleman who wished to see him.

"Show them into my sitting-room," said MacIver, "and I will be with them immediately."

Presently, when the Colonel entered his apartment, he found a tall, fair, handsome man, who rose and said:

"My name is Baird—Sir David Baird—and I must apologise for this intrusion, but hearing by accident that there was a Scotchman in the town, I believed I might venture to ask his assistance out of a difficulty."

"Certainly, Sir David," replied MacIver; "how can I help you?"

"Well, Colonel, I have just landed from my yacht, having Lady Baird and her maid with me, and I came to see if you could assist me to get a conveyance on to Athens."

MacIver at once assured Sir David Baird that he

would do all that he possibly could to be of service to him and his lady, remarking that he considered himself a countryman of the baronet. He also insisted that Sir David and Lady Baird should make use of his sitting-room until he could make arrangements for ensuring them a safe journey to Athens. The baronet gladly availed himself of MacIver's courtesy, and then the Colonel was introduced to Lady Baird ; and subsequently in a chat with her husband he discovered that he and the baronet had met before in India, during the Mutiny, when Sir David was a lieutenant, and serving on the staff of Sir Colin Campbell.

MacIver then proceeded to the Commandant of the town and told him who he was, and that he must have an escort for a countryman of his—a Scottish senor—and his lady, to pass them safely the few miles across the isthmus. At first the Greek officer was inclined to refuse, but the Colonel insisted, and threatened that if anything happened to Sir David and Lady Baird through his (the Commandant's) neglect, not only his own, but the British Government would hold him responsible.

This frightened the Greek into a ready consent, and he not only agreed to supply a sergeant and ten troopers as an escort, but to strengthen the infantry pickets which were stationed at intervals along the route across the Isthmus of Corinth. The Commandant promised, too, that his men should be prepared to accompany the Scottish senor and his lady at any moment, and further that the escort should be so placed as to give no alarm to Lady Baird.

MacIver then returned to the hotel to report to Sir David the result of his mission.

After arranging the preliminaries for the journey, and seeing that a conveyance was in readiness, the Colonel entertained Sir David and Lady Baird with such refreshments as he had to offer. The baronet and his wife were greatly obliged by his efforts on their behalf, and the former, at parting, gave his card to MacIver, and asked him to see his brother, Captain Baird, of the Royal Navy, who had taken the yacht round to Missolonghi. This the Colonel promised and did not fail to carry out on his arrival at that port. He and Captain Baird spent such a jovial evening together that they sat in the yacht's cabin far into the small hours, and did not part until the next morning when the Colonel crossed the gulf in a small steamer to Zante.

Sir David and his party crossed the isthmus without meeting any interruption from the brigands, but no doubt they owed their escape to having fortunately met MacIver. The latter heard from Colonel Corroneus on his arrival at Zante that a plot had been hatched by the brigands to capture the baronet and his lady, which was only prevented from being carried out by the escort and from the strengthening of the pickets.

No doubt, knowing that Sir David was a rich man, they had anticipated enforcing a large ransom, had they succeeded in getting him and his party into their power. Colonel MacIver has had the pleasure of meeting the baronet and his wife more than once since then, and likewise his brother, the captain, when he commanded the *Swiftsure*, and subsequently when he had become an admiral.

From Zante, Colonel MacIver passed over to the mainland, and proceeded direct to the frontier to operate against the brigands, who each day were becoming more daring and impudent in their aggressions. It was not only peaceable travellers that they attacked, robbed, and frequently murdered, but emboldened by numbers on their sides, and the smallness of the parties of Greek troops, they had even dared to assail the latter on various occasions.

Still, as a rule, they were terrible cowards, these picturesque-looking rascals, stabbing in the dark, or shooting from behind rocks, and at the same time inflicting the most horrible cruelty upon their prisoners, unless they were ransomed—cruelty and disfigurement that too often ended in death. When prisoners were taken, especially if supposed to be rich, they were strictly guarded until their friends were communicated with. Then if there was any delay in the ransom being sent, an ear of the victim was cut off and forwarded to the relations or connections of the captive as a slight reminder of what was to follow. If still slow to remit the amount demanded, after waiting another day, the nose or the hand would arrive as another terrible reminder of the fate that would surely be the end of the captive did no ransom arrive.

Sometimes the friends were not able to raise the exorbitant sums demanded, however anxious they might be to release their friends, and the head of the unransomed person might in all probability be expected as a proof that all further negotiations were at an end.

Although we have a proverb that there is honour amongst thieves, these Greek brigands did not always keep faith with the friends of their captives, for more than once cases had occurred where money had been duly forwarded, and after receiving the money they had assassinated their prisoners. But who could wonder that up to this time these rascals had committed their crimes and aggressions unpunished, when it was rumoured—and it was supposed with too much of truth—that the brigands were in secret communication with some of the Greek senators, and with others in high official authority at Athens, and for whom they acted as political agents.

True or not, however, King George was determined to suppress brigandage if possible, and he could not have sent a better man for the purpose than Colonel Corroneus: and no doubt the old Spartan knew well what he was about when he asked that his friend MacIver might accompany him. The latter was instructed to operate in conjunction with Captain Machiea, and these two speedily commenced their reprisals against the robbers. Carrying a rifle like the men under him, MacIver entered heartily into the work, trudging over the mountains, or through dangerous passes, and peering into caves and other dark holes and corners in the hunt for brigands.

The outlaws in many cases fought fiercely enough when brought to bay, for they knew that, if taken, no quarter would be given to them, and that they would be instantly shot by the soldiers. Despair therefore gave them obstinacy, raised their drooping courage when it was wanted, and, moreover, made them contend fiercely to the very last.

Frequently, however, when tracked to their lair, they managed to escape, as they had a series of secret signals in use amongst themselves, that gave warning in time for the band to fly The chirping of birds and the cries of animals were imitated to perfection by the brigands, and, although readily recognised by their own men, the sounds were so true to nature that the soldiers could not distinguish between the real and the false.

Arrayed in Greek costume and leading this rough and perilous life was at first much to the taste of Colonel MacIver. He soon, too, became noted, not only with his men, but amongst the brigands, for his excellent shooting, and for being ever foremost at the point of danger. The old Spartan Commandant often gave a grim smile of satisfaction at the zeal of his young lieutenant. Many a narrow escape and many a hand-to-hand encounter did he have during those two months of brigand hunting; but at length these pests to civilised life were so far got under that there was little or nothing more to do.

Still, Colonel Corroneus was retained in command of that department, but now that the excitement was over MacIver found the life very monotonous, so he made up his mind to leave, although it was with regret that he severed himself from Corroneus.

The old Spartan, moreover, was very sorry to lose his young friend, and, to show his appreciation of MacIver's merits, he sent on a report to Athens, recommending that he should receive the Cross of Our Saviour — the principal decoration for Greece — before retiring from the service of the Hellenic Government. MacIver after bidding farewell to his friends went on to Zante, and from there took the steamer to Corfu. At the latter island he found several friends, principally amongst the officers of Her Majesty's ships *Lord Warden* and *Royal Oak*, whom he had met previously at Piræus.

These gentlemen had heard of him in Greece, and congratulated him on his exploits against the brigands. The Colonel remained at Corfu for about six weeks, and during that time frequently dined with the officers of the *Royal Oak* and *Lord Warden* at their mess, receiving many kindnesses from these hospitable sailors. From Corfu he at length took the steamer to Brindisi, and after staying for a day in Paris, on his way to England, proceeded straight to Glasgow.

His restless spirit, however, did not permit him to remain long in the great centre of Scottish industry, for, after staying for a short while in Glasgow, he once more took ship for America, from whence he had heard rumours that made it not improbable that he might find employment for his sword. There was nothing particular to record during the passage out to New York. He enjoyed the usual pleasant life which is to be found on board an American liner during fine weather, where the table is always good, all the appointments about the great ship perfect, and, as a rule, the society met with not only agreeable, but amusing.

CHAPTER XXIX.

THE CUBAN EXPEDITION—APPOINTED TO THE COMMAND OF A CORPS OF OFFICERS—FAILURE OF THE FIRST ATTEMPT TO REACH CUBA

On arriving at New York, Colonel MacIver found that a large body of men was being raised in the city, for the purpose of freeing the Cubans from the yoke of their Spanish masters, and for establishing their independence. He had no particular sympathy with the cause, but in the end, like a good many Confederate officers whom he knew, he joined the intended expedition, and was appointed to an important command.

This was not the first attempt by many which had been made to release the long-suffering Cubans, under what was called the Junta Cubana, from the Spaniards, but which attempts hitherto had resulted in disaster, owing either to jealousies existing among the leaders, a lack of concert of action, or serious mismanagement. After so many failures, the friends of Cuba began to despair of success in ever getting a force to sea.

At length, however, General Domingo de Giocouria was empowered by the Junta to fit out another expedition, and a sum of one hundred and fifty thousand dollars was placed at his disposal. The General's first device was to centre about him all the Cubans in New York willing to leave and participate in the invasion, and the encouragement he met with led to the recruiting of a force which was subsequently known as the "Battalion de Cazadores de Hatnez," under the command of Colonel Luis Del Christo. This latter officer had served with great distinction in Mexico, and his name, as the leader in the popular rising against Spanish tyranny in 'fifty-two, in the Vuelta Abijo district, now inspired all Cubans with a true military spirit.

The weekly steamer brought from Cuba numerous refugees, and the recruiting was so brisk, that Del Christo's battalion was soon filled up. Although General de Giocouria's instructions were, that none but Cubans should be enlisted, Colonel Del Christo accepted all men fit for service, irrespective of nationality, and the result was that early in September, 'sixty-nine, he had the finest organisation ever raised in New York for foreign service. Amongst his officers were several prominent South Americans, who had before fought against the Spaniards.

Colonel MacIver was led on by his friends to join the expedition, and his services were gladly accepted by General de Giocouria, the Commander-in-Chief of the expedition. He was at once appointed chief of the cavalry to be organised in Cuba, and in the meantime given the command of a picked body of men, most of whom, it was intended, should subsequently be made into commissioned officers. During the progress of enlistment, General de Giocouria left for the South, and established his headquarters at Atalanta, with the object of enlisting a regiment of veterans from the late Confederate armies, Colonel MacIver remaining in New York with Colonel Del Christo, the second in command.

The latter had now raised six hundred men for his battalion, and early in September, learning that the steamer *Lilian* was ready to take her departure from New Orleans for Cedar Keys, in Florida, where she was to take on board the troops, he gave orders to his command to be prepared for embarkation. But the first of the series of misfortunes which the expedition was to meet with, now came. The *Lilian* having sailed from New Orleans, encountered a great storm on the coast of Louisiana, and was so disabled, that she was compelled to put back for repairs. At length, however, the time came for the troops to embark from Cedar Keys, and the following general order was issued :

"Liberal Army of the Republic of Cuba, Cedar Keys, October 3rd, 1869. The following Order will be observed for the organisation of the expeditionary division that departs from Cedar Keys to-morrow :

"First—The expeditionary body shall be composed of one division from the battalion of infantry, under the command of Colonel Luis Edwardo Del Christo ; one company of artillery under command of Robert Dohine ; another company of artillery under the command of Captain Mercer ; having this force under the immediate command of General Samuel E. Williams.

"Second—The exploring company under command of Captain H. C. Puryear ; the body of engineer officers under the orders of Colonel J H. Keats, and the body composed of individuals that are not attached to any organised corps of the division will go under the command of Colonel MacIver, who will immediately report to the General commanding the department. Lieutenant Alberto Giocouria of the Engineer Corps is relieved from the same with the knowledge of the Commander-in-Chief, to operate hereafter as Assistant Inspector General. By order of the Commander-in-Chief.

"Domingo de Giocouria."

A later order issued on board the *Lilian* four days subsequently again referred to MacIver, in the last paragraph. It said: "The chief of the staff of Colonel Del Christo was formed under the idea of establishing a brigade under his command. The change that has taken place compels the appointments of the officers to be cancelled. They will be transferred to the command of Colonel MacIver's corps of officers not commissioned."

Colonel Del Christo originally had been appointed to the command of a brigade, but, having been superseded in favour of General Williams, he was so displeased that he gave up the Battalion de Cazadores de Hatuez, and retired from the expedition, hence the transfer of his staff officers to MacIver's corps.

It was not anticipated by General de Giocouria that the *Lilian* would be allowed to proceed on her voyage uninterrupted, and he not only expected some interference from the American cruisers, but that he would be chased by Spanish men-of-war. These fears, however, so far proved to be groundless, as not a vessel was sighted except the British brig *Amelia*. All went well on board for a while, but after a few days' sail the *Lilian* was reported to be short of coal, and as there was no chance of the authorities at Nassau in the island of New Providence allowing her to take in fuel, the matter was very serious, affecting as it might do the success of the expedition.

At length, the ship, having reached the Bahamas, could proceed no further, and the expedition had to land at one of the small islands a no great distance from Nassau, with the hope that they should be able to cut a sufficiency of wood to enable the *Lilian* to proceed on her voyage. The troops were at once landed and preparations made for their remaining on the island for a while. Some were set to cut up wood, and others drilled; as much advantage as possible, in this latter respect, being taken of the temporary release of the men from shipboard. Many, of course, had little or no experience in the art of war, so that although the delay was vexatious the time lost was not ill spent.

Colonel MacIver made himself so valuable to the expedition as to earn the special commendations of General de Giocouria, who said that for ability in tactics and as an organiser, he was one of the most brilliant young officers he had ever met. This was no small compliment, coming from the lips of De Giocouria, who was an old and experienced officer in the Spanish service.

While the *Lilian* was detained at the island waiting for fuel, the British authorities at Nassau were taking immediate and stringent measures to put an end to her voyage. By some means the English Governor of New Providence had got wind of the affair, and had learnt the particulars of the sailing of the steamer from Cedar Keys, and her presumed destination. As the representative of a power at friendship with Spain, this official had but one course

P

open to him, and he lost no time in carrying out what he believed to be his duty to his Government.

In the meantime the drilling and wood cutting went on satisfactorily. In about a week after landing so much wood had been collected that it was expected two or three days more would enable the steamer to resume her interrupted voyage. Although there were plenty of willing hands, the refueling of the ship had been necessarily slow, as the number of axes at command were but limited.

However, as it proved, they might have saved themselves all the trouble and hard work, for fate was against them. When everything was nearly ready, and preparations were being made for re-embarking the troops, a British ship of war appeared upon the scene, and put an end to the voyage of the unlucky *Lilian*.

CHAPTER XXX.

SEIZURE OF THE "LILIAN"—TAKEN TO NASSAU—MACIVER SICK UNTO DEATH—LEAVES FOR CUBA—AN ORDER FOR HIS ARREST, AND A NARROW ESCAPE

On the arrival of the English frigate at the island her commander at once confiscated the *Lilian*, her stores, and arms. Putting a prize crew on board, he took her and General de Giocouria's expeditionary force back with him to Nassau. At this port fortune again frowned on the supporters of Cuban independence. Yellow fever broke out amongst the troops, and a large number were stricken down, amongst whom, after a time, was Colonel MacIver.

In the end a great many of the expeditionary force died of the fever, including Colonel Keats, of the Engineers. Fortunately for MacIver he fell into good hands, and was nursed carefully to convalescence. His was a very bad case of fever, and it was only by great attention that he was pulled through.

In the meantime, the Cuban expeditionary force, after being detained a short time in New Providence, had been shipped off to America, and returned to New York. A few only remained behind in Nassau, and amongst the number MacIver. Thus for several weeks the Colonel stayed at the Bahamas, and enjoyed life amongst the islands. When he was well enough he was taken for a cruise through a part of this wonderful group, which is said to be five hundred in number, and amongst other spots went on shore at San Salvador, the first land discovered by Columbus in 1492.

In the meanwhile he learnt that General de Giocouria had again sailed from America with a considerable force, and at length had effected a landing in Cuba, where he was carrying on the war of independence. When this news reached him, Colonel MacIver decided to take passage for Cuba at the first favourable opportunity which should offer for landing at some convenient port. He knew well enough it must be at some out-of-the-way spot, or his immediate arrest would follow as a matter of course.

Besides his late connection with General de Giocouria, and what he felt besides was his duty to the cause he had espoused, he was curious to see for himself how the war was being carried on, and how the Cubans would fight for that independence which they had so long been anxious to obtain. But probably the chief incentive that moved him to leave again for the Spanish island was the craving to be where strife was going on. Yet, although he had made up his mind to attempt to join General de Giocouria, the carrying out of that design was not so easy. More than once he could have found a passage from New Providence to Havannah, but to land there would entail suspicion, if not arrest, and he knew that if once suspected it would be next to impossible to reach Giocouria's command.

At last, when he was almost beginning to despair, he heard of a small brig that was leaving Nassau for Cuba, and he took a berth on board her. The master promised to land him at a small seaport near Cienfuegos, which was so unimportant a spot that it was but little frequented except by fishing craft and traders along the coast. As soon as the brig had completed her cargo, MacIver went on board, his departure being known but to few, and after a quick and pleasant run he landed safely in Cuba. To his gratification his appearance at the port seemed to be taken little or no notice of, and he took care to be very careful in his movements for a few days, so that no cause might arise as to his motives for visiting the island, except those which he had announced—pleasure, and a change of scene and air, after a long illness.

Although he had landed in Cuba without interruption, to make his way to that part of the island where General de Giocouria was contending for

Cuban independence against the Spanish Royalist troops under General Caballero de Rodas, was no easy matter. He had not only a long distance to travel, but must perhaps pass through the Spanish lines before he could attach himself to De Giocouria's troops.

Nothing daunted, however, he set out on his perilous journey, and after twice nearly falling into the hands of the enemy, and having also to undergo a considerable amount of privation, he at length succeeded in reaching the Cuban forces. On reporting himself at headquarters he was received with much *empressement* by General de Giocouria, who, to tell the truth, was just then so hard pressed that the advent of a daring and dashing young officer like MacIver was a matter of no small importance to him.

When the expeditionary army had been organised in New York, Colonel MacIver had been appointed chief of the cavalry, but now that he came face to face with the enemy, he found that there were no cavalry to command. The troopers might be there— or the material out of which they were intended to be formed—but there were no horses to mount them. General de Giocouria explained this somewhat apologetically on his first interview with MacIver at the seat of war. The following day he appointed him instead to the command of a body of infantry, composed in the main of natives of the island, and officered principally by Cubans.

It made little difference to our friend what nationality he led, so that they fought well before the enemy, and from the appearance of his new men they looked a likely enough set of fellows. It was not long, however, before he was to have the opportunity of trying their metal in the field. Three days after joining the Cubans, it was reported that the enemy was advancing in force, and shortly afterwards some of the vedettes came in with the news that General de Rodas had occupied a wood not far distant on the right with a strong body of Royalist troops.

Colonel MacIver was ordered to the front to, if possible, dislodge this advanced party of Spaniards, and moved forward with his command without seeing anything of the enemy until he was within some quarter of a mile of the wood which they were reported to have occupied. His men stepped out briskly enough, and apparently highly elated at having the chance of a brush with the Royalists. Presently the enemy commenced his ball practice from his shelter in the forest, but his firing was but desultory, and did little harm to the Cubans, who advanced boldly to the charge.

It had been Colonel MacIver's intention to drive the Spaniards out of the wood at the point of the bayonet, and hitherto he had not wasted a shot upon an enemy that he could not see. Now as he advanced to closer quarters, the enemy's fire became steady and well directed, and his men began to drop before the hail of bullets. Suddenly, to his chagrin, he saw that there was a want of steadiness in the ranks, and that some of his men were beginning to waver. To have halted even for a moment would have been fatal, and he gave the word to charge, dashing forward himself sword in hand, and a few moments later had crossed blades with a Spanish officer, a tall, powerful fellow, and moreover a good swordsman.

But only a few of the boldest of the Cubans had followed their Colonel into the wood. The rest were in a state of disorganisation and had halted in spite of the efforts of some of the company officers to urge them on. After a fierce contest of a few brief seconds MacIver had to fall back before the mere weight of overpowering numbers, and although on rejoining the main body of his men he tried both entreaties and threats to induce them to follow him in a second dash upon the wood, his words were useless. Finally he had to retire as best he could, cursing the Cubans both loud and deep for a set of cowards.

General de Giocouria came galloping up as MacIver commanded his men to retire within the shelter of their own lines. The General, a grand old soldier, who had seen much service formerly in the Spanish Army, was as furious as the Colonel at the want of pluck shown by the Cubans under fire, although, probably, he did not express himself in such strong and indignant terms as the latter.

MacIver sternly declared—which was no doubt true—that had the Royalists in the wood taken advantage of the opportunity, and charged in their turn, they must have cut his men down almost to a man. The disaster, too, was all the more annoying, from the fact that the wood which the Spaniards occupied might be said to be the key to the position, as so long as it was held by the enemy, they might seriously harass the Cuban force.

After looking through his field-glass for a few seconds, General de Giocouria turned to MacIver, and said, "The enemy must be dislodged from that post at any risk."

"I will undertake to carry it," replied the Colonel, "if only a handful of brave men will follow me."

The words of both officers were spoken aloud and heard by many. Immediately a number of volunteers crowded round MacIver, most of them Americans, and many of them officers. In less time than it has taken us to write, the gallant little band, shoulder to shoulder, moved forward to the attack. Presently the bullets of the enemy began to whistle about them. Then the quick step was changed into the double, and with a ringing cheer they dashed into the wood. The conflict was sharp and short, and in a few minutes the Spaniards were seen flying before the swords and bayonets of the undaunted men, whom they must have outnumbered by four to one.

The dashing charge, although it more than repaid MacIver for his previous failure, did not prevent the fortune of the day going against the Cuban forces. General de Giocouria had little or no artillery, and in this and in other respects he was at considerable disadvantage. The Spaniards, too, not only outnumbered him, but they were better organised, and armed, and better found in every respect; and as he was compelled inwardly to confess, more courageous under fire than the majority of his Cuban soldiers.

The unfortunate De Giocouria did his best with the material at his command, but on this, Colonel MacIver's first engagement against the Spaniards, as on many previous occasions, the brave General had to fall back before the victorious Royalist commander, and make a speedy retreat. The disasters which had lately attended De Giocouria might have had something to do with disheartening the Cubans, for they certainly fought worse and worse.

Still the Spaniards did not have it all their own way, and their records of killed and wounded were very heavy. Amongst the insurgent forces were many strong-hearted and strong-armed soldiers of the Anglo-Saxon race, who possessed all the courage and dogged obstinacy of the men of that Mother Country, of which they were worthy sons. These might be defeated, but only when they had done all that man could do, and who—those that were left of them—were as ready to fight again on the morrow, as though disaster had never come.

In the meantime, while this fierce contest was going on between the Cubans and their Spanish masters, the commerce of Cuba, "The Pearl of the Antilles," as the Americans called it, was being ruined, and the rich plantations of sugar and tobacco laid waste. For months had the native forces been engaged in the deadly conflict with the home power, and everything had been neglected but terrible war. In the eloquent words of Mr. Senator Sumner spoken at the time, "The beautiful island was fast becoming a desert, while the nation to which Columbus gave the New World was contending for its last possession there."

CHAPTER XXXI.

CUBA AND HER CLAIMS—THE INSURRECTION—DISASTER

At the time the natives of Cuba first rose in arms against the Spaniards, whom, in spite of being of the same blood, they regarded as oppressors, they no doubt anticipated that they would have the assistance of a great power, their near neighbour, whose own example in casting off the home yoke they were in a smaller way but attempting to imitate.

That the Cubans had suffered great injustice—nay, cruel wrong—from Spain, was a matter of history; and it was little to be wondered at that a down-trodden nation, the inhabitants of an island seven hundred miles long by eighty broad, should wish to sever themselves from an effete power, that ruled by the aid of soldiers, and with a grip of iron. But, however great was the desire for freedom, it is a question if the Cubans would ever have rebelled against the home rule, however unjust, had they not hoped and believed that they would have the armed assistance of the United States. The Americans, who had wrested their thirteen colonies from Great Britain and established their independence, could not, they thought, stand idly by whilst Cuba struggled to be free.

That the sympathies of the majority of the Americans were in favour of the Cuban insurrection there was little doubt, and if the feeling of the vast mass of the people could have had its way it would have made but short work of the pretensions of Spain to retain her West Indian island. But there was one little awkward matter standing in the way of help from her great neighbour upon which Cuba had not reckoned.

The Government of the United States, however much they might desire to see the independence of Cuba proclaimed, could scarcely go to the gross inconsistency of assisting her with armed intercession at the very moment when they were making a grave complaint against Great Britain for merely proclaiming neutrality and recognising the rights of belligerency to the Confederate States at the outbreak of their own recent and unhappy civil war.

The United States were therefore compelled to retain a position of neutrality in the struggle going on between Cuba and Spain, but they went so far as to endeavour to help the insurgents by tendering friendly offers to the home power for her voluntarily giving up the island of Cuba. This Spain as promptly declined to do, although at this, the first period of the insurrection, when General de Giocouria was opposed by General Dulce, the fortune of war appeared to be greatly in favour of the former commander.

Perhaps we shall better understand the persistency with which Spain clung to Porto Rico and Cuba when we remember that they were the last of the vast and rich possessions which she once possessed in America and on its coast. Had it not been for this, one would scarcely conceive, proverbial as is said to be the pride of the Castilians, that the Spanish nation, with trouble and conflict at home, would have cared to waste money and men over an island which at the best could be of no great benefit, and in fact has cost her more in keeping up than it has ever benefited her. However, with persistent obstinacy, Spain did her best to put down the insurrection, and any advantage which the Cuban forces at first gained speedily slipped from their grasp. Reverse followed reverse, until at length the insurgents might be fairly said to be brought to bay.

Still General de Giocouria and the principal officers —such men as Colonel MacIver—fought on, even after all hope of success was at an end. Had the Cuban forces been formed of such material as the Commander-in-Chief and a few of his followers were made of, no doubt the result of the war would have been very different, and Cuba now a free and independent nation. But much as they desired liberty, and strong as might have been the first determination of the natives to release themselves from Spanish rule, when brought to the test the flesh was found to be weak in that most essential point, being able to stand the fire of the enemy.

At length the end came. General de Giocouria was signally defeated in a final pitched battle against the Spanish forces, and his command almost cut to pieces. The few who remained fighting to the last, and escaped death or capture, had to fly for their lives as hunted fugitives. Amongst the handful of men who were staunch to their chief until all was lost was Colonel MacIver, and although in the heat of the *mêlée* whilst it lasted, he was not only uninjured, but succeeded in evading the attempts made to capture him, fighting his way to freedom with one or two others.

When night set in he found himself alone, and

uncertain which way to take to ensure his safety from arrest. To seek the shelter of any house for the present he knew was like rushing into the lion's den, although, worn out as he was by fatigue, he would have been glad of a resting-place, however humble. He was hungry, too, and knew not where to procure food even with the aid of the Spanish gold in his pocket. However, he did not despair of concealing himself until the first hot pursuit was over, for during the war the tillage and cultivation of the country had been so neglected that there were plenty of spots which were almost deserted, and in one of these sparsely-inhabited districts he hoped to find not only concealment, but probably help from some Cuban Samaritan.

That the search for fugitives would be carried out through the island, with all the craft and ingenuity of which the Spaniards were capable, he knew, but he determined to evade them if possible, by any means, or if the worst came, to sell his life dearly, and to die rather than be taken. He left his sword as a now useless weapon in a deserted sugar plantation through which he passed, as he had his revolver, loaded in all its chambers, safely about his person. He found relief to his hunger, too, in a few canes of sugar which he broke off, and then, resolving to put as much distance as possible before morning between himself and the scene of the late disastrous battle, he walked on as fast as his tired limbs would carry him.

Long before daylight, however, but when he believed he must have covered a good score of miles, he came upon some small cottages, and on turning aside to avoid them he found that he was at the edge of one of those dense forests so common in the island. It occurred to him that he could not find a more secure hiding-place than this wood, the intricacies of which might bid defiance to all but a most persistent and thorough search. Under ordinary circumstances he would not have cared to venture within the recesses of such a place after dark, for there was always the chance of being bitten by one of the venomous snakes that abounded in the forest, and whose sting was at all times highly dangerous, and frequently fatal in its effect. But venomous serpents were little to be dreaded in comparison with the man-hunters who now were scouring the island far and near, and MacIver, without hesitation, plunged into the depths of the forest, oblivious of everything but his present safety, and the discovery of some quiet spot where he could find a resting-place for his weary body.

For nearly a week did the Colonel remain in the forest, not daring to venture forth, and subsisting on such edible roots and fruit as he could find, and a drink of water taken up from a rivulet in the palm of his hand. On two or three occasions during that first week of his sojourn in the wood he saw parties of Royalist soldiers scouring the country, and once they searched for fully an hour in the forest where he was concealed, and came within a few paces of his hiding-place. At length his hunger became so difficult to bear, and his craving for food so overpowering, that on the seventh day that he had been in the wood he determined to venture forth in search of something more substantial and satisfying than the fruit and roots upon which hitherto he had managed to subsist.

For the last day or two he had seen no Royalist soldiers, and that morning, as on previous occasions, he had noticed four men take their departure from the cottages, as if going to their work. The hope dawned upon him that none but females might be left at home, and that if he could communicate with one of them unobserved by the others, he might enlist her sympathy so far as to be able to induce her to give or sell him some food.

With cautious steps, and many a look in each direction around him, Colonel MacIver stole forth from the wood, and, making a detour, he managed to approach within fifty yards of one of the cottages without seeing or meeting a soul, and as he fondly hoped without being observed himself. Sheltering behind a low bush he waited patiently to see if any one should come forth. Nearly an hour seemed to have elapsed, although it was probably not more than half that time, when to his delight he saw the door of the cottage nearest to him open and a young girl come out of the house.

She carried one of the earthen vessels used by the Cubans for holding water, and was evidently going to some well or spring close by. She approached, too, in the direction where the Colonel had crouched down, and for fear that his sudden appearance might startle, and cause her to rush back in alarm ere he could communicate with her, he allowed her to pass by the bush before he disclosed himself.

Then he whispered a few reassuring words in the best Spanish he could command, and raised himself from his crouching position. For a moment the girl seemed inclined to turn and fly, and the Colonel was afraid, too, that she was about to scream. With his finger on his lip he motioned her to keep silence, and the girl must have realised at once that he was a fugitive, and have read aright his look of entreaty, for quickly suppressing her first alarm, she glanced pityingly at the half-famished stranger.

As briefly as possible MacIver told her who and what he was, and begged her to procure him some food, entreating her at the same time not to betray him. The girl asked him in a soft musical voice to remain where he had been concealed behind the bush until she returned from the well, when she would bring him some food.

Presently she again passed on her way to the cottage, and shortly afterwards brought him out a loaf of coarse bread and some slices of cooked meat, and what was almost equally acceptable, some leaf tobacco. The Colonel offered her a gold coin in return, but the girl shook her head and refused anything but his thanks. She told him, too, with a look of pity, that he had better not venture near the cottages again, as the Spanish soldiers had been frequently in the neighbourhood of late, and added, in her simple way, that they would kill him. She, however, promised, if possible, to contrive to come down to the forest on the following morning, and to bring with her some more provisions; and a little wine if she could procure it, or if not, some milk.

Anxiously enough next day did the Colonel look out for the approach of the kindly young Cuban who had so nobly befriended him, but hour after hour went by without her making her appearance. At length it grew so late that he had given up all hope of seeing her for that day at least, as in an hour or so it would be dark. But at length, true to her promise, she came tripping along from the cottages, although not alone, for a handsome Cuban youth accompanied her, carrying with him a rough kind of wicker basket.

CHAPTER XXXII.

FRIENDS IN NEED—A LOVE AFFAIR AND A QUARREL—FLIGHT AND A LUCKY ESCAPE

At first Colonel MacIver looked with some suspicion on the young Cuban who was the girl's companion. He seemed like a peasant, and by his dress was probably employed at one of the copper mines in the neighbourhood. When the fugitive officer came to talk to him, he seemed a straightforward, honest sort of fellow. He brought with him provisions that would last for a day or two, and a bottle of wine, and promised that whenever it was safe he would venture down to the forest with a fresh supply. At the same time he warned the fugitive that Royalist soldiers were in the vicinity, and were hunting in every direction for officers and stragglers belonging to the late insurgent army. Like the girl, he refused a money reward.

It was nearly a week before the peasant again visited him, and MacIver had scarcely been disappointed at his non-appearance, as the Spanish troopers had not only again passed by the forest, but had actually searched it. Thus, with occasional visits from one or both of the young Cubans, nearly two weeks sped by, and the Colonel still remained concealed in the forest.

One day when his friends came, he heard with regret of the death of his old chief, General de Giocouria, who, they told him, had been executed by order of the Spanish Government. MacIver, on learning this, determined to leave the forest and make his way down to Cienfuegos, with the hope of ultimately being able to escape from the island. It was necessary, however, that he should be disguised, and the young Cuban undertook to purchase the clothes and other requisite articles.

At length he bade farewell to his two faithful young friends, and, unsuspected as he believed, made his way boldly down to Cienfuegos. He had not long arrived there, however, before he nearly got himself into another duel—this time with a Spanish noble—the cause being a fair Cuban, with whom the Colonel established an incipient flirtation as innocent as it was amusing to both parties.

The girl kept a cigar shop in a very narrow street abutting on the footpath. This box of a place was so circumscribed as to space that it was scarcely possible for two people to pass each other within it, but here were vended for sale the choicest of cigars and tobacco leaves. The fair shopkeeper who presided was as remarkable for her beauty as for the excellence of her tobacco, and her customers were not only numerous but aristocratic.

There was no window to the shop, and during the hot hours of the day a curtain was suspended to keep off the fierce rays of the sun, which would have been injurious to the delicate goods exposed for sale, and probably also to the complexion of the fair seller. Into this miniature warehouse MacIver used often to drop in for a cigar and a chat, thus enjoying his smoke and improving his Spanish.

There was a small counter, with little pyramidal heaps of cigarette packets and cigars of genuine Havannah brand heaped upon it, and behind where the fair Cuban sat to serve her customers was a glass-fronted case, with bundles of precious tobacco leaves tied up with the brightest of yellow ribbon.

The girl who owned this establishment was as good and modest as she was handsome, which caused her to have all the more admirers, high and low. One of these would-be lovers, a certain Don Pedro Diaz, not only took offence at MacIver's frequent visits to the cigar store, but was foolish enough to show it in a manner that our friend was about the last man to submit to, especially in the presence of a woman.

On the occasion to which we refer, almost before he could realise what he had brought upon himself, the Spaniard found his noble person bundled out of the shop, and pitched on to the opposite side of the narrow street, from whence he gathered himself up with many threats of vengeance. The result, of course, was a challenge, but before the duel could come off, Don Pedro was shot whilst in pursuit of some of the unhappy Cuban outlaws.

Singularly enough, MacIver met at this tobacconist's a Spanish Royalist officer, who proved to be a brother Mason, and this gentleman was the means of doing him a very signal service, by saving him from a great danger which threatened his liberty, and possibly his life. By some means the Spanish authorities began to suspect MacIver, and through their secret agents discovered that he was an Englishman, who had formerly held an important command in the expeditionary force which sailed from Cedar Keys. The instant this was known an order was given for his arrest.

Fortunately for the Colonel, the knowledge of what was about to take place came to the ears of his brother Mason, the Royalist officer, who immediately gave MacIver warning of the danger that threatened him, and moreover, at great risk to himself, kept the stranger concealed in his own apartments until a favourable opportunity presented itself for his leaving the town unobserved. The noble Spaniard, too, provided him with a supply of food and wine that would last for some days, and one night, about an hour after midnight the Colonel succeeded in leaving the town and getting clear away into the open country.

Although he had evaded the Spaniards for the moment, he was still in great peril, for whilst he remained in the island, his life was not safe, and how he was to get away from Cuba he could not conceive. He walked on until about an hour before daybreak, and then coming to a large tobacco plantation, he hid himself in an old hut or shed which had the appearance of not having been used for a length of time. Here, after he had refreshed himself with a draught of wine and a few mouthfuls of bread, he threw himself down in a dark corner, and spite the danger of discovery was soon sound asleep. He had walked long and fast, and he was so tired that he slept until nearly three o'clock in the afternoon without awaking.

He was aroused by the sound of voices, which appeared to be close at hand, and he started up, grasping his revolver, and anticipating momentarily to see the speakers, whoever they were, enter the hut. Contrary to his expectations, however, he was not disturbed, and, on looking through a crack in the wall, he saw that the people whom he had heard were three negroes, who were at work in the fields, amongst the tobacco plants. To his satisfaction they kept moving further away, and very shortly he lost the sound of their voices altogether. He neither saw nor heard anything more of them during the afternoon, nor did any other person come near him. As soon as it was quite dark he left the hut, but before starting he made a substantial meal to prepare him for his long night march.

The country through which he was travelling, being not far from the sea coast, was pretty level, and fruitful as was the soil, large tracts of it were lying now idle. He passed one or two sugar plantations, and another of tobacco in cultivation, but these he skirted so as to avoid coming in contact with any of the inhabitants.

At length he came to a large forest, the trees of which appeared to be principally cedar, and although it yet wanted a couple of hours to daylight, he decided to seek shelter under their friendly covering, and to take a few hours' rest. For greater safety, he managed to scramble up into the branch of one of the large trees, where he found a secure and not uncomfortable resting-place. He feared to sleep, however, lest he should slip from the branch, and tried to keep awake until it was light enough for him to get a good view of the country around. If, as he more than half suspected, he was in a part but little frequented, he could close his eyes for a while in peace, and then push on again during the daylight, shielded from sight by the wood.

As he had already imagined, when day broke he saw no sign of anything human about him. Some part of the country had evidently been recently under cultivation, but was now wild and neglected, having probably been deserted at the outbreak of the war. As the sun rose, the forest in which he had taken shelter was fairly alive with birds and insect life. It seemed, too, to abound with game of various descriptions, as did the land around. A rivulet ran close to where he had taken shelter in the tree, and the sight of the cool, clear water was a great relief to him, as his mouth was parched and his face and brow hot and feverish.

When he had drank freely, and thrown some of the cold water over his head and face, he felt much refreshed, and returned to the forest, where, on a bed of dry leaves, he was soon fast asleep. Before noon, however, he was again on his feet, and had resumed his journey. By keeping within the forest, he concluded that he could walk for the remainder of the journey without scarcely a chance of meeting any one or of being seen, and when night came he might rest, if in the meantime he had not found some means of escape along the coast.

His plan of action was to reach the shore, with the hope that he might discover some small vessel about to sail, or, failing that, that he should find a boat in which he could put to sea and trust to being picked up by a passing ship. It was, he knew, a desperate resolve, but anything was better than being arrested by the man-hunting soldiers of the Spanish tyrant who ruled over the island of Cuba. There was, too, he felt, another danger before him, that of being lost in the forest, but he fancied he should be able to guard against this, by keeping as near as possible on the edge, and from which, by the shadow of the sun, he could easily judge his distance.

CHAPTER XXXIII.

LOST IN THE FOREST—DANGEROUS NEIGHBOURS—ALONE ON THE WIDE ATLANTIC IN AN OPEN BOAT

MacIver must have travelled through the forest for some hours, when the idea forced itself upon him that he had returned to a spot which he was certain he had passed at least an hour before. This was where a large cedar tree had become uprooted by age, or by tempest, and had partly fallen, resting in peculiar position against another giant of the forest. Entwining round the living and the dead tree, and as it were uniting them, was a mass of tall, luxuriant creepers, covered with blossoms of the most gorgeous hues, which, as they hung from branch to branch, assumed the shape of a cascade.

The moment his eyes rested on this tree for the

second time—for that he had seen it before he could not doubt—he came to the disagreeable conclusion that he must have lost himself, and got away from the skirt of the forest. Although at spots he had had to force his way for a short distance through the undergrowth, the route that he had travelled had seemed like a path, which, if not recently trodden by man, had often been used.

After a few minutes of consideration, MacIver thought the wisest course for him to adopt was to retrace his steps, for it was evident that he had not only gone wrong, but that he had wandered further away from the edge of the forest than he had supposed, as the trees grew so thickly together that he could not catch even a glimpse of the sun, which, on looking at his watch, he found must be now fast sinking to the western horizon.

Although he had travelled far, and was weary, the thought of being benighted in the forest made him step out with renewed briskness; but he wandered on and on without any sign of an opening in the thick mass of foliage above and around him, whilst each minute the surroundings seemed to become more gloomy Night was beginning to set in, and it would soon be too dark to attempt to proceed further, and he felt that he must look about for some convenient nook in which he could rest until daylight.

Although the enemies whom he most desired to avoid were men, he was by no means certain that the forest might not contain foes even more deadly to him. However, the Colonel had no choice but to remain where he was, and at length he seated himself with his back to the trunk of a cedar, and placed his revolver on the ground, ready to his hand. He had still a little of the wine left, of which he drank about half, and then lighted a cigar. But he was so tired and worn out with walking and the want of proper sleep, that he could not have taken many whiffs of the fragrant Havannah before it dropped from his mouth and a deep slumber overpowered him. He slept so soundly, that it was already broad daylight when he awoke, nothing having disturbed nor, as far as he knew, approached him during the night.

MacIver made a frugal breakfast, for his supply of food was getting low, and he knew not where he should obtain more. He was compelled to drink his last drop of wine to quench his thirst, but he kept the bottle so that he might fill it with water at the first opportunity. In better spirits than the night before, but somewhat footsore, he again commenced his journey, yet quite uncertain where his steps would lead him. More than once he diverged to the right or left where the trees appeared thinner, in the hope that the edge of the forest was near, but only to be disappointed. The day was about half spent when, much to his delight, the trees became perceptibly further apart, the light brighter, and the ground clothed with a carpeting of grass. Immediately he hurried forward, and in a few minutes stood on the verge of the forest. And there, oh, glorious sight! stretching before him, and but a couple of miles away, was the broad expanse of the Spanish Main. He saw, too, that there was a small port, the houses and the masts of the vessels being sharply defined against the background of sea and sky.

But whilst he still gazed enraptured by the view,

another sight met his eyes, which did not please him so well. About half-way between the forest and the port, but advancing in a direction towards where he stood, was a small body of men, which his practised eye at once perceived to be soldiers, and whom presently he made out to be Royalist troops. This was indeed a dilemma, and he drew quickly back into the forest, where, concealed behind the trunk of a tree, he could unseen watch their movements.

Were it not impossible that such could have been the case, it might have seemed that they knew that he was there, for they marched straight on towards the spot where he had first emerged from the forest. This armed party appeared to number about a score, and was under the charge of an officer. No doubt they were searching for others like himself, whom the Spanish Government were anxious to arrest. However, he had had enough of the forest, and determined, at whatever risk, not to plunge again into its depths; he therefore looked about him for the most likely spot to conceal himself until the soldiers had passed by, and chose a huge tree covered with dense foliage, into the branches of which he managed to scramble.

Much to the dismay of MacIver, when the Royalist troops arrived within about thirty paces of where he was hidden, the Lieutenant in command halted his men, and presently they unstrapped their haversacks, and made preparations for their midday meal. From his elevated resting-place, the Colonel not only looked down into their midst, but occasionally could catch the meaning of the words they uttered, which latter confirmed his suspicions that they were watching the line of coast to prevent the escape of Cubans, or others recently fighting for the independence of the island. He feared at first that they might take it into their heads to remain for some hours until the heat of the day was past, when by some unfortunate accident he might be discovered. Luckily, however, their stay was short, and they departed, happily for him, oblivious of the fact of how near they had been to effecting an important capture.

When they had gone, the Colonel descended from the tree, and found that they had left behind them some pieces of fine white bread and also a bottle containing a small quantity of wine. These were very welcome, and he valued the bottle almost as much as the wine which it contained, for if he should have to trust himself alone on the sea in an open boat, as he believed would be his only chance of escape, it would prove invaluable when filled with water. He decided, however, not to venture down to the coast until it was dark, as the risk which he must run would be too great, and the attempt might end in his capture; even then he determined to avoid entering the town if possible. How anxiously he waited for night to set in can be well imagined.

At length the time came when he could venture. He had already been down to a brook and drank as copiously as it was safe for him to do, rinsing out also and filling his two bottles with water, and washing his hands and face. The night was anything but dark, the heavens being brilliant with myriads of stars. Leaving the port on his left, he struck down towards the beach, which he reached in about half-an-hour, being then a good mile away from the town; but though he looked searchingly along the water's edge, as far as he could discern on each side of him, he could see no sign of a boat.

He was at a loss now what to do. If he walked further along the coast there was less chance than ever of finding a boat until he came to some other seaport or fishing village, and if he ventured into the town near him, and succeeded in getting some small craft, he probably might be seen as he put out to sea—unless he waited until a very late hour. However, to delay was perhaps more dangerous than the risk of discovery, and of the two alternatives, whether to go further along the coast, or to turn towards the town, he chose the latter.

MacIver walked cautiously, without meeting or seeing any one until he was within a quarter of a mile of the nearest house, when he came to a little rivulet, which discharged itself into the ocean. This was most likely the same stream at which he had filled his two bottles, higher up, and at its mouth, to his delight, he found a small boat moored to a stake. On closer inspection, too, he discovered that she had a sail and mast and a couple of oars. He next looked to see if he could find a keg, or anything that would hold a supply of water, but here he was unsuccessful. Placing his two precious bottles in the stern-sheets, where they were not liable to be upset or broken, he unfastened the painter and stepped cautiously into the little craft, pushing her off as noiselessly as possible.

Colonel MacIver was now afloat on the broad Atlantic, in a frail little boat which, although safe enough so long as the weather kept fine, would probably founder or be capsized at the first appearance of a storm. However, he gave little thought of that at present; his chief anxiety was to get away from the shore, and, if possible, out of sight of land before morning. There was a slight breeze off the land, but he could not for a while venture to step the mast, and put the boat under sail, as the risk of being seen was too great. He knew that if discovered he would be chased, and in all likelihood speedily overhauled. But getting out the oars as silently as might be, he pulled slowly out seaward, leaving a bright line in his wake from the phosphorescent water.

More than once he ceased rowing, listening intently, and looking towards the harbour, but although sounds came on the night air, they were not those indicative of an alarm being given. Gradually the shore receded further and further away, until at length he lost sight of the low line of coast. Then unshipping the oars he stepped the mast, and with a full sheet, was soon bowling away before the breeze, the sea calm, and with a vast, cloudless canopy of blue and gold around and above him.

CHAPTER XXXIV.

A DREARY VOYAGE—GHASTLY COMPANIONS—PICKED UP BY A STEAMER.

ALL night did the breeze serve, and when day at length broke the little boat in which sat the Colonel was still making good headway. Anxiously did he scan the horizon, but there was naught to be seen but the vast expanse of trackless ocean. He had fully expected to find himself out of sight of land, but he had hoped at the same time that some passing ship might have rewarded his searching glance.

After sunrise the breeze gradually died away, until the boat lay becalmed and almost motionless upon the sea. The Colonel had not tasted food since the previous afternoon, and he now took a morsel of bread and a drink of water. He next proceeded to examine his stock of provisions, which was small indeed. He calculated that he might keep himself from actual starvation for three or four days, and if he limited himself to about half a pint of water a day, his supply of that might last for about the same period. As to his escape from the boat, his only chance was of being picked up by some passing ship. If he had been on the other side of the island he might probably have reached one of the Bahamas, but now the only islands that he knew of where he would find safety were the Caymans and Jamaica; and even if his food and water would hold out long enough to enable him to reach any of these, he knew not in which direction to steer.

But what the Colonel dreaded more than anything else was that a storm should arise, as he found that the boat was very old and far from being watertight. Twice during the night he had had to bale her out, and he felt certain that in a rough sea she must inevitably founder or go to pieces.

As the sun rose higher in the heavens, it beat down upon him in a fierce heat that was almost unbearable, and this unfortunately engendered a burning thirst which he dared not quench. After a time, however, it occurred to him that he might make the boat's sail serve as an awning to keep off the glare, and from that, and laving his hands and face in the sea water, he found immediate relief.

To attempt to row the boat with the oars he considered would be useless, as he would not only have to expose himself to the sun, but could expect to make but little headway. At all events, he decided to wait until evening, with the chance and in the hope that a breeze would again spring up. In the meantime he forgot his danger and late troubles by dropping off into a quiet slumber, and slept soundly for some hours, he, the solitary man and his frail little craft, being left alone to the mercy of Heaven. When he awoke he again looked anxiously around with, it must be confessed, but a faint hope of seeing the smoke of some ocean steamer. His chances of escape, he was compelled to acknowledge, were very small, for unless he fell in with an American or English vessel he might as well perish in the boat. If picked up by a ship under Spanish colours, he knew too well what his fate would be.

As these thoughts flashed through his mind and he turned his gaze from the often anxiously scanned horizon, his eyes happened to rest on the sea about a dozen yards astern of the boat. There, rising above the water, was the dark fin of a huge shark, as the monster lay basking in the sunlight. For a minute or two it remained stationary, and then with a slow gliding motion it approached close to the boat's gunwale, so near, indeed, that MacIver could actually discern the ghastly glare of its horrid-looking eyes.

Suddenly as he gazed, half fascinated with the basilisk glance, the shark sank from view, and he saw no more of it for the present, nor of any of its fellows. Its appearance, however, reminded him of the stories he had heard of the persistency with which these monsters are said to follow shipwrecked men when in an open boat, waiting for a horrid meal of the first human body which should be cast into the sea.

Towards evening the Colonel ventured to partake sparingly of food, and to drink a little water. The latter, however, tasted warm and brackish, and although it relieved, it did not quench his almost intolerable thirst. But as the sun went down the air became cooler, and presently a breath of wind again sprang up. First it came with a few gentle puffs, and then settled down into a three or four knot breeze, and, almost at once, MacIver felt reinvigorated.

Judging by the direction of the setting sun, he headed the boat to a course which he believed, if held, would eventually bring him between the island of Cuba and that of Jamaica, where he concluded he had the best chance of falling in with a British or American ship. In fact, he cared not what flag she sailed under so that it was not Spanish. Much to his satisfaction, too, although the breeze freshened towards midnight, the ocean kept wonderfully calm. The little boat, spite of her unseaworthiness, sailed well, and he took care to keep her in good trim by baling when necessary, lashing the tiller on such occasions so as to keep her to her proper course.

After night set in, he had been much struck by

the peculiar appearance of the sea in the wake of and around the boat. Bright flashes of greenish light scintillated for a short space on every side, which, for a time, he attributed to the highly charged phosphorescence of the water. Presently, however, he realised that this beautiful effect was produced by the sharks which had given him their company The discovery was anything but a pleasant one, for if some huge monster amongst them should by accident or design strike the rotten planking of the boat, there would be a speedy end to his voyage. However, although they followed him all night long, and at times approached dangerously near, no such mishap as he feared occurred.

Judging by the previous night, he had expected the breeze to die away at break of day, or shortly afterwards; but, contrary to his anticipation, there was enough of wind to give the boat headway until a couple of hours past noon ; so that he must have covered a considerable extent of mileage when at length the sail hung idly against the mast, and the boat floated almost motionless on the ocean.

Neither had he felt the heat so much as on the day previous, and the small quantity of water which in his prudent economy he ventured to drink, seemed for the time to satisfy in a measure the requirements of nature. Now that the boat was again becalmed he took a few hours' rest, first baling her dry, and then sheltering himself from the sun with the sail. A bath in the cool sea would have been most acceptable before sleep, but that was out of the question where sharks literally swarmed.

His slumber was but brief, and even then disturbed. He awoke with a start, and at once glanced quickly around him. Whether it was reality or only fancy he could never tell, but in the far distant horizon to the south-west it seemed that there was a faint line as of smoke from a steamer. He sprang from his seat, and, with his eyes shaded with his hand, gazed long and anxiously in the direction, and for a moment believed that he could make out smoke distinctly. Then it faded and vanished, and he saw it no more. What would he have given at that moment for his field-glass!

A breeze sprang up earlier than usual, and the sun that night went down with an angry-looking glare that MacIver thought threatened a change of weather. There was a slight swell, too, of the ocean which made the boat roll until he got the sail on her to steady her.

The breeze also had chopped round into a different quarter, but as near as he could judge the Colonel endeavoured to steer the boat in the same course as on the previous night and during the morning, although with the wind on her beam she did not make nearly so much headway, and strained somewhat badly, as was proved by the necessity for more frequent baling. But the heavens were still brilliant with their myriads of stars, which shone brightly throughout the night; and although the morning broke with a hazy mist upon the sea, it cleared off as the sun like a great ball of fire rose in gorgeous splendour.

Once more did the Colonel glance anxiously around him as the fog lifted, and now his heart gave a great bound of delight, for not more than three or four miles away was a large steamer. She was dead astern of him, and at first he feared that she had passed him in the mist, or was steaming in an opposite direction, but presently he was able to make out her bows, and to decide that she was fast overhauling the boat.

He was about to lower his sail when it occurred to him that if the watch on board the steamer had not already made out his small craft, they were more likely to do so when she was under canvas, so that he still kept on, but bringing his boat a point or two more up to the wind. It was indeed providential, he felt, that this steamer, whatever she might be, had not passed him in the night. An hour earlier, and in all probability he would not have seen her himself until it was too late, and might then have been left to perish of hunger and thirst.

He was not long in doubt as to being seen. The sight of a solitary boat so far from land had caused a great commotion on board the steamer. As soon as the news of a boat being in sight spread through the ship, passengers and crew crowded on deck to have the first glance at this strange and startling object, and he could soon make out the eager faces, as the large steamer first eased her engines, and then stopped to pick him up.

Colonel MacIver was very kindly received on board, and everything that was possible was done by the officers to make up for his late discomforts and privations. He found, too, that the steamer was bound direct for Nassau. He had had a very narrow escape for his life, for not half-a-dozen hours after he was picked up by the steamer a violent tempest arose, which in its first fury must have swamped his frail little boat. As he watched the lightning and listened to the fierce blasts of the storm as they roared around him, he fully realised that he had indeed cause to be thankful for his merciful deliverance.

When he landed at Nassau he was received by those whom he knew as one from the dead, as in the news of the suppression of the Cuban insurrection, the execution of their General, and the flight or death of most of the officers, he was supposed to have been one of those who had perished.

CHAPTER XXXV

AN AGREEMENT WITH ISMAIL PASHA—MACIVER RECEIVES HIS COMMISSION AS COLONEL OF CAVALRY — JOINS THE EGYPTIAN ARMY

AFTER remaining for a week or two in the island of New Providence, Colonel MacIver took leave of the numerous friends that he had made there and embarked in a schooner for Baltimore. The vessel in which he left Nassau made a very quick and pleasant run to the mainland, and after a somewhat lengthened absence, our friend found himself once more in the United States, free to offer his sword and services whenever and wherever an opportunity should arise.

From Baltimore he went to visit some old Confederate friends in Maryland, but on the Pennsylvania line, with whom he remained until he received a plentiful supply of cash. After which he journeyed on towards Philadelphia, through Pennsylvania, at which city he took the train to New York.

Shortly after his return to the latter city Colonel MacIver entered the service of his Highness the Khedive and proceeded to Egypt, but this, to be the better understood, will require a short preliminary explanation.

At this time there was in the Egyptian Army a General named Thaddeus P Mott, who had formerly been an officer in the Northern Army during the war with the Confederate States, and who had suddenly become the military adviser of Ismail Pasha. General Mott after the conclusion of the American struggle had gone to Europe in a mercantile capacity, being the representative of a firm of gun manufacturers, and amongst other places had proceeded to Constantinople, there to endeavour to trade with the Turkish Government.

At Constantinople he made the acquaintance of a Greek lady, whom he shortly afterwards married, and then went to Alexandria. It has been always believed that this gentleman's subsequent career was owing to the influence of his wife and her mother with the ladies of the harem of his Highness Ismail Pasha, and that by their interference General Mott obtained his commission in the Egyptian Army, and his power in the councils of the Khedive.

Mrs. Mott and her mother, it appeared, had been for some years employed in supplying the ladies of the harem with fancy articles of the toilet, and in such business were reputed to have made a large fortune. Besides having free access to the palace of the Khedive, they were said to have no little power over the minds of its fair inhabitants, and that this influence was turned to account by the General's wife and his mother-in-law in procuring for him the especial favour of Ismail Pasha.

At least so ran the story, and, whether true or not, undoubtedly General Mott was speedily held in high esteem by the Egyptian Sovereign, and his advice taken on all matters pertaining to his own profession. After being appointed a General of Division in the Khedive's service, Mott grew so rapidly into favour that he received permission to entirely reorganise the Egyptian Army.

In his new position as reorganiser of the forces, General Mott suggested to the Khedive that he could procure many useful and experienced officers in America who had served in the Federal and Confederate Armies. This appears to have been so favourably received by his Highness, that his adviser was at once vested with full power from the Egyptian ruler to proceed as his representative to New York, there to select and engage what officers he required. General Mott was armed with absolute authority to act in the Pasha's name, and it was officially announced that any undertaking entered into by him was to be as binding as if made personally by Ismail. Further, the new officers were to receive their commissions immediately on their arrival in Egypt.

Fortunately for General Mott, he could not have arrived in America at a better time for the successful carrying out of his scheme. There were then staying in New York, Generals Lowring, Reynolds, and Sibley, Colonels Cannon, Reynolds, and Jenifer, Captain Hunt, and a few others, late Confederate officers.

These gentlemen, having lost all their property, and having been ruined, or nearly so, during the war, had gone to the Northern city to try to better their condition by any mercantile or professional pursuit that might offer. Of course these officers and many like them were only too glad to have their services and swords sought for by the Egyptian Government.

Shortly after General Thaddeus Mott had landed in New York, Colonel MacIver arrived in the city, just fresh from his Cuban expedition. The General was busy at work at the moment engaging officers for the Khedive, making no distinction between North and South, so long as their previous reputations were distinguished.

Colonel Skinner—a Virginian officer—and one or two others highly recommended MacIver to the notice of Mott, and the General at their first interview offered our friend a commission as colonel of cavalry in the Egyptian service. The proposal was somewhat tempting, but MacIver took a little time to consider before giving his decision. The engagement in the Khedive's service was for five years; the pay was very high, commencing immediately. Many of his friends were joining, and, moreover, there were several other advantages; and yet for a while he hesitated. What decided him in the end to accept General Mott's offer was the rumour current, that the real purpose of the reorganisation of the Egyptian Army was to free the Khedive from the yoke of the Sultan of Turkey and to declare Egypt a free and independent nation.

At length, MacIver having given in his acceptance of service to Mott, a regular legal document was drawn out, representing, on the one part, his Highness the Khedive of Egypt, and on the other part, Colonel Henry Ronald MacIver. We have this agreement now before us, and it is a curiosity in its way.

It is dated on the 23rd March, 1870. After appointing the said Henry Ronald MacIver a colonel of cavalry in the Egyptian Army, it engages his services in that capacity for five years, or at the option of the Khedive to a further term of five years. It further enjoins that he (the Colonel) shall make, wage, and vigorously prosecute war against all the enemies of his new sovereign, and that he shall follow and enforce all orders of the Minister of War.

It provides, also, that should the engaging officer be ill through the effects of the climate, he shall have power to resign his commission, and to receive two months' pay and the expenses of his return journey to his own country. There are liberal clauses, too, as to pay; one-fifth extra being allowed if on active service in the provinces, and, in case of injury, additional allowances; whilst, if dying from natural causes, one year's pay to legal representatives; or if killed or dying from wounds received in actual warfare, a pension to widow or children of one-half the pay of the deceased officer.

Suitable quarters, rations, and the necessary horses were likewise to be provided free, and each officer was to receive a gratuity of a month's pay on signing the agreement; besides, a handsome amount for expenses of passage to Egypt. The document, which is duly stamped, witnessed, and attested, is signed by Thaddeus P Mott, General of Division, on behalf of his Highness the Khedive of Egypt. Then comes the following declaration:

"I, Henry Ronald MacIver, the person named in and who executed the foregoing agreement, do sincerely and solemnly swear and declare in the presence of the ever-living God, that I will in all things honestly, faithfully, and truly keep, observe, and perform each and every of the obligations and promises above enumerated, according to their spirit and letter, and that I will in all other respects discharge the duties connected with the office of a colonel of cavalry to the utmost of my ability, and endeavour to conform to the wishes and desires of the Government of his Royal Highness the Khedive of Egypt, in all things connected with the furtherance and the maintenance of his throne.

"HENRY R. MACIVER,
"Colonel of Cavalry."

Very shortly after this agreement for service had been signed, Colonel MacIver and most of the American officers whose names we have before mentioned, took the steamer from New York to Liverpool. Those who did not then sail followed ultimately with the last batch, accompanied by General Mott. On their arrival in Liverpool, our friend and his companions immediately proceeded to Paris on their way to Marseilles, at which latter city they joined the steamer for Egypt.

At Alexandria, much to his delight, MacIver met his friend, General Corroneus, the old Spartan officer who had been engaged in the Cretan affair.

The General had gone to Egypt to offer to the Khedive, in case he declared his independence, a large contingent of Greeks. This visit of Corroneus only confirmed MacIver in his hope that Egypt intended to throw off the Turkish yoke, which had been his principal reason for taking service with the Khedive's Government.

It was well known that there had been something brewing between the Sultan and the Khedive for a considerable time, and most people expected that it would end in the latter asserting his freedom from Turkish rule, and in a declaration of war between the two countries. How these expectations were fulfilled — or rather how they fell through — is now well known. General Corroneus, at their first meeting, showed how much pleased he was to again see his *protégé*, and congratulated him on his present position as colonel of Egyptian cavalry.

However, they had not much of each other's society, as MacIver with the rest of the officers was ordered on at once to Cairo. There by the direction of the Minister of War, they were conducted to their different billets, but had to wait for nearly a week before their uniforms, horses, etc., were supplied to them. Everything, however, was done in the meantime to make comfortable these new adherents of his Highness, and there was nothing to complain of in any respect. The people, too, were very kind and courteous.

MacIver's experience personally was a very pleasant one. Servants were detached for his use, and the Minister of War presented him with two beautiful Arab horses. At length he received his uniform, and a very handsome one it was. It consisted of a blue tunic with gold spangles, and embroidered in gold up the sleeves and front, neat-fitting red trousers, and high patent leather boots adorned the continuations, whilst the inevitable fez completed the gay costume.

Colonel MacIver had been but a very brief time in Cairo—in fact had only just received his commission—when he was appointed Inspector-General of Cavalry. His new duty was simply to inspect the different troops and squadrons of Egyptian horse, and occupied but little of his time. This was a somewhat idle life, and he would have liked more to do, but the pay was good, and he had every luxury that the heart could desire.

Thus three or four months went by, and still there was no sign of a fight with Turkey. The Colonel's leisure hours, which were many, were principally spent in visiting and amusements, amongst which latter might be included flirtations with the fair Greeks and Armenians. These love-makings, however, created no end of jealousies amongst the Egyptian officers.

In fact, through his susceptibility in favour of a fair face he had one or two little quarrels with certain gentlemen whilst in Cairo, but they ended, we believe, amicably, for he escaped duels during his sojourn in Egypt.

CHAPTER XXXVI.

THE CLIMATE AFFECTS COLONEL MACIVER'S HEALTH, AND HE RESIGNS HIS COMMISSION—LEAVES FOR CONSTANTINOPLE—INTENTION OF JOINING THE FRENCH IN THE WAR AGAINST GERMANY

LATER on, the climate of Cairo began seriously to affect the health of Colonel MacIver. If there had been any fighting going on, or even if he had had more to do, he might not have suffered so much from its baneful attacks, but the idle life, combined, perhaps, with the free living in which he had been indulging of late, made him feel very unwell indeed.

As his health got worse, he determined to resign his commission, which he had power to do under one of the clauses of the agreement entered into with the Khedive, providing against the effect of the climate. His discharge from the Egyptian service bears date Cairo, October 6th, and speaks of his honourable retirement from the Egyptian Army on the previous 28th of September. It is signed by General Stone, as Chief of Staff.

This General Stone, who subsequently was raised to the rank of Pasha, was until quite recently in the Egyptian service. He was said to have worked General Mott out of the favour of the late Khedive, although Mott had been the means of procuring him his position. Stone Pasha was formerly a Federal officer, and had been defeated in one of the battles in Virginia by General Jenifer, who accepted service in Egypt at the same time as MacIver. The latter and General Stone were no friends, and they had a quarrel before they separated. In fact, there were several disagreements between the Northern and Southern officers in Egypt, who could not forget their old enmity, and, consequently, had frequent bickerings, and seldom got on well together.

It was not, however, without great regret that MacIver was leaving Cairo, where he had made many friends. It was his intention, if his health served him, to enter the service of France, and to join in the Franco-Prussian War, then going on. Several of his acquaintances in Cairo were French, and from these he received numerous letters of introduction.

The Marquis E. de Bassano gave him one to his Excellency Monsieur Crémieux, the French Minister of the Interior at Tours, and another to the Marquis de Boisthierry, at the Château Rénault. In the former Monsieur de Bassano says, "It is to serve the good cause of France that Colonel MacIver quits the lucrative service of Egypt." MacIver had also letters of introduction from Count A. Morosine, and one from Colonel Waldemar de Becker, a Russian Fin, whom he had formerly known in Athens, and had again met in Cairo. We shall have more to say subsequently of this gentleman, who turned up in Servia at the same time as MacIver.

After leaving Cairo, MacIver proceeded to Alexandria, intending to take the boat from thence direct to Marseilles, but not finding a steamer, as he expected, he went on to Constantinople, where again he was detained for some ten days. Whilst in the Turkish capital he met Hobart Pasha, whom he had formerly known as a blockade runner in America.

The celebrated Turkish Admiral, who had heard

something of MacIver's previous career, seemed glad to again meet him, and when he found out that it was his intention to join the French Army, congratulated him on the change he was making, saying that the Egyptian service was not fit for an active officer like him.

Subsequently Admiral Hobart Pasha introduced him to the Grand Vizier, and paid him a great compliment in the most flattering terms, saying that if he (the Admiral) were in an intricate position where he required a gallant officer to lead a forlorn hope, there was no man whom he would sooner choose than Colonel MacIver.

The Turkish Grand Vizier received our friend with marked politeness, and during the conversation said that, if the Colonel would like to return to Turkey after the Franco-Prussian War was at an end, he should be only too glad to offer him a command in their own service. The Colonel, however, had no sympathy with the Turks, and merely bowed his thanks. Little did he think at the time that ere long he was to be actively employed against their flag.

The night following his presentation to the Vizier, MacIver met with an adventure which is, perhaps, worth recording. He went to a café chantant, where there was singing going on by some French "artistes." Whilst listening to one of the lady singers, he noticed that her voice did not seem to please one or two of the Greek and Armenian gentlemen, who principally occupied the front seats. To one of these, who appeared more boisterous than the rest, MacIver turned round, and, addressing him in French, said it was a cowardly, contemptible, unmanly action of which he was being guilty, as the poor girl was doing her best, and he was trying to take her bread from her.

Immediately upon this, a very dark and fancifully-dressed gentleman took up the quarrel, and asked the Colonel if the words he had just spoken were meant to apply to him also.

"Yes, sir," replied MacIver, "or to any one else who is guilty of such a cowardly act."

Starting up, this man pulled out his card, and asked MacIver for his, but before exchanging cards with his opponent, the Colonel turned to one of the bystanders, and said: "Does this person hold the position of a gentleman? If so, I shall give him any satisfaction he may require; but if not, I shall immediately kick him out of the place."

At this, the person who had taken up the quarrel looked furious, but the gentleman to whom MacIver had appealed replying satisfactorily, he exchanged cards, saying:

"I am at your disposition, monsieur."

The matter then dropped, but he subsequently learned that the dark gentleman was represented to be a bit of a duellist. In due course, on the following morning, the Colonel had a visit from his second, demanding satisfaction. MacIver at once agreed to meet his principal with pistols, and referred the second to Captain Edenborough, who now held a captain's commission in the Imperial Turkish service, but who had been formerly a lieutenant under Garibaldi in Italy This was the same officer who was present when MacIver had a dispute with Colonel Peard.

MacIver immediately sent for Edenborough, and explained to him all that had taken place the previous night at the café chantant, and asked the Captain to take up the quarrel. To this he agreed, and Edenborough had only just got back to his rooms when the foreign gentleman's second waited upon him and stated his business.

"Yes," said Captain Edenborough, "I am prepared to discuss the preliminaries; but may I first ask if your principal is a particular friend of yours?"

"Yes, Monsieur le Capitaine," replied the other. "I love him as my brother."

"Then, sir," said Edenborough, "I should advise you to tell your dear friend to apologise to Colonel MacIver, for, as sure as he is a living man to-day, you will not be able to call him so to-morrow."

"Sir!" ejaculated the Armenian.

"I mean what I say," said Edenborough, "and am as certain as that I am now sitting here that Colonel MacIver will put a bullet through him if he goes out. You know me, monsieur, and I assure you that I am not romancing."

The second then retired, and, no doubt, told his friend all that had transpired. About a couple of hours afterwards, the two—principal and second—came to MacIver's rooms in the Rue Glavani and offered an apology The Colonel, however, said, before he could listen to their proposal, they must first apologise to the poor French "artiste." This was done, and the matter there ended.

MacIver sailed from Constantinople in the middle of November, from Marseilles, and was favoured with other letters of introduction from French gentlemen resident in the Turkish capital. One was to Count Kereatry, General-in-Chief of the Army of Brittany, from Monsieur Jules Despecher, who was attached to the French Embassy.

MacIver had a pleasant passage to Marseilles, his health being much improved by the voyage, and, perhaps, from mixing with the agreeable society he met on the steamer. Of course, the great topic of conversation was the Franco-Prussian War, there being a number of French people on board; the officers and crew also being of that nationality.

CHAPTER XXXVII.

THE CLOSE OF THE FRANCO-GERMAN WAR—ARRIVAL OF MACIVER IN FRANCE—JOINS GENERAL CHANZY, AND IS WOUNDED AT THE BATTLE OF ORLEANS—THE BATTLE OF ST. QUINTIN—LIFE IN PARIS AFTER THE COMMUNE

THE history of the Franco-Prussian War is too well known for it to be necessary for us to refer to it here, except as regards that part of the struggle in which Colonel MacIver played a part. Four months before he sailed from Constantinople, France had thrown down the gauntlet which declared war, and Prussia, as eager for the fray, had immediately sent forward her troops to the frontier. How rapidly were to follow the great battles of August, the fight at Sedan, the fall of the Empire, Napoleon the Third in exile, and the election of a Government for National Defence.

Colonel MacIver, on his arrival at Marseilles, proceeded at once to Tours, the then seat of the Government, where he presented to Monsieur Crémieux, the Minister of Justice, the letter of introduction so kindly given by the Marquis de Bassano. The Minister received the new comer with much courtesy and consideration, and gave him a letter to General Chanzy, who was then at the front with the Army of the Loire. MacIver lost not a moment in delay, starting at once for Orleans, where he arrived on the first of December, and found that hostilities had again commenced that morning. General Chanzy, who commanded the left wing of the French line, had been sent forward into action to operate against the right wing of the Germans, which for a time was weakened by the rather considerable interval which separated the forces of Von der Tann from those of the Grand Duke of Mecklenburg. Before he had an opportunity of closing with the Duke, the Bavarian commander had been fiercely attacked by Chanzy, but the Grand Duke moving up to the assistance of Von der Tann, the French had to fall back with considerable loss.

MacIver, before the day was out, had an opportunity of delivering to General Chanzy Monsieur Crémieux's letter, and, whilst welcoming the Colonel, Chanzy promised an immediate appointment as soon as the necessary arrangements could be made, and said that in the meantime MacIver could remain with his staff.

On the following morning the Germans, under Prince Frederick Charles, the Grand Duke, and Von der Tann, moved forward in full force, and a general action ensued. This might be said to be a battle of divisions, and when night set in both armies had suffered severely. In the morning the fight was renewed, and MacIver, as on the day previous, moved forward with General Chanzy's staff, but this time he was not to escape scatheless, as shortly after the commencement of the action he received a bullet wound in the shoulder, which placed him *hors de combat*.

At the conclusion of these two days' fighting of what is known as the Battle of Orleans, the French were thoroughly beaten, with an immense loss in killed and wounded, and had to evacuate the city, which again fell into the hands of the Germans.

Being wounded, MacIver was told by General Chanzy that it would be better that he should go on to Bordeaux until he had recovered from his hurt, and to which city the Government for National Defence had removed from Tours. There he could be communicated with, when necessary, and when fit for duty could join any ocmmand to which he might be appointed.

Although by his consummate generalship and obstinate courage, General Chanzy, after the battle of Orleans, was able to hold the Germans in check for four days, on the night of the tenth of December he was compelled to fall back, but making a masterly retreat in the direction of Creteval. So cleverly had this march been carried out, that it was not until the second day after the departure of the French from the neighbourhood of Marchenoires that the Grand Duke of Mecklenburg discovered that General Chanzy and his army had stolen a march upon him, whilst he, the Duke, supposed them to be waiting for a renewal of the fight.

s 2

Following in rapid pursuit, the Germans came up with General Chanzy, and his equally gallant second in command, the brave sailor, Admiral Jaurequiberry, at the small town of Fréteval on the fourteenth of December. The commanding position of the French, and the obstacles which the broken ground offered to the passage of the German troops, made the advance very difficult—especially in the face of a heavy and well-sustained fire from General Chanzy's guns. But the successful Germans, although more than once repulsed, could be stopped neither by the natural formation of the country, nor the cannon and bullets of the French, and after two days of fierce fighting on both sides, General Chanzy was compelled to fall back on Le Mans.

Three days later, hastily as had been his retreat, General Chanzy was compelled to fight another rearguard battle, having encountered the Germans—who in the meantime had taken Vendome—at Epinsey. Chanzy's force outnumbered the Prussians, but the French soldiers would not fight, and after suffering severely in killed and wounded, the gallant General and the equally brave Admiral, who had fought so many losing battles, had again to fall back.

This time they succeeded in reaching Le Mans, after a rapid retreat, which they entered on the twenty-first of December. Chanzy's command had been so cut up since his retreat from Marchenoires, that but a fragment of his army remained. He had, so to speak, contested every inch of the road, from the time that he was compelled to fall back to the day that he entered Le Mans, and in each action his expenditure of men had been terrible. It subsequently was estimated that the entire loss of the French on the Loire during the first ten days of December was not less than fifty thousand men killed, wounded, and missing. And as there was a week's hard fighting after that, it must have exceeded that number by many thousands. Of the German loss there is no record, but it must also have been very heavy.

We must now refer to the French Army of the North, which had its headquarters first at Lille, and subsequently at Arras. On the twenty-fifth of November the Prussians, under General Manteuffel, had taken the city of Amiens, and on the fifth of December the victorious troops of the same commander captured Rouen. The day following the fall of this latter city, the new Commandant of the French Army of the North, General Faidherbe, issued a stirring proclamation from Lille, and prepared to meet the enemy. Faidherbe had for his lieutenant another very able officer, General Farre, but his army, although strong in number, was weak in material, being made up largely of men from the Garde Mobile.

It was not, however, until the second day of the new year that General Faidherbe fought a pitched battle with the Germans. This occurred at Bapaume, which commands the high road from Arras to Peronne. The action lasted all day on the second of January, and was renewed again with equal ferocity on the third. The second day's battle of Bapaume lasted from eight o'clock in the morning until six in the evening; and although the fortune of war was against the French, the Germans had no less than three thousand men *hors de combat*. So fiercely was the action contested, that in one part of the field the Prussians under Prince Albrecht maintained a nine hours' fight with two hostile army corps.

We must now return to Colonel MacIver, who, as the reader knows, had gone on to Bordeaux until he should recover from the wound which he had received at the battle of Orleans. On his arrival at the former city, he at once reported himself to the Director-General—General Trosy—who promised that his commission as Colonel of Cavalry in the French Army should be made out in due course.

MacIver's wound — although by order of the surgeons it incapacitated him from active duty for a short while—did not prove to be a very serious affair, and in a day or two after his arrival in Bordeaux he was able to go about in his usual manner with the exception of having his arm in a sling. He was almost a stranger in the city, but through the kindness of the Minister of Justice, Monsieur Crémieux, he was introduced to other members of the Delegate Government, and made the acquaintance of several persons who extended to him their hospitality. Thus his brief stay in Bordeaux was passed much more pleasantly than he could have anticipated, and those days are still remembered by him with pleasure.

He chafed, however, somewhat at the delay in joining the army of France, and in not participating in the fighting going on, the news of which from time to time reached him, and made him long the more to be at the front. The month of December was drawing to an end—Christmas Day being past —and he had not yet received his commission in the service of France. Fortunately for his patience and temper, he had not much longer to wait, and two days before the new year he received an official-looking envelope, which contained his commission in the auxiliary army of France as a Colonel of Cavalry, and of which the following is an exact copy:

"Ministère de la guerre.

"Le Ministre de la guerre informe Monsieur Henri R. MacIver ancien Colonel de Cavalerie en Amerique et au Service Egyptien qui par décision de ce jour il est nommé Colonel de Cavalerie hors cadre dans l'armée auxiliaire et mis à la disposition de Monsieur le Général Commandant en Chef la Région du Nord.

"Bordeaux, le 28 Décembre, 1870.
"Pour le Ministre et par son ordre,
"Le Général Directeur par interim,
"(Signé),   "TROSY."

The next morning the accompanying order was sent to him from the War Office:

"Ministère de la guerre,
"Bordeaux, le 29 Décembre, 1870.

"Ordre,
"Monsieur le Colonel H. R. MacIver mis à la disposition de Monsieur le Général Faidherbe le rejoindre à Arras, les autorités civiles et militaires devront donner toutes facilités à Monsieur le Colonel MacIver.
"Le Général Directeur.
("Signé),   "TROSY.
"à Monsieur le Colonel MacIver."

The journey from Bordeaux was a tedious one, as he had to take steamer to England and then cross to Calais. He was also the bearer of despatches to General Faidherbe from the Minister of War. At length, however, he managed to join the army, and report himself to his new commanding officer. He was received with much courtesy, but for the present General Faidherbe had no position to offer him. The Major-General at the same time told MacIver that he would shortly make arrangements for giving him a responsible and permanent command.

The Prussians under General von Goben, who was looked upon as the Von Moltke of the future, were advancing in great force, and a general engagement between them and the French was expected. When Colonel MacIver joined the Army of the North, every effort was being made to strengthen the latter by fresh drafts of men from the ranks of the Garde Mobile. These citizen soldiers, however, were but poor substitutes for the trained soldiers who had marched to the frontier but a few months before, and most of whom had fallen in the fierce conflicts with the enemy. They were to fight, too, against troops which were in better condition and more thoroughly organised than when they first took the field.

But what was even worse, the French soldiers were getting sick of the hardships of war, and were only too glad if they happened to be taken prisoners by the enemy. Nothing, in fact, was more common than to see two or three Prussian troopers riding at the head of a batch of prisoners fifty or sixty strong, who followed their captors like a flock of sheep.

On the 18th of January Faidherbe encountered

BATTLE OF ST. QUINTIN

the Prussians under Von Goben, near St. Quintin, and a general engagement took place. The French were posted in a fairly strong position and awaited the approach of the enemy, who were the first to open fire with their field guns.

MacIver, who was attached to the staff of the Major-General during the battle, was from almost the first in the very thick of the fight, for General Faidherbe was not the man to be chary of his person when danger threatened. He knew, too, by experience that the raw troops at his command might at any moment be seized with a panic, which only his presence could check. The veteran troops of France fought with great courage and dash at the battle of St. Quintin, as they had always fought throughout the war. For a time the Garde Mobile followed their example, but as the fire became hotter and the serried ranks of the Prussians advanced like walls of steel, the Mobiles began to waver, then to become disorganised, and finally to give way.

It was in vain that the officers tried to stop the panic that was seizing these raw troops. Appeals and threats were alike useless, and soon most of the Garde Mobile were in full retreat, if not actual flight. MacIver, amongst others, did all that he could to save the honour of France, by stopping these runaways, galloping into their ranks, and exhorting them to continue the fight. Addressing them in French he told them that he, a foreigner, was giving his sword, and was willing to sacrifice his life for their country, whilst they, who were Frenchmen by birth, were afraid to meet the enemy in defence of their hearths and homes.

Nothing, however, could now retrieve the day, and General Faidherbe was compelled to retreat with terrible loss before the victorious soldiers of Von Goben. The French loss was said to have been fifteen thousand, including eleven thousand prisoners, and besides which the town of St. Quintin was retaken by the Germans. The result of this disastrous battle was that the French fell back in full retreat on Cambrai, and subsequently to Valenciennes and Douai. General Faidherbe, however, did not despair, and hoped before long to retrieve the fortunes of war.

After the action at St. Quintin, the Major-General despatched MacIver to the city of Lille for the purpose of raising and organising two squadrons of scouts, which were much needed at the time. The following complimentary paragraph, a translation from a Lille newspaper, refers to the visit of MacIver to that town :

"We have to announce that Monsieur H. R. MacIver, Colonel of Cavalry, commissioned by the Government for National Defence, has arrived in Lille to render a service to General Faidherbe. This distinguished officer intends to give to our country the aid of the squadrons of cavalry which he is now organising, and which are to be used as advanced scouts. Colonel MacIver was much distinguished during the Confederate War, and will be welcomed in the North. He will render a signal service to our army, which is known to be short of cavalry, and, without doubt, our General and his officers will appreciate his experience and his sword."

MacIver, obeying his orders, commenced raising

the proposed squadrons immediately on his arrival in Lille, and, from the numerous applications which he received, he anticipated but little difficulty in carrying out the instructions of General Faidherbe. All went on very promising; but on the fifteenth of February he received the following order from the Major-General's staff quarters, which, of course, at once put a stop to all further steps in regard to the scouts. The instructions were in English and were signed by Captain Williardy, who, like the gallant sailor, Admiral Jaurequiberry, who had fought so many losing but persistent battles, under Chanzy, was of English extraction on the mother's side.

"Army of the North.
"Lille, 15th Feby., 1871.
"Major-General's Staff Quarters,
"No. 2987 G.
"MY DEAR COLONEL,
"By an order received from Bordeaux, it has been ordered to dissolve the Franc corps, and consequently it is impossible to create another one.

"I should advise you thus to address yourself to Bordeaux.

"Receive, my dear Colonel, the assurance of my perfect consideration.

"The Colonel-Adjutant to the Major-General.
"Signed (Captain) WILLIARDY."

Having received his order direct from General Faidherbe, it was, however, useless for MacIver to address himself to the Provisional Government at Bordeaux. Besides, there was the probability that the war would be at once at an end. In fact, any day, any hour, might bring about such a desirable event. On the twenty-ninth of the previous month (January) Paris had capitulated to the Prussian monarch, whilst the Army of the North, pressed on every side, was preparing to fall back on Havre as a last resource. So that the Colonel had good reason for believing that the unhappy struggle would soon cease.

Before long came the welcome news to a suffering nation that peace was proclaimed. Then followed the evacuation of Paris by the Germans, and on the eleventh of March the Assembly held its last sitting at Bordeaux, under its president, Monsieur Thiers, when it was announced that the first meeting at Versailles was appointed for the twentieth of the same month (March). But before the day on which the Government had arranged to assemble at Versailles, Paris was to be subjected to a visitation almost as terrible as the war which had for the time being laid waste the fair provinces of France.

On the night of the seventeenth of March the insurgent Communists, who had established themselves in a camp at Montmartre, heard of the failure of their leaders to arrange with the Assembly at Versailles for a political Convention. As the night advanced, the streets of Paris began to fill with armed citizens preparing for that terrible struggle which in a few weeks was to culminate in scenes of savage butchery and wanton destruction, unparalleled in the records of history.

After the fall of the terrible Commune, MacIver entered Paris with the army of MacMahon, and was an eye-witness of many of the terrible scenes which followed. To the Colonel, who had so frequently visited the beautiful city in former days, the change which had been wrought by the Prussians and the Communists made it scarcely recognisable. Where had been palaces, stately public buildings, and elegant mansions, were nought but heaps of unsightly ruins.

But it was strange how soon Paris seemed to settle down into her normal state. A great war had almost ruined the country, and an empire had passed away. The Louvre, the Tuileries, the Hôtel de Ville, and other national buildings had been given to the flames, the historical Vendôme Column had been destroyed, the highest dignitaries of the Church had been shot like dogs, and yet in a few days people were seen going about their usual occupations of life with as little apparent concern as if terrible war and the more terrible Commune had never been.

Whilst at Versailles, MacIver had made the acquaintance of many pleasant people of position, several of whom were of high rank under the Empire or the more ancient House of France. Amongst the latter he had been especially well received as an "Ecossais." In Paris these friendships were further cemented, and tended much to make his stay in the gay capital enjoyable. Amongst others whom he knew were the Duke and Duchess de Gramont, and Comte de Fleury, of the old *noblesse*. The Count, who lived in the Place Vendôme, appears to have taken a great liking to MacIver, as he frequently invited him to his house. In fact, so high did he stand in the old gentleman's favour, that he presented him to a very charming young countess; but, for some reason or another, Comte de Fleury's kindly wishes with matrimonial intent in this instance were not gratified.

Although Sedan had lost Napoleon the Third his throne, party spirit still ran high in favour of the ex-Emperor, and one day, when MacIver was at the house of the Minister of War, he was asked whether he was for the Empire or the Republic.

"Gentlemen," he replied, "I am a soldier. I came to fight for France, not for a party."

The Colonel intended merely what he said, but there was immediately a meaning smile on more than one face present, crediting him with being an accomplished diplomatist as well as a soldier.

For a considerable time he led a quiet Parisian life, going more than once to England for a few days, and returning again to France. Altogether he enjoyed himself thoroughly There was the usual round of dinners and balls, and one or two small flirtations with grand dames, but little that was worth recording.

By the way, we must not forget another person well known to him, who happened to be in Paris at this time—Madame la Comtesse de la Torre. This lady, whom he had had so much cause to remember in Italy during the Garibaldi days, made advances for a renewal of their old acquaintanceship. Warned, however, by his past experience, and by the reputation which she now enjoyed of having acted as a friend of the Germans, the Colonel fought shy of the fascinating Countess.

CHAPTER XXXVIII.

COLONEL MACIVER PRESENTED TO THE WIFE OF DON CARLOS IN SWITZERLAND—RETURNS TO ENGLAND AND ESTABLISHES THE CARLIST LEAGUE—JOINS DON CARLOS ON THE SPANISH FRONTIER

COLONEL MACIVER was in Scotland in the autumn of eighteen hundred and seventy-two, as we see, from a newspaper dated the 3rd August of that year, that he was present at a very influential meeting of "The League of Scotland," held in St. Mary's Hall, at Edinburgh, and, in speaking, mentioned that he hoped soon to be in the field in the vanguard of his Majesty Charles VII. of Spain. The hour it seemed was at hand when he was to be once more actively engaged, and to serve under another flag, that of Don Carlos de Bourbon.

Through the Honourable Mr. Kenyon, who married a daughter of Lord Hay, the Colonel was introduced to Monteith of Carstairs, and also was presented to Fletcher of Fletcher, in Argyllshire, the latter being a great friend of the late Pope. Subsequently both these gentlemen did all that they could to forward his interest with the Prince Don Carlos, with whom they were intimately acquainted.

Early in the month of August MacIver left England for Switzerland with influential letters of introduction to the Donna Marguerite, Duchess of Madrid, the wife of Don Carlos: the rightful Queen of Spain, as she was styled by the supporters of her husband. This illustrious lady, formerly Marguerite de Bourbon, Princess of Parma, had then been married to the Pretender about five years. She was the daughter of Charles III., Duke of Parma, and niece of the late Comte de Chambord.

Before leaving London, MacIver also received letters to several other people of distinction. From the Count Saraiva, he had one to General Cabrera, Conde de Morella — Don Carlos' Minister — and another to his brother-in-law, General Polo, as well as one for General Elio.

To General the Baron de Cherette, who had formerly commanded the Pontifical Guards, the Chevalier O'Clery wrote, "I desire to introduce to you Colonel MacIver, a distinguished officer under General Lee in the American war, and under Generals Chanzy and Faidherbe in the late war against the Prussians. Colonel MacIver is an ardent supporter of the Legitimist cause throughout Europe, and as such, a true representative de l'ancienne Garde Ecossaise. He desires to place his sword at the service of his Catholic Majesty King Charles VII. of Spain, and will you, General, kindly aid his efforts to reach the headquarters of his Majesty?"

Don Carlos was not in Switzerland when MacIver reached there, but he at once sought for an interview with the Princess, his wife, the Donna Marguerite, presenting his letter of introduction to her secretary, Vicomte de Benaesa. On the next day he received the following note from the Viscount, appointing a time for his interview with that illustrious lady, at her residence.

"Monsieur le Colonel MacIver,

"S. M. la Reine informée de vos desirs me charge de vous prévenir qu'elle sera heureuse de vous recevoir demain, mardi, à une heure.

"VICOMTE DE BENAESA.

"Bocage, 19 Août."

In accordance with this gracious message MacIver presented himself in due course at one o'clock on Tuesday, and was received by her Highness the Princess with much courtesy and kindness of manner. Afterwards she entered into conversation with him with charming frankness.

He took occasion to explain to the Princess a plan which had occurred to him for forming a Carlist organization in London, with which her Majesty, as in courtesy we must call her, was so pleased that she at once commissioned him to carry out all the necessary details for the establishment of a League similar to the one which he had suggested. The Donna Marguerite also told the Colonel that she should write to her husband, Don Carlos, recommending him highly to the consideration of her royal spouse. Further, as an especial mark of her favour, the Princess presented MacIver with her portrait and autograph. It was arranged, too, before he took his leave that he should return to England for a while to form the Carlist organization and appoint the necessary officers, and that when this was carried out he should proceed to Spain to take part in the war.

After his interview with the Princess Marguerite the Colonel communicated his plan to the Comte d'Albanie—Charles Edward Stuart—who had been a major in the Austrian service. MacIver had met the Prince, as he was frequently called, on previous occasions in society in England and elsewhere, and the son of the Scottish Pretender now entered very warmly into the projected Carlist organization.

Before leaving Switzerland on his return to England, MacIver received letters from the Donna Marguerite to her friends the Misses Monteith of Carstairs, which he was to deliver to these young ladies personally on his arrival in Scotland. Her Highness, too, in a final interview again expressed her gracious thanks for the efforts he was making to forward the Carlist cause.

MacIver spent some time in Glasgow and London, carrying out the details for the working of the new league. When he had done all that he could for the benefit of the cause in the former city, he arranged that the Count D'Albanie should take offices in London, and act as honorary secretary to the organization. This was accordingly done, with the expectation that the Legitimists would give assistance to the Carlist cause; a belief which subsequently was fully justified, as a number of eminent men at once lent their names and aid to the committee.

Having organised the League, Colonel MacIver was named as its president. Hard, however, as he had worked for the cause, good faith was not kept with him in this respect, for General Kirkpatrick was afterwards made the president, owing, we believe, to the interference of Prince Alfonso; for no better reason, it seemed, than the idea that the name of a General would sound better, and carry more influence than that of a Colonel.

Early in March, 1873, MacIver started from England on his way for Spain, having to break his journey for a short time in Paris to transact some business with the President of the French Legitimist League. But with as little delay as possible he was again on his way. He carried with him letters of introduction to the Carlist Commander-in-Chief, Prince Alfonso, to General Saballs, and to several other distinguished officers. Amongst other recommendations was one from a general officer, then in England, to Captain Thio, Chief of the Staff to the Army of Tarrigoha, and which spoke of him in very flattering terms.

"My friend, Colonel MacIver," it said, "who served in the United States of America during the Confederate War, and who was a Colonel and Chief of Staff in the Army of Egypt, and Colonel of Staff in the late French War, is about to join the Army of Charles VII. in Catalonia. The Colonel will join the Prince Alfonso, or perhaps Captain-General Tristany. I have given Colonel MacIver a letter to General Saballs, and he has letters to other chief officers, in the six provinces. The Colonel speaks some Spanish, and will have no difficulty in that respect. He's a most excellent officer, and will, I am sure, be a great acquisition in the field, as he has been here, to the cause of his Catholic Majesty Charles VII. As you speak English well, I hope that you will extend to my friend every favour that may be in your power. While doing this you will place me under personal obligations."

Whilst waiting in Paris, too, he received the following interesting communication from the Comte d'Albanie, which was dated 12th of March, 1873, from the Legitimist League Office, Northumberland Street, London.

"My dear McIver,

"Just received your letter of the 11th inst. and in answer to your suggestion about the Legitimist League in Paris, I have to state that we are as yet in no communication with them, but that we intend to get necessary information as soon as possible, but at present we have so much to do. We shall have to go to the King very soon, and have much to arrange beforehand. Yesterday we had a large meeting, Sir G. Bowyer in the chair, the particulars of which you will see in to-morrow's daily papers. We receive so many letters from abroad—particularly from France and Belgium—that we have not left the room hardly, except for refreshment, from half-past ten in the morning until about the same hour at night, but we hope to get on now, as the plan is open to us through Lord P———m and Sir———. My father will honour the committee representing the Legitimist League to-day with his presence, and Lord R——— has also done so.

"I am now going to drink your health, and with Kirkpatrick's and De Prez's best regards,

"I remain, ever yours faithfully,

"Charles Edward Stuart,

"Comte d'Albanie, Colonel,

"Honorary Secretary."

The De Prez alluded to in the letter was the treasurer of the League, Lieutenant-Colonel Comte de la Crouel de Prez. Ten days later the Count of Albany, secretary to the Carlist Committee, wrote again to MacIver in Paris, from which letter the following extracts will be found, we imagine, not without interest:

"I think it is a list of the names of the Carlist Committee that you require. If so, it will be sent to you. As soon as the consent of certain lords and peers is obtained to the publication, we shall send the list to the public press. There are some members of the committee who are Members of Parliament, and others are holding high offices under the Government, therefore they are backward about allowing their names to be made public. However, we will furnish the list soon. Will you be good enough, my dear Colonel, to hand the enclosed letter to the President of the Carlist Committee in Paris. Please write us also immediately, and tell us all particulars of what you are doing."

After leaving Paris MacIver proceeded direct through France by the nearest route to Bayonne, where were assembled the Junta. Subsequently he crossed the frontier at St. Juan de Luce, but before entering Spain he had an interview with Monsieur Lemas, the principal Minister of Don Carlos. After once crossing the frontier, although he had but to proceed to the first station from France, his progress was attended with considerable personal danger both from the guerilla followers of Don Carlos and the outlying Republican troops. The former, who were not very particular as to whom they fired upon, were just as likely as not to favour him with a chance shot, and he had to keep a sharp look-out for friend as well as foe. At length, however, he reached the front unhurt and in safety, and had an opportunity of tendering his services to the Prince, Don Carlos, who received him with much *empressement,* and thanked him cordially for the service which he had rendered to his cause by establishing the Carlist League in England and Scotland.

But as to giving him then a command in his army, the Prince was in a difficulty which MacIver understood readily enough afterwards. There was, it seems, great jealousy amongst Don Carlos' supporters as to the military appointments, and the Prince felt that if such were conferred upon a foreigner, it would not only give offence to the Spanish grandees, but lead him to no end of trouble. Thus Don Carlos—king as he claimed to be—was not his own master, and had to bend to the will of others.

On the twelfth of April, the day after his first interview with the Prince, Don Carlos, he received an official letter, which is now before us written in French, from Don y de Ypanayaire, the Secretary de Compana to the "King." In this the Minister, whilst thanking MacIver most sincerely for the offer of his military services, at the same time regrets that for reasons previously personally explained to the Colonel by his royal master, those services have reluctantly to be declined.

Although unattached to the Carlist army, MacIver remained on this occasion for some short time at the front, and once or twice was under the enemy's fire. But at best they were small affairs that he witnessed, and did little harm to either side. He could not fail, however, to be struck with the coolness displayed in action by Don Carlos, who seemed to have no thought of danger. This probably would not have been so much noticed by him but for the doubts which he previously had heard thrown out elsewhere as to the Prince's personal courage.

On the fifth of May, 1873, MacIver received a somewhat important communication from Monsieur Lemas, the chief Minister and confidential adviser of Don Carlos. In it reference was made to the former letter sent by the Secretary de Compana, in which regret had been expressed as to the inability of the Prince to appoint him to a military command. Now, through his minister, Don Carlos asked the Colonel to give him his services in carrying out an important affair in connection with the Carlist Committee in England, and where, on his arrival, he was to act for the Prince.

What that mission was we are not at liberty to state, but we may mention that at an interview which took place between Monsieur Lemas and MacIver, previous to the latter leaving Spain, the Minister promised that if the matter was carried out satisfactorily and certain important services rendered, he should receive a marquisate of the kingdom of Spain. This was to be a reward in part, and of course was conditional on Don Carlos being successful in winning the throne of his ancestors. We need scarcely say that this high honour was never conferred upon the Colonel. Subsequently, however, through this same Minister, he received the Cross of a Commander of the Order of Isabella the Catholic.

MacIver having consented to accept the post offered to him, left Spain without delay, *en route* for

England. The war at this time was being persistently carried on, and some extracts from a letter received by him two or three months after his departure from the Spanish frontier will be interesting as a record of the Carlist struggle. The epistle was written by a gentleman, who for certain reasons must be nameless, and was dated from the Hotel Baudot, Eaux Chaudes, Basses Pyrenées, and addressed to his friend the Colonel. It commenced as follows :

"I write this on the chance of your being in London. The King is going to Bilboa, and when it is taken, its instant defence from the sea will be all important, as the Republicans will attack it at once if they have any pluck in them. Torpedoes are ordered, I believe. If that is being arranged by you, on no account be short of wire covered with gutta-percha; other things can be made easy enough, but that is difficult to extemporise successfully. These things are not contraband of war, but it would be as well to head them up in casks. I wrote a note to —— the other day, with some advice to you about difficult things. Have you seen him lately ? The 'spotting' Bilboa Harbour would be a little holiday to me, but I cannot join you actively, being on leave and bound by rules I have accepted. I may, however, come back and report myself, and then return to Spain. No one knows that I am there or at the Langham, and no one need care. Answer this here if you are in town, if with the army in Spain, send your letter to the Hotel d'Angleterre, Biarritz.

"I was told that the King was coming here yesterday, intending to strike the frontiers more to the eastward. I don't think it likely that he will enter

France again if he can avoid it. The last time they were all sold. The Prefect got an anonymous letter, I am told, that sent him with troops to the eastward, when his Majesty crossed quietly from Bayonne. I reckon the insurgent frigates won't care to do much more than lie at their anchors, but if any of the ironclads are commanded by men sticking to the new order, the torpedo arrangement is vital to the success of the whole business. That port open, there is room for all the prodigal sons of Europe to make a pilgrimage.

"There are a number of people that invent torpedoes, &c., in England. If you can get across any of these fellows, explain the chance they have now of making a contact (not contract). Nothing would raise the invention so much as sinking an ironclad, without loss to your friends, off Bilbao. Bring out a chart of that town on a large scale, in fact, it would be as well to get a complete set of charts for the whole of the Spanish ports, and good plans of the towns on a large scale. The chances are that you would not find them so good at Bilbao as in London; they are to be got in the Poultry. Before you leave, appoint an agent to forward letters, &c. A sea-port may vastly extend the King's affairs. Answer this at once if you are in town, or if you are coming out I'll move on to Biarritz a little earlier."

The attack on Bilbao, here suggested, was ere long to become an accomplished fact, and the Spanish Government to have before them the prospect of losing that important port. But this was not until the following year, when so closely was it besieged by the Carlists that Marshal Serrano, who was considered the only man in Spain likely to cope with the victorious troops of the Pretender, was despatched in great haste from Madrid to the seat of war.

What fighting had been carried on during the year 1873 had been mostly in favour of Don Carlos, but early in 1874 his attempt to gain the throne began to look much more formidable by the entry into Spain of the partisan troops under General Ollo by the pass of Beras-vagni. Besides other able officers, Ollo had for his lieutenants Yoaquin Zubini, his nephew, and Perula, the cavalry leader.

The fighting commenced at Irun, the first station on the frontier from France, and went on with but little breathing time, the Carlists having the best of it. The Spanish Government became alarmed at the successes of the enemy, and appointed Marshal Serrano to the chief command of the army operating against the partisans, and he started for Madrid on the twenty-seventh of February.

The second day of May witnessed the relief of Bilbao (besieged by the Carlists) by the troops under Marshal Serrano, which gave some hope to the Republican Government, but everywhere else Don Carlos' partisans were victorious. Toledo had been twice beset by the latter, and Estella taken after a smartly-sustained siege.

But the great fight of that campaign was on the twenty-eighth of June at Dicastilla, near Estella, which ended in the defeat of the Government troops and the death of Marshal Concha, their Commander-in-Chief. But the Carlists, too, sustained a great loss, for their General, Ollo, was also killed there.

Colonel MacIver returned to Spain and joined the Carlist army at Irun. During the campaign, amongst others whom he knew, he again met Frank Vizetelly, the English artist, and John Augustus O'Shea, the war correspondent of the *Standard*. There were other Irishmen with Don Carlos besides O'Shea; notably Edmund O'Donovan and Majors Leader and Sheehan. O'Shea was a very old friend of MacIver, and Frank Vizetelly he had known during the American War and previously. The latter gentleman and poor Edmund O'Donovan, both kind-hearted gallant fellows, have died at their duty recently whilst attached to Hicks Pasha's expedition to the Soudan.

MacIver speaks now in high glee of the *sang-froid* under fire of O'Shea, who was out in Spain all through the war. The Colonel tells how the famous special of the *Standard*, whilst the bullets were zipping around him, used to go on with his writing with as much coolness as he may now be seen strolling up Fleet Street, or along the Strand. Occasionally his glasses would go up to his eyes, then he would give a knowing look and an extra shake of his head and scribble away at his notes at a great rate. John Angustus O'Shea, however, has been in so many campaigns, that we imagine he has become pretty well used to the whistle of bullets from both friend and foe.

The campaign was not without its amusing incidents. There was a Carlist officer named Lizzaraga, a General of Brigade, who was a regular fire-eater, and who was always fighting against his old schoolmate Loma, a Republican General. The troops under the respective commands of these two seemed continually meeting and having a pitched battle.

For the greater part of the year Don Carlos had met nothing but success, but on the tenth of November, the Republican troops encountered the Carlists before Irun, and routed them with great loss. This was followed by other reverses, but the great blow to Don Carlos' cause was struck on the last day of December, 1874, when Prince Alfonso, son of the ex-Queen Isabella, was proclaimed King by the Spanish troops as Alfonso XII. The Carlist campaign might be said to be then virtually at an end, although the Prince and many of his faithful followers continued the struggle in a small way for the next two years. Always gallant, they occasionally met with success, but the contest—at least for the time—was a hopeless one, and at length gradually died out.

Colonel MacIver remained a loyal supporter of Don Carlos de Bourbon, so long as his services could be of any use to the Prince, the assistance, however, that he had been able to render was more civil than military in character, and it was as a soldier that he desired to be recognised, so that when his mission could tend to no further benefit to the Carlists, he was not sorry to withdraw from an engagement which, whatever might be his sympathy with the royal claimant, afforded but little prospect for the use of his sword.

CHAPTER XXXIX.

A NEW LOVE AFFAIR—A RIVAL AND A QUARREL AT THE CAFÉ RICHE—A FATAL DUEL—THE HERZEGOVINIAN STRUGGLE

MacIver had been frequently in Paris during his service under Don Carlos, and had kept up an intimate intercourse with his French acquaintances, especially with his friend the Comte de Fleury, at whose house he knew he was ever a welcome guest. Amongst others to whom he had been introduced after the days of the Commune was a young lady—a Countess—and something like a love affair was the result of that introduction. This fair lady was rich and beautiful, and in every way would have been a desirable wife for him. He had also the best wishes for his success from his friends, and the Countess seemed to fully appreciate his attentions, but somehow the match did not come off; probably the Colonel did not then feel inclined to enter the bonds of matrimony, being too much wedded to his profession. It seems, however, he had more than one rival with the Countess, and his attentions to the young lady not only gave rise to jealousy, but ended in a serious quarrel between him and one of the other aspirants to her hand and fortune. This gentleman was a French Count who appeared to have formed a bitter hatred to MacIver, which he only waited the opportunity to vent.

He was a noted duellist, too, and had the reputation of having nearly always killed his opponent. He was a man of middle age, handsome and accomplished, but with a peculiarly supercilious air, that, without being actually offensive, made him disliked by many. To the Colonel, hitherto, he had been particularly polite, although MacIver knew that at heart he was his enemy.

He was a man, however, to whom the Colonel gave but little thought, although he frequently met him in society, as he was generally to be found dancing attendance upon the young Countess when she appeared in public or at the house of mutual friends. But with all this the Count did not press his attentions, and seemed to be contented to remain an admirer at a distance, so that had MacIver have had even a thought of picking a quarrel with him—which he had not—it would have been difficult to say where the cause of offence lay.

A fire of revenge it appeared had long been burning in the Count's breast, and one evening it burst forth in an intentional offence aimed at his rival. This was in April, eighteen hundred and seventy-five, after the Colonel had retired from the service of Don Carlos. He strolled one evening into the Café Riche in the Boulevard des Italiens to while away an hour, and as he passed along to a vacant table, he noticed that the Count was seated with some friends.

Suddenly MacIver heard his own name uttered by the Count, coupled offensively with that of the young Countess. The Colonel at the moment was in the act of drawing off one of his gloves, and instantly turned on the Frenchman. Striding up to the table where the other was seated, he struck the Count full in the face with his glove, and then cast it down under foot as though it had been contaminated by the touch. MacIver's action was perhaps more irritating than the actual blow, and the Count, in an uncontrollable rage sprang to his feet, as if about to measure his strength with his rival, but his friends restrained him and held him back.

"Monsieur le Comte," said MacIver, quietly placing his card on the marble slab, "you know where to find me, and I shall be at your service whenever and wherever you require me."

Bowing to the other gentlemen, the Count's friends, he turned on his heel and walked towards the table where he had intended to seat himself and called for what he required.

Early the next morning, as from the first he had anticipated, a gentleman called upon him at his hotel with a hostile message from the Count, and a request for the name of MacIver's second. The latter referred the bearer of the challenge to a friend whom he knew would be ready to act for him, and in whose hands he was safe as to future arrangements. Of course a duel was inevitable. An insult had been offered, and a blow given, and nothing but fighting could afford satisfaction. The seconds of the Count and the Colonel decided that the meeting should take place on the Belgian frontier, and that swords should be the weapons used.

The quarrel at the Café Riche had been so public, and the Count and the Colonel were both so well known in Parisian society, that the affair became much talked about and commented upon. The former was not only a noted duellist, but an expert swordsman, and there were not a few who feared for MacIver's chance of life, and regretted his embroilment with the

Frenchman. The evening before the meeting took place a friend told the latter that the Count had boasted of his intention to mortally wound him. At the same time he had remarked that this would be the first Englishman whom he had killed in all his duels, and that he was glad now to have that opportunity.

Although it was known that a duel must come off, the time and place of meeting was kept a profound secret by the friends of both principals, and every precaution was taken that no particulars should leak out. The necessity for this caused some short delay, but both parties crossed the frontier at different points, making for the rendezvous which was on the road to Waterloo, and within a few miles of that celebrated battle field.

It was a lovely spring morning, not long after sunrise, when the Count and the Colonel, each attended by two seconds and a surgeon, met to settle their quarrel. The spot was in a long avenue of trees, bright in their first blossom of verdant green, and there was not a sound but that made by the chirping of the birds to break the silence.

MacIver's opponent, though not so tall as himself, was an athletic man, with broad, but somewhat rounded shoulders, and a lithe, active frame. Whilst the length of the swords was being tested, he stared directly at the Colonel as though measuring his calibre, and with the usual supercilious, half sinister smile on his dark yet handsome face. As they took their places on the short turf and were about to cross swords, MacIver quietly remarked in French:

"Monsieur,—J'ai entendu dire que vous avais l'intention de tuer un Anglais ce matin. Vous avais tort. Je ne suis pas Anglais, mais je suis des Montagnes de l'Écosse."

The next moment there was the ring of steel, and the glances of the swordsmen met. The instant MacIver caught the eye of the Count, those who were present, saw that a pallid hue spread over the face of the latter, and that there was a slight yet perceptible shudder. But the Count quickly recovered himself, and with deadly purpose used all his skill to get the better of his antagonist. He was a perfect master of fence, but he had met a man scarcely less proficient as a swordsman, and with muscles of iron, besides the advantage of being cooler than he. Thrice he tried a lunge which he thought was known only to himself, and the last time it proved fatal to him.

Twice before had MacIver skilfully parried the intended death-stroke. On the third occasion, he lunged forward with his left shoulder, at the same time receiving his adversary's sword under his arm; then instantaneously stepping forward with his right foot, he ran the Count through the body, mortally wounding him.

As the Count fell back the surgeons and his seconds rushed forward to raise him, but it was soon seen that help was of little avail, and that his end was near. He was carried to the carriage which had conveyed him to the fatal field, whilst the Colonel and his friends, who could do no good by remaining, made their way on to Brussels.

Till the end of the year eighteen hundred and seventy-five, after MacIver had disconnected himself from the Carlist cause, there were no dissensions

U

amongst foreign nations nor State affairs to enlist his sympathies. Then the revolt of the Herzegovinian chiefs and people against their oppressors, the Turks, seemed to open out to him a fresh field for action. He determined to proceed to the seat of war, but more in a civil than in a military capacity. Before leaving England, he arranged with Captain Hamber, then the Editor of the *Hour*, to represent that journal as its special correspondent at the front.

From London, the Colonel first went to Malta, where he remained for a short while. Leaving that island on the twenty-first of December, he took steamer for Syra; thence he started on Christmas Day—his birthday, by the way—for Piræus, which he reached the next morning at four. Here he was once more amongst friends, and received a hearty welcome. Amongst others whom he found at Athens was the old Spartan, now "General" Corroneus, with whom and his niece he dined the same day, and afterwards passed the evening with General Artemis.

He could not afford the time for a lengthy stay in Greece, but he remained long enough to see the old year out and the new year in. On the last day of December there was a very heavy fall of snow, and everything looked dull, cold and miserable, so much so, that he went to bed low-spirited, and out of sorts. But the sun broke so bright and smiling on New Year's Day that it seemed a good omen of the future, and, under its cheering influence, the despondency which he had felt on retiring to rest quickly disappeared.

The next morning he sailed from Piræus for Kalamaki in the steamer *Paunnellinien*, at which latter place he arrived at daybreak, and whence, as the reader will possibly remember, he had, when in the Greek service, found a safe conduct for Sir David and Lady Baird. Crossing the isthmus, he left Corinth at ten on the following morning by a fresh steamer for Corfu. He visited the Masonic Lodge here (Corfu), and took part at the installation of a New Worshipful Master—Woodley

However, being anxious to reach the seat of war as quickly as might be, MacIver left Corfu at once, by an Austrian steamer, and arrived off Duratzo at six o'clock on the morning of the tenth of January.

The weather had been very bad, and the storm still continued, but he proceeded on to Ragusa, which he reached late next evening.

There was a number of Herzegovinian refugees here, who had been housed and cared for, and to whom in his capacity of "special," he paid a visit the morning after his arrival. He met also, and made the acquaintance of Mr. Stillman, the *Times* correspondent, who, besides himself, was the only representative of the English newspapers at the war. Being desirous of seeing how matters were going on, he subsequently started for the front, but returned to Ragusa again, on the morning of the fourteenth.

Somehow the Colonel, with his hasty temper, managed to get mixed up in a quarrel, which seemed fair to end in another duel. His difference was with an Italian Count, who, however, disappeared the next morning. It was a fortunate termination, for although an affair of honour might be looked on with tolerance in the case of a cavalry soldier, it was scarcely compatible just then as the representative of an English journal.

Four days after his first visit to the army, he again returned to the front, where he made the acquaintance of several of the Herzegovinian chiefs, amongst whom where Covacivich, Josef, and Papao. The weather was very fine, and the hostile armies occupied a beautiful hilly country. The war had been going on for some time before the Colonel reached Herzegovina, and since his appearance on the scene there had been somewhat of a lull in active operations. But on the eighteenth of January, at three o'clock in the day, the fighting commenced in earnest.

The native soldiers fought well and gallantly, and the Montenegrins especially were conspicuous for their steadiness, pluck, and dash. The short winter's afternoon was soon at an end, but before darkness set in, the Turkish forces had been beaten, and had to fall back with considerable loss. Fighting was resumed on the following day, when MacIver visited the wounded.

On the twentieth both Turks and Herzegovinians were as eager as ever for the fray, and a fresh battle was commenced. It was early in the morning when he heard the firing, and he started at once for the field. Fighting was going on furiously on both sides, and MacIver, in his desire to see the most of it, was nearly hit several times by a passing bullet. Fortunately, however, he escaped unhurt, and returned to Ragusa the same evening to write his letter to the editor of the *Hour*.

This last fight must have been nearly a drawn battle, for both armies were at it again next morning at daybreak as obstinately as ever. MacIver, who and returned to the front, looked on for awhile as a spectator, but finally became so excited that he felt he must do a little fighting himself for the pure love of the thing. Shouldering a rifle he joined one of the battalions as a volunteer.

Subsequently, whilst engaged in a charge with his new comrades, he was nearly captured by the Turks. Luckily for him, however, several of the gallant Montenegrins rushed to his assistance, and after a brief hand-to-hand fight, effected his rescue. Over four hundred were killed on this day, and the Turks, having a much greater strength in the field, had the best of it, although they suffered severely. MacIver still speaks in high terms of the courage the Montenegrins displayed during the time he was in Herzegovina. They were a fine body of men, and most excellent soldiers. The Herzegovinian troops, too, fought very gallantly.

Mr. Stillman, of the *Times*, in his position as war correspondent, seemed to have no thought of personal danger, and was always to be found where fighting was going on.

The war was now fast drawing to a close. The Turks, overpowering in numbers, gained the victory, and, before the month of January was out, the end had come. MacIver had now nothing further to keep him in the country, and went on to Corfu. In the middle of the month of February he left Corfu for Brindisi, where he caught the express train for Naples.

In the Neapolitan capital he met several friends whom he had known in the old Garibaldian days, but left the same day by steamer for Marseilles, *en route* for Paris. Staying in the latter city for a fortnight he then returned to London, where he arrived early in the month of March. Shortly afterwards he again crossed for the Continent and took up his quarters in the gay French capital for a month or so,

CHAPTER XL.

COLONEL MACIVER LEAVES ENGLAND FOR SERVIA—RECEIVES HIS COMMISSION AND RAISES A FOREIGN LEGION OF CAVALRY

THE struggle of the Servians for independence from the galling yoke of the Turk, speedily enlisted the sympathy of Colonel MacIver, and in July, eighteen hundred and seventy-six, he determined to offer to their Prince his sword and his services. With that purpose in view, on the twenty-fourth of that month, he started from England, and making all speed reached Belgrade four days later, on the evening of the twenty-eighth.

He had with him letters of introduction to Doctor Humphrey Sandwith, C.B., who was then in Servia, engaged in the benevolent mission of affording assistance to those in distress during the war. Doctor Sandwich very kindly introduced him to M. Christich, who is now the ambassador from Servia in England. By these two gentlemen he was presented to the Minister of War (Colonel Nicolics), a fine, handsome, soldier-like fellow, who received him very kindly, and at once offered to him a commission as Colonel of Cavalry.

It was proposed that MacIver should organise a legion of cavalry to be composed of foreigners, and this he consented to do. On the sixth of August he received his commission as a Colonel in the Servian Army, and with his usual energy commenced his new duties. In fact, he had been busily engaged during the previous week enlisting men, and when his commission arrived he had already enrolled about one hundred.

But although quarters had been promised, he could not get his men housed, and most of them were scattered about the town, and some without rations. The Colonel was furious with the officials, but he could get no satisfaction. With his usual determination, however, he carried the day in a most unexpected manner. He assembled his men, and, much to the chagrin of those negligent understrappers who had failed to carry out the instructions of the War Minister, announced that he was going to march his recruits to Colonel Nicolics.

In vain the officials expostulated. True to his word, MacIver now moved his men off, four abreast, and marched them through the streets on his way to the War Minister. They were incongruous enough as to nationality, these troopers without horses, but they were a fine body of men. Some were in Greek costume, others in the various dresses of the great German Empire, but they looked well and made a good show. On their arrival Colonel Nicolics was astounded to find his order had not been carried out. Pointing to his men, MacIver said:

"I have received, sir, my commission, with orders to raise a Cavalry Brigade. I have in part executed them. Here are some of the men. I want tents, horses, uniforms, and rations."

The War Minister, much displeased that his orders had not been carried out, immediately granted all that had been asked, and Colonel MacIver triumphantly marched his men off to some capital tents, which were allotted to him. Proper rations, too, were issued, and subsequently he was taken to the stables to select what horses he required. In a few days uniforms also were served out, and the promptitude with which their Colonel had seen their wants attended to, made him at once very popular with his troopers.

This was not the only occasion on which MacIver was indebted to his friend the War Minister for prompt action when he had to complain of any dereliction of duty on the part of the officials. Colonel Nicolics was not only a most able and efficient Minister, but the most kindly and courteous of gentlemen.

In a few days more nearly a hundred men had been enlisted, horses being at once provided as they were enrolled. Amongst others who joined Colonel MacIver's squadron was Prince Nica, a Roumanian cousin of the King. Although recruits flocked eagerly around him, his task was no easy one, for many difficulties had to be surmounted. He had material to work on, but it was raw and untrained, for many of his men were exchanging the reaping hook for the sword. But, nothing daunted, the Colonel kept steadily to his work, getting his troops into shape. Twice daily he mustered them for parade and drill, and in a very short time they were in readiness to proceed to the front when called upon.

In connection with this part of General MacIver's career we are, by the kindness of two gentlemen—one of whom, however, does not wish his name to appear—enabled to publish some amusing extracts from private letters. The writer of the first is the well-known war correspondent, Mr. Robert Coningsby, who, in the struggle between Turkey and Russia—which may be said to have grown out of the Servian campaign—represented the *Times*, first at the Turkish headquarters, and afterwards with the Russians. In one of these deliciously gossiping epistles to which we have referred, Mr. Coningsby, dating from the "Crown" at Belgrade, writes:

"'Such larks!' as Mr. Joseph Gargery would observe if he were here, but first I must warn you to abandon all notions of making this your happy holiday hunting grounds. If Mrs.—— knew half what I do about these piggy wiggies, she would insist upon you pulling up sharp and short at Vienna. Not an inch further east, my dear boy, should any respectable father of a family of three-and-a-half, who values his character, ever dream of venturing. As for me, I am deteriorating by whole pounds avoirdupois. Why, I actually laughed this morning when an American friend, who was my *compagnon de voyage* on the way here, told me his trouble, and what do you think it was? Why, this only! While he was tubbing in room number eight, which has no lock on the door, in walks the chambermaid, after having demolished the barrier of chairs with which he vainly thought he had securely fastened himself in. Young Bousted, that is his name, although 'Gosling' would fit him far better — yelling out in the American tongue, which is the only language he recognises, did his best to frighten the young person into a speedy retreat before she should have time to notice that he was only clothed in a mantle of water drops from the sponge he was 'squizzing.' But I regret to say that the forward young woman burst into a silvery laugh, and instead of retreating, actually called aloud in Serbish for her fellow-servant to make haste and come and see the sport. Which she did."

After referring further to the troubles of his American friend, Mr. Coningsby goes on to write: "How small the world is! When I got as far away from you all as Pesth, I said to myself, 'Poor Pill Garlic will never look upon a familiar face again unless he lives to return westward.' It is true I had met an old chum at the 'Hotel Metropole' in Vienna, but then Vienna is only the next street like to London, and one expects to meet people there—but as I was going down the staircase of the 'Queen of England,' in the Hungarian capital, I was mentally bewailing the impossibility of coming across anybody who knew me very far away from —— Square, when a cheery voice cried out from the first landing, 'What, Coney, old man, what the deuce brings you here?' It was my old fellow-Savage Seyd, who had brought his wife for a run up the Danube, and they were both staying at my hotel. We had jolly times, you bet. Then again, upon reaching here, the very first man I set eyes on as I walked into the garden of this hotel, was your friend, little Kelly, my old comrade during the Franco-Prussian kick-up. He is here for the *Times*, and is as fierce a warrior and daring a horseman as ever lawyer was. Then there is Boyle for the *Standard*, and Forbes for the *Daily News*, and there are two ladies whom I have met in London, Miss —— and Miss ——; also young Lamson,* a clever and amusing American doctor, whose father, a parson, and I have become very chummy in London since his son and I were in the Franco brush together. Last, but by no means least, we have that redoubtable warrior, of whom you have heard me speak, MacIver, of Italian and Spanish war renown. He is organising a cavalry corps, or something of that sort, with which he declares when he 'once gets those rascally Turks on

---

* Afterwards hanged at Wandsworth for the murder by poison of his brother-in-law.

the run he'll let the blackguards know who is after them, and no mistake!' I for one believe him. It is wonderful what a knack that man has of turning up in out-of-the-way places. I believe I shall meet him one day in Heaven—at least, I hope so. He is everywhere where one is not expected."

Another letter of Mr. Coningsby's amusingly refers to his young American acquaintance, Mr. Bousted, who, being short of money and unable to get a commission in the Servian army, finally became a trooper in MacIver's squadron of cavalry.

"I have got Master Bousted thoroughly on my back," says Mr. Coningsby. "His *motif* in coming all these thousands of miles is, forsooth, that he had 'a quarrel with his girl!' He is utterly helpless, and until he hears from his father, will not have money enough to pay his hotel bill. He seems to have had the coolness to think that the Servian people would be so delighted to see him, that they would fall on his neck and make him a field-marshal, or something of that kind, on his arrival here. I took him to the Archbishop yesterday, and solemnly dedicated him to the Servian cause, hoping that that handsome tip I told you of in my last letter* would induce 'Michal' to get the poor devil a commission, if it were only as major-domo. The prelate, however, was too many for us. He had absolutely no influence in military matters. Such as he had he freely gave, to wit, his blessing, and oh! such a sounding kiss, which made poor B. absolutely squirm again. What is to be done with the unfortunate boy I can't think! He

---

* This refers to a sum of two hundred pounds Mr. Coningsby was requested by some friends of the Servians in London to take out with him for the sick and wounded.

tells me he is only eighteen, and he may be, but he looks, at least, four or five years older. One does not like to cut even a travelling acquaintance as soon as you find he hasn't nary a red cent, even if he has been laughed at by some saucy chambermaids, and kissed by a live Archbishop! *Eureka*. The very first thing after breakfast I will take the young man up to MacIver's camp, which is about two miles from here, and I'll take anything for him the General likes to stand, if it is only a liquor. He says he can ride, and that accomplishment, might, perhaps, come in handy, although, to tell the truth, there are at present, to the General's infinite chagrin, but very few horses for MacIver's cavalry.

"The deed is done, and he looks quite nice in his new clothes. I want him to call and show himself to the Archbishop, but he says he will see the old gentleman blessed first! The uniform is rather a becoming one. It is a short brown jacket, similar in shape to that now worn by our own linesmen, with crimson facings, the pantaloons crimson, and the cap not unlike a Glengarry in shape. The officers wear a brown cloth jacket, similar in shape to that worn by the men, but of better cloth; blue pantaloons, with a narrow red stripe down the seams. On the collar, which is of scarlet, is displayed the different badges of rank by silver or golden stars. General MacIver is an awful swell. As he rides into town with a smart and soldierly-looking orderly after him, you might take him for the Commander-in-Chief, at least. We have become very thick since I have turned recruiting-serjeant for him, and I have made the acquaintance of most of his officers, who are all first-rate fellows, chiefly Austrians. When I went up to dine with the General yesterday, poor little Bousted, who is only a full private trooper as yet, was doing sentry duty outside the General's tent, and as he presented arms upon his commanding officer's appearance, he gave me a most gruesome wink, as much as to say, 'You've done this for me, you know.'"

In another letter, after much gossip on private matters, Mr. Coningsby says, "Upon my word MacIver ought to be very grateful to me. I've taken him up another recruit. A 'Captain' S—— from Cheshire, a rather good-looking, gentlemanly young fellow, arrived the other day, and was walked straight off to the 'jug' before he had been in Belgrade a quarter of an hour. This is how it came about. My attention was called to the youngster's pickle by the German-speaking waiter here, who came running to me in the garden, where I was enjoying a quiet cigar, with the sensational intelligence that an Englishman had been found with treasonable documents on him, and that they were about to shoot him right away. I went quickly to the post office, and asked my friend Spooner if he had heard anything of the affair. Yes, he had seen the arrest, which took place at the post office itself. A letter of introduction to the pretender to the Servian throne, Prince Kara Georgivitch, had been found upon the unfortunate youth and nothing could save him.

"Spooner, who speaks Serbish as fluently as he does English—having been here for the last twelve years—went with me to the prison, and with great difficulty we obtained an interview with our unfortunate fellow countryman. He naturally looked rather scared, but we did our best to cheer him up. A 'lady' in Paris had, it appeared, given him the introduction, telling him that the illustrious Prince, who was under obligations to her, would give him a commission for her sake, and that he had better lose no time in seeking an interview on his arrival in Belgrade. Following that advice he had gone straight to the post-office on landing, and asked the scared officials for the *address of Prince Kara Georgivitch!* Tableau, a procession of police, soldiers, and howling citizens from post to prison. My friend, the Archbishop, was now very useful. He happened to have influence with the civil powers, and after convincing them that our ignorant young friend had been merely the victim of a stupid practical joke, he was delivered to us. As I have already told you, I took Mr. S—— up to my regular white elephant shop, and had him provided for *toot sweet.* MacIver has promised to get him a commission shortly, as he has seen service in some militia or yeomanry corps at home; but, of course, he is enlisted as an ordinary trooper. In future I mean to enlist everybody who comes here to bother me, so tell K—— that he had better think twice before he turns up here once."

The gentleman alluded to above, Lieutenant S——, proved indeed a white elephant to MacIver, for he scarcely knew what to do with him during the time that he remained under his command. On his return to England, too, he published a book on his short experience in Servia, in which he was so foolish and unjust as not only to throw out innuendoes against his late commanding officer, but to cast aspersions against the army of Servia, and her entire people. This latter calumny, emanating from one so little capable to judge of them as a nation, brought forth an indignant denial and a long statement of facts, signed by a number of distinguished Servian officers, a copy of which was forwarded to the Horse Guards, and another to the Colonel of Lieutenant S——'s militia regiment.

As to Colonel MacIver's relations to Mr. S——, he had, having private quarters of his own in Belgrade, giving up his own tent to the Lieutenant, when introduced by Mr. Coningsby. A few days afterwards the Colonel presented him to the Minister of War, and at his (MacIver's) urgent request a commission as Lieutenant in his own squadron was given to the young Englishman. This favour was not obtained from Colonel Nicolics without great pressure, as, from his want of knowledge of languages, Mr. S—— was unfitted for the position of an officer in the Servian Army. Subsequently he quarrelled with several of his comrades, and was only saved from the consequences by the intercession of his commandant. On one occasion, too, MacIver had to take his sword from him and place him under arrest; but, subsequently, wishing to avoid even the slightest cause for scandal as between two foreign officers, the Colonel passed over his subaltern's want of discipline, and returned Lieutenant S—— his sword.

Most of MacIver's officers were capital fellows, and several of them old soldiers. There was one, however, who was almost, as one might say, his second self. This was his adjutant, Lieutenant Shwagroffski, a fine, strong, well-built young fellow of twenty-three, a Bohemian by birth. He had commenced life as an officer in the Austrian Navy, and had led a wild, adventurous life. Shwagroffski was devoted to MacIver, and the latter had a great liking for his Lieutenant. Amongst other peculiarities of the Bohemian, he carried an enormous two-handed sword, which bore a date on its blade of a year early in the seventeenth century. This weapon, which he highly prized, played a most important part during the war, and it reminds us of a duel between its owner and an Austrian newspaper correspondent at Belgrade. The following racy description, from another letter of Mr. Coningsby, will, however, more vividly bring it before the reader than any words of our own.

"I must tell you that I have enlisted another bore. A Scotch doctor this time. Sawney brought a letter of introduction out to me; and, bless you, before he could say 'lancet' MacIver had him as right and tight as a tourniquet. Only for the war, of course. He'll naturally be shot if he attempts to desert before it's over, as I told him, just to cheer him up. But I must leave the doctor, for I have a duel to describe to you. Three or four hundred yards from the Cavalry Camp—which, by the way, is beginning to look quite business-like now that the horses are coming in—is a pleasantly-situated little hostelry. Here the officers and non-commissioned officers of MacIver's *corps*—of the latter of whom *Corporal* Bousted is a bright and shining example—spend a good deal of their spare time in smoking and tasting the wine of the country, or sipping *sleebervitch*, or plum brandy, which is the national drink. I occasionally assist in the performance of these arduous duties, so I happened to be present, the day before yesterday, when an Austrian war correspondent, who has been in the Austrian Army, and Lieutenant Shwagroffski, also an Austrian, and one of MacIver's best officers, must begin first arguing and then quarrelling. One word brought up another, until the newspaper man committed the unpardonable sin of sneering at the cavalry *corps*, and the warrior, of course, in return sneered at the Press. Then they called one another names, and so on, until there was only one way out of it. The newspaper man took me on one side and asked me to be his friend, but I told him bluntly that I thought he had been the aggressor, upon which Lieutenant Shwagroffski came up, and asked me to walk with him to Colonel MacIver's tent to obtain his permission to fight.

"Walking being more in my line than either fighting or 'seconding,' I consented, not without a hope that by a series of nods and winks behind the Lieutenant's back, I should be able to persuade MacIver to refuse his consent. The great man, however, neither gave nor withheld it. He would not interfere with his officer's private affairs, and so forth; but the Lieutenant would have been a bigger fool than he is, if he had not seen plainly. that if the newspaper man did not kill him, neither would his Colonel. So the matter was arranged. The scribe soon found another scribbler to back him, and a brother officer did the same for the Lieutenant, and the result of the conference was that it was to be sabres, not pistols. My contribution to the fun was to gallop as hard as my horse would carry me into the town and bring a doctor back with me, as my last present to the Colonel was away, having leave on some urgent private affair connected with a post-office order for forty shillings.

"Two or three English sawbones very properly declined to return with me when I explained the secret, but an enterprising young German, whom I lured from his dinner with an awful whopper about a poor fellow who was lying badly hurt at the Cavalry

Camp, packed up his tools, and jumped into a carriage with me without suspicion. As we were entering the camp I nervously let out the truth upon which he joyfully assured me that I could not have found a properer person in all Servia, inasmuch as he had attended dozens of such meetings, and was quite at home in them."

Mr. Coningsby then goes on to describe the adjournment to a barn, where the principals, the seconds, the doctor and himself as a witness, find themselves in the evening. The surgeon places his instruments and bandages ready for use on the floor in the corner, and then the two six-foot combatants divest themselves of boots, socks, coats, vests, shirts, and everything in fact but their inexpressibles, which are kept in their places by the braces being twisted round the middle. "Upon my word, it is awfully catching, and I am in a good mind to pull the doctor's nose, so we two can have a little lark to ourselves, while the giants are settling their scores. Now comes the tug of war. Each hero receives a sabre from his friend, and bowing stiffly to the gentleman he is about to make mincemeat of, if he can, gracefully feels his blade, bends it a little, first by the hand, and next by sticking the point in the ground, and then they stand on guard.

"Now they are at it, while I make myself as small as I can near the door, for as the infuriated swordsmen chase each other this way and that, and the flashing fireworks fly about all over the shop, I have more than half a presentiment that it will be my head which will come off first. Nevertheless, I should like to have a turn outside with the doctor. I feel quite sure I could manage *him*. But now the seconds, with drawn swords in hand, have rushed between the fighters. It is nothing but a slash across the Lieutenant's nose. The blood runs freely down my friend's chin and chest, but as there is still a good deal of nose left, honour is not yet half satisfied. Away they go again, and presently the journalist's left shoulder is opened most artistically, and when the swords are knocked up again he is in a worse state than our man: I really must have a turn at the doctor. Now both foreheads are chipped and bleeding, but honour is still quite hungry. Still the men's strength is evidently giving out, and the doctor rather fussily picks up his bandages, as if he knows the end is near. After two or three chest gashes which are taken no notice of, our man, who it is clear from the first is the better swordsman, suddenly swings his blade with lightning rapidity from number two to number three, and smash! the other's body opens, and he falls into the arms of his friend.

"I am truly horrified, for it seems to me that the man is dying. 'Brandywein,' shouts the doctor, who kneels down by the man, who has swooned. Of course nobody has a flask with him, and away I rush faster than I ever ran in my life to MacIver's tent. I am utterly winded and speechless when I arrive, but seize a bottle, and am just able to gulp out the word 'victory' to the astonished Colonel, as I rush off back again to the barn. Now, my dear ——, you know all about how honour is satisfied, and I am happy to end this lengthy rigmarole by telling you that the newspaper man is reported to-night as being likely to recover. At the same time I am truly thankful that I did not pull the nose of the little doctor, for I have learnt this morning that he is a demon swordsman, and can shoot away a thaler balanced edgeways on the thumb of a friend."

After this terrible duel MacIver gave every possible attention to his faithful Lieutenant, Shwagroffski, who, spite some ugly cuts, was soon ready again for the saddle. The Austrian war correspondent, too, recovered in course of time. On the fourth of September, Colonel MacIver received orders to proceed to the front. He had a march before him of four or five days at the least, even if the distance covered each day was extended beyond that usual for cavalry.

The route was through some of the grandest scenery in the Servian territory. On either side mountains flanked the path, many of them verdant and fruitful with the vine and the melon gardens, whilst others were crowned with dark and sombre pine forests. Rustic-looking villages smiled upon the traveller from sheltered nooks or from picturesque spots on the mountain side, and here and there a white spire stood out clearly against the cloudless background of sky.

After a short halt soon after leaving Belgrade, the squadron pushed on until, from the extreme heat of the day, the Colonel deemed it advisable that the horses and men should enjoy two or three hours' rest, and avail themselves of the screen from the fierce rays of the sun which the shelter of a little village afforded. At sunset the march was resumed. The delicious coolness that followed made travelling very pleasant. Soon the Danube was neared, with a vast plain stretching away on the opposite side, and from the hill over which the squadron was passing could be seen, six or eight miles away, the spires of the churches in the town of Semendria, which was to be their halting place for the night.

A lovely moon was shining from the starlit heavens as MacIver's men rode up the principal street after a thirty-six miles' march, and were welcomed by the citizens with loud acclamations. His troopers were scarcely yet used to a soldier's duties, and he took care that every man groomed, fed, and made his horse comfortable for the night before going to his own billet.

At the hotel the Colonel found Doctor Sandwith and Captain Carter, late of the 43rd Light Infantry. Here he learnt, too, that the Circassian and Egyptian cavalry had cut the road between Razanj and Deligrad. This was rather important news, as Razanj was a village but a short distance from Deligrad, and lay between that town and the squadron, and in two or three days would have to be passed over.

At half-past six the next morning the troopers were in the saddle, and shortly after leaving Semendria, passed a battalion of Servian infantry on the march. The morning was deliciously cool and fresh, and enabled the cavalry to push on rapidly until at two o'clock in the afternoon they halted for the day, after covering twenty-five miles, at Oraschia. By five the following morning they were again on the march, and when they halted at Jagudina at seven in the evening fully thirty-five miles had been ridden during the day, and MacIver's troopers were white with dust. They had met several waggons carrying wounded men during the day, and also one conveying Turkish prisoners to Belgrade. They now found the town filled with troops of all descriptions, and it was some time before the Commandant could find quarters and rations for his squadron.

Even when this was done there was no leisure for the Colonel; nearly the whole night was taken up in dictating or writing orders and letters. Amongst other telegrams which he despatched was one to General Tchernaieff, the Russian Commander, stating that although he (MacIver) understood that the country lying between them was in the hands of the enemy, he should march at five in the morning for Deligrad, unless he received orders to the contrary. Between three and four came a telegram in reply, ordering him to advance with his command at all speed.

Before five o'clock the trumpet sounded "Boot and Saddle," and soon afterwards they were on the move. Darkness had set in some time before the march was ended, which, contrary to expectation, was uninterrupted. After passing the little village of Razanj they had to ascend a hill, and ere they had marched to the top, both officers and men were struck with the particular redness of the sky, as though from some vast conflagration. This was soon found to arise from the numerous watch-fires in the different positions which were spread over the country for ten or a dozen miles. In addition to these watch-fires, however, there were one or two villages in flames.

When they were near to General Tchernaieff's headquarters, the Colonel halted his squadron and then, accompanied by two of his officers, proceeded to report himself to the Russian Commander-in-Chief. This distinguished officer received MacIver very cordially, and during the interview, which lasted nearly an hour, told him that very probably there would be an action the next day.

MacIver's squadron had to bivouac as best they could on the low-lying ground by the river, and, as they imagined, within half-a-mile or so of the enemy's outposts. To make matters worse it had commenced raining heavily, and they had to picket their horses, and themselves lie on the bare wet ground; besides which the men had been without food since the previous night. But, in spite of all this, most of them managed to sleep soundly, for they had marched one hundred and thirty miles in four days, and thirty-six that very day, and were thoroughly tired out.

On the following morning a couple of waggons came into MacIver's camping ground with the rations, which consisted of loaves of brown bread and meat, and in the afternoon General Tchernaieff paid a visit, accompanied by his staff. He was on a tour of inspection, and rode down the ranks of the foreign squadron, which was drawn up on foot to receive him. He was a fine, soldierly-looking man, and seemed young for the rank which he held, and for the distinguished position which he had gained. There was a little improvement as to sleeping quarters that night, some rough huts having been erected. The next morning the camp was changed on to higher ground, and where it was well sheltered by trees from the piercing rays of the sun, which was intensely hot during the days, although the rain fell heavily at nights.

On the morning of the eleventh of September the Turks made an attempt to cross the Morava in the vicinity of Alexinatz. As cavalry operations were not required, MacIver gladly embraced the opportunity of personally testing the qualities and capabilities of the Servians when in action. From line to line the command re-echoed, and, in response, led by Russian officers, they charged the enemy right gallantly, not, perhaps, with great enthusiasm, for they were a quiet people, but with a steadiness that considerably raised his opinion of the military qualities of the race when properly organised.

A terrible cannonade went on all day, and the valley was so enveloped in smoke from the musketry and great guns, that it was almost impossible to see what was going on. But towards evening Tchernaieff, who was in the front, with the aid of two fresh batteries of ten guns, drove back the Turks with great slaughter. The loss, however, was very great on both sides, that of the Servians alone being, it was said, two thousand men.

Mr. Winholt, an English gentleman, who had come to Servia more for amusement than anything else, had accompanied the squadron to the front, by permission of MacIver. He now decided to return to England, and left again for Belgrade, much to the regret of all. A day or two after this Colonel Hamilton, late a British cavalry officer, but then of the Lanarkshire Volunteers, paid a visit to the camp of the Foreign Squadron, and stayed a night in the commandant's hut. The bill of fare that MacIver had to offer was not that, perhaps, which he would have wished, but it was the best he had to give, and seemed to be enjoyed by the guest. On this day, which was the fifteenth, the Servians were said to have sustained a loss of two thousand men.

The commandant of the cavalry had another visitor to his camp at this time, to whom he had previously been opposed as an enemy on the battle-field. This was Major-General Upton, of the United States army. The two now, however, met as friends, and MacIver, with his usual courtesy, did all he possibly could to make the American General's visit to the Servian army agreeable. He placed his horses at his disposal, for which he received the thanks of General Upton, both personally and by letter. Taking advantage of the week's armistice, which was signed on the sixteenth, Upton went round all the positions.

On the 16th of September, which was Sunday, an event occurred which caused a great sensation. The troops at Deligrad, which included some five thousand Russian volunteers, proclaimed Prince Milan King of Servia. Their officers assembled and came to General Tchernaieff to announce this declaration. The chaplains or regimental priests of the army also consecrated it with a solemn religious service. The General formally accepted this important act and communicated it to the officers commanding at Paratjin and elsewhere, besides sending an account of it to the one most concerned, Prince Milan, whom he saluted as king.

The Servian Government, however, under the direction of M. Christich, the Prime Minister, did not think fit to accept the responsibility of such a change of title, however gratifying it might be to the national feeling of Servia. At least such an important matter required mature consideration. It would not only stand, M. Christich considered, in the way of a possible peace with Turkey, but might be displeasing to the Emperor of Russia as well as to the other Foreign Powers. On the very day that this proclamation had been made, a seven days' armistice had been arranged with Turkey, through the intervention of the six great Foreign Powers — Great Britain, Russia, Austria, Germany, France, and Italy—and the friendly negotiations which were expected to accrue might fall through by this direct act of defiance to the Porte.

Colonel Gourley, the member for Sunderland, late of the Durham Militia, also visited the Servian camp and received a hearty welcome. General MacIver often speaks of him in high terms, as he does also of his brother member for the same borough, Mr. Storey.

NOTE.

As we have referred to several gentlemen who visited the Servian camp, it would, perhaps, be as well to give here an extract from General MacIver's pamphlet alluding to these visits. He says :

"Going to another subject, there is a little matter that I deem it my duty to mention here. It concerns an assertion made by the *Times* special correspondent, stating that an English officer (Colonel Hamilton) had been expelled from the headquarters of General Tchernaieff's army. I embrace this opportunity of repudiating that assertion, and briefly state the real facts of the case. Colonel Hamilton arrived at our headquarters at Deligrad on September the 15th, and was most kindly received by General Dochtouroff, who introduced him to General Tchernaieff, who, in his turn, invited him to dine with him the same evening. Afterwards he came to my headquarters, a distance of about a mile, and there made the acquaintance of my officers (principally Russians), who treated him with the courtesy and respect demanded. Our bill of fare was not, perhaps, that of a West-end club, but what we had we shared, soldier with soldier. I had not a feather-bed to offer him, but such as I had I gave; he shared my own—a little straw in my hut, and I think Colonel Hamilton rather enjoyed his night in camp. Early next morning, after taking a little *sloveich*, he left us for headquarters. The same day, in the afternoon, I met him again at headquarters, when he informed me that the General could not permit him to go to Alexinatz. I most emphatically deny that he was expelled from the camp, and I may add that I make this statement upon the authority of General Dochtouroff himself. Colonel Hamilton, as a soldier, must acknowledge that at certain times it is requisite, and even essential, for a commander to prohibit strangers, especially foreign officers, from visiting private and stratagetic points and positions. In conclusion, I must add that Colonel Hamilton must also acknowledge that while in camp he was treated as an officer and a gentleman, and I can call upon other gentlemen, including the names of Messrs. Story and A. Winholt, and Colonel Gourley, M.P., to testify concerning their reception and the treatment they received among us.

"The names of these gentlemen remind me of an incident which it will, perhaps, be profitable for the English public to know. During the visit of the aforementioned gentleman and others to our camp, I pointed out to them through my field-glasses a distant object, a short distance within the enemy's lines, and proffered them horses that they might ride over and see it for themselves with their naked eyes. It was the charred remains of an aged woman, who had been fearfully outraged. Her breasts had been cut off, her throat severed, and other abuses committed on her unfit for publication; and after these she had been secured to a post and burnt alive. But this cruel outrage is only one speck in the great black sand of atrocities which has fallen upon Servia and its sister provinces."

CHAPTER XLI.

APPOINTED TO THE STAFF OF THE COMMANDER-IN-CHIEF—RECEIVES THE ORDER OF THE TAKAVO—MISSION TO ENGLAND—THE END OF THE WAR.

WHILE the armistice was still in operation, Colonel MacIver was transferred to the staff of General Tchernaieff. The Commander-in-Chief, it appears, had been most favourably impressed with the soldierly qualities of MacIver, and by his (the General's) particular request, he consented to give up the command of his squadron. In his new position he was to take rank as Chief of Cavalry, which was equivalent to that of General of Brigade. This change was the means of bringing about a most intimate and lasting friendship between himself and the Russian commander.

MacIver's new position on the staff gave him greater facilities for witnessing and studying the character of the Russian and native officials. Nothing could possibly exceed their hearty hospitality, nor the kindness and consideration he received from them.

Some days before the termination of the armistice

intelligence was received at headquarters that the Turks were actively engaged in erecting a bridge across the Morava, which bridge was actually completed before the conclusion of the truce. Nevertheless, strictly maintaining his honour as an officer and a commander, General Tchernaieff with a forbearance that was most noble, refrained from interposition until the armistice had expired.

Immediately, however, upon its close, under cover of the night, a detachment of troops, commanded by Colonel Andrieff, advanced and fired the bridge. Their intentions, however, were speedily discovered by the Turkish outposts, but too late to be of any advantage to them, as the bridge was already in flames. The enemy's batteries opened fire, but with no success, and though volley after volley of musketry was fired, it only resulted in the loss of one man. We mention this fact to show that it was the Turks and not the Servians who first infringed the laws and regulations of the armistice.

Nothing worthy of note occurred until the evening of the twenty-seventh of September, when, at midnight, preparations were commenced along the whole line for the morning's attack. When darkness closed General Tchernaieff with his staff moved from Deligrad, and bivouacked close to the village of Ravinch. Before daybreak each division and brigade commander had received orders to be in readiness for the attack, which was to be carried out by a given signal shortly after daybreak. Just as each position was reached, the report of the signal gun announced that the fight had commenced, and at the same time the Servian artillery opened fire along the whole line. The Turks made a good reply, and for upwards of an hour the roar of artillery and the explosion of shells were mingled with the cries and groans of the wounded and dying.

In about an hour the fire slackened, and the Servian right wing, commanded by the gallant Harvatovich, pressed onward. About nine o'clock an explosion announced the blowing up of one of the enemy's batteries. The Servians still pressed on, the enemy's first line giving way before them. Then began a conflict that was deadly. Down upon the Servians came a perfect deluge of fire poured from masked batteries and repeating rifles, yet, notwithstanding that the native troops were insufficiently armed—many of them carrying old rusty muzzle-loading, and even ruder weapons—they still pressed on, and before midday succeeded in capturing two redoubts, and one of the enemy's batteries, carrying also their second line of defence. Scarcely had these gallant fellows done this when the Turks were heavily reinforced; and the Servians, finding that sufficient support could not reach them, were compelled, after a stubborn resistance, to fall back to their previous position, on account of a cross-fire maintained unremittingly by the enemy.

Upon this eventful day the Servian losses included some sixty officers and one thousand five hundred men, the majority of the former being Russians. The few prisoners captured were kindly treated and transferred to Belgrade. That day, at least, must undoubtedly be recorded a Servian success. Nothing could exceed the heroic courage shown by both officers and men, or the gallantry of the Russian and Montenegrin troops. But for the heavy reinforcements of the Turks, the day would have been for the Servians a signal one of triumph.

The following morning was devoted to caring for the wounded and burying the dead; in fact the last sad offices were interrupted on the morning of the thirtieth by the Turks opening fire with a heavy volley of musketry, followed by artillery. The Servian infantry immediately formed line of battle to receive the enemy's attack. In fact, the engagement might be regarded as an infantry battle. The Servians fought well, but MacIver has told us that in the rear of the Turks he could discern lines of cavalry urging on their men with drawn swords. He further added that throughout the day the gallantry displayed by both Russian and Servian officers and men demanded the highest praise, especially as two-thirds of the Servian infantry were armed with wretched fire-arms against the most improved weapons of the period.

The battle continued with unremitted fury the whole of the day, and the Turks were driven back with great slaughter, the Servians still maintaining their position and one of the captured redoubts. At night, however, the Turks were heavily reinforced, and they came down upon the Servians in such overwhelming numbers that, before repeated charges, the latter were compelled to retire. So, contesting every inch, the Servians slowly fell back to the line occupied in the morning, yet obliged to leave a portion of their wounded upon the field. Their losses during the two days were estimated at two thousand five hundred men and eighty officers killed and wounded. Yet, nothing daunted, the Servians renewed the attack at dawn on the first of October, and, after a desperate struggle, charged and recaptured the redoubt and defence line lost—and yet so bravely—the night before.

So highly did Colonel MacIver distinguish himself during these engagements, that General Tchernaieff conferred upon him, on the field of battle, the Gold Cross of the Takavo, taking the Order from his own breast and fastening it on that of MacIver. Subsequently he was made a Commander of the same Order of the First Class. About the third of October he left the front to return to Belgrade, having, at the request of Prince Milan and General Tchernaieff, consented to go on a special mission to England.

Previous to leaving Belgrade, for the purpose of carrying out these instructions, a very interesting ceremony took place, in which he was the chief character. A lady in England had embroidered with her own hands a silken banner and presented it to the Colonel of the foreign Squadron. It had only reached him on his arrival in Belgrade, and he determined to offer it to the Servian nation.

The following letter, however, sent to the secretary of "The League in Aid of the Christians of Turkey," and which appeared in different English journals, will describe it more graphically than we should do It is dated Belgrade, October 10th, 1876.

"Belgrade, Oct. 10th, 1876.

"DEAR SIR,

"In reference to the embroidered banner so kindly worked by an English lady, and forwarded through the League to Colonel MacIver, I have great pleasure in conveying to you the following particulars:

"Colonel MacIver, upon returning from the front on Friday evening, found the flag awaiting his arrival, and on Sunday morning the following interesting ceremony took place. The flag having been previously consecrated by the Archbishop, was conducted by a guard of honour to the palace, and Colonel MacIver, in the presence of Prince Milan and a numerous suite, in the name and on behalf of yourself and the fair donor, delivered it into the hands of the Princess Nathalie, who graciously received it. The Prince and Princess were highly delighted with the exquisite workmanship and effective beauty of the unique gift, and expressed their heartfelt thanks to the considerate donor, who sympathised so kindly with the Christian cause— now struggling for independence. The gallant Colonel wore upon the occasion his full uniform as Brigade Commander and as Chief of the Cavalry of the Servian army, and bore upon his breast the Gold Cross of the Takavo, which he received after the battles of the 28th and 30th September, in recognition of the heroism and bravery he displayed upon those eventful days.

"The beauty of the gift was enhanced, and its value increased, by the significant circumstances of its bestowal, for on the evening of the battle of the 30th, as the officers returned to the camp, General Tchernaieff approached Colonel MacIver, and, unclasping the cross from his own breast, he placed it with his own hands upon that of the Colonel as a testimony alike of his and Servia's appreciation of the undaunted courage and untiring perseverance of the gallant Colonel in the Servian cause.

"The flag, I learn, is to remain at the palace, and it has become the most popular object of interest in the Servian capital.   "With kindest regards,

"I am, dear Sir, very truly yours,

"(Signed)   Hugh Jackson,

"Member of the Council of the League in Aid of the Christians in Turkey."

During Colonel MacIver's mission to England he visited Manchester, Liverpool, and several other large towns, where he not only met with a very enthusiastic reception, but did much to aid the movement that was then on foot for assisting the distressed Servians. In Manchester and Liverpool alone upwards of fifteen thousand pounds was raised for this good purpose. We append a letter referring to Servia and the Christians in the East, which was received by him during his visit to England, and which we doubt not will be read with interest :

"L'Etat Major Général de l'Armée Serbe.
"Belgrade, October 9th, 1876.

"Monsieur le Colonel,

"Inspired by a deep sympathy for the noble and just cause of the Slavonian people of the Balkan Peninsula, you came to place yourself under the flag of the Servian army, and have aided it in the defence of our territory and of our sacred rights. The services you have rendered as a loyal soldier and able officer are appreciated and recognised, and we now expect new services from you in the cause for which you have so nobly fought.

"The British nation, free and enlightened, has always regarded with interest the accomplishment of events which were likely to seriously influence the fate of struggling nationalities. It has always known how to appreciate them judiciously, and has, up to the present, invariably pronounced in favour of civilisation against barbarism, for justice and humanity against iniquity, for the free enjoyment of the sacred rights of man against oppression and brute force. It cannot be otherwise to-day than it has been in the past, and that is why Servia may, we hope, reckon on the sympathy of your generous and noble compatriots.

"But to obtain that hearty sympathy it is necessary that the British public should be well informed as to the real state of things, not only in the interior, but also at the theatre of military action. We know well what dependence can be placed on the communications of correspondents, how very far they are sometimes from the truth, and how frequently they misrepresent facts which cannot be contested. You, Colonel, who have lived with us and fought in our ranks, will be able to refute mis-statements, and picture the situation as it really is. Tell your countrymen that Servia, which counts no more than one million of inhabitants, has undertaken this war with the sole object of compelling the Porte to ameliorate the sad state of our brethren in Bulgaria, Bosnia, and Herzegovina; that, menaced by the armed force of a considerable Empire, Servia has defended herself successfully for more than three months against the invasion of a numerous hostile army; that the entire male population is under arms; that the country is deserted, the crops are destroyed, the fields are uncultivated; that there is not a Servian who has not brought to the common cause his share of material sacrifices, the total of which for a country so young and so poor as ours, surpasses almost the limits of belief; and that, nevertheless, Servia will continue the contest, as she believes firmly in the triumph of her cause, which is that of justice and humanity.

"If the Great Powers cannot or will not intervene in our favour, we shall expect from the peoples, and above all from the English people, moral support and encouragement. It will not refuse us when it shall be enlightened in the true state of things. Whatever the nature of the assistance, it will be precious to us, as it will be a clear proof that the English people, the most enlightened and the most humane in the world, at length appreciate at their true value the heroic efforts of the Servians. We do not doubt you will accomplish your mission with that chivalrous devotion you have always shown in the performance of your duties, and we hope that with the blessing of God your efforts will be crowned with success.

"Accept, my dear Colonel, the assurance of my distinguished consideration.

"Le Chef d'Etat Major Général
"l'Armée Serbe
"(Signed)   L. IVANOVITCH.
"M. le Colonel MacIver,
"Chef de Cavalerie, Armée Serbe."

During the time General MacIver was in England he published a small pamphlet on his experiences of the war in Servia, which was dedicated by permission to the Right Hon. W. E. Gladstone, M.P. The sufferings of the Servian people, described with a graphic pen, and the atrocities committed by the Turks, so vividly portrayed by one who had been an eye-witness, created at the time a great sensation. It brought the author, too, in contact with many influential and agreeable acquaintances.

Amongst others was Madame Olga Novikoff, who was then staying in London, at Symonds' Hotel. This lady was the sister of Colonel Kiveef, who was about the first officer to fall in Servia, as he was leading on his battalion. He had formerly been one of the aide-de-camps to the Czar, and was a very brave and accomplished man. Madame was the wife of a Russian ambassador, and was a great linguist. She took so much interest in the Slav cause, and was so moved by General MacIver's representations of the cruelties practised by the Turks, that she had his pamphlet translated into the Russian language and published there. Madame Novikoff spoke highly of the flattering terms in which the General had been mentioned in the Russian newspapers.

Another lady known by MacIver very intimately at this time was Mademoiselle Sophie von Doer'per, who was a great friend of Madame Novikoff, and staying with her. This young baroness was an ardent supporter of Servia, and took great interest in all matters relating to her struggle against the Turks.

After carrying out to a successful termination the mission which had brought him to England, MacIver at once returned to Servia. It was on his second arrival in that country that he was decorated with the Commandership of the Order of Takavo by King Milan. For services in Servia, too, he received the gold and silver medals for valour. This Cross of Takavo was instituted by Prince Michel in honour of his father, Miloch—that Prince Miloch who fell when fighting against the Turks in eighten hundred and fifteen. Takavo is a little town in Servia.

The Colonel, or the General as we must now call him, for he held the rank of Chief of the Servian Cavalry, again went to the front, and remained on the staff of General Tchernaieff until the close of the war. Of his old Commander, who is now Governor-General of Turkestan, he held a very high opinion, not only as a soldier, but as a thoroughly conscientious, high-principled, Christian gentleman.

We cannot, however, do better than quote MacIver's opinion in his own words: "Of General Tchernaieff, the Commander-in-Chief of the Servian Army, I will say he is a man whose presence alone must command the respect and admiration of all around him. To those who know him I need not say he is a gallant officer and a true friend; but to those who do not know him I repeat that there is not a braver or more nobler hero living than that glorious, devoted champion of the Servian cause. I will give one instance of kindness and humanity which renders him so thoroughly beloved by those around him.

"On the first of October a man was brought into camp who had deserted his regiment three times. Considerable difficulty had been experienced in effecting his capture; indeed, he had deliberately shot one of those who attempted it, dead. As a rule, the punishment for desertion is death; and so, when the details of this case had been heard, the man was condemned to be shot, and urged to prepare himself. The sentence had scarcely been pronounced when the man's wife appeared, weeping piteously, and bearing in her arms a little child, to implore the General to spare her husband's life.

"It was a sight not soon to be forgotten. The woman's anguish was terrible, as she prayed for a life that seemed very dear to her; but I think the wistful, pleading look of the little child did more than the mother's cries. A deep feeling of sympathy was perceived on the General's face as he saw that little mute appeal, and in a voice that was not clear, he ordered the execution of the deserter to be stayed and commuted to twenty years' imprisonment."

Writing of the Russian General Dochtouroff, MacIver says: "Of his courage and gallantry I will not speak—they are too well known to need any comment here. But of his courtesy, of his kindness, and his consideration for those about him, which of all the virtues in his heart are the most marked in his daily life, I will say that they render him beloved by all who come in contact with him."

Referring to the Servian people, General MacIver again remarks: "Of simple habits, they are kind, honest, and generous. The very grasp of a Servian's hand speaks a Servian's heart; and I bear testimony that for piety, sobriety, gratitude, and unselfishness, they are surpassed by no nation upon earth. Like the other Christian populations of the Balkan Peninsula, they have now arrived at a degree of enlightenment and refinement sufficient to make them feel acutely a degradation which they have suffered for four hundred years; and while there is a drop of Servian blood unshed, or a Servian arm with strength to wield a sword, they will struggle on with assistance, or without assistance. That just and noble cause must exist, until that last drop of blood is shed, and that last arm is powerless—or the accursed yoke of the Turk is broken."

On his return to Belgrade from the front, MacIver tried his best to get into a quarrel with a Captain Kooper, a Prussian, who was supposed to be in the secret service of Prince Bismarck. But whatever he was, he turned out to be a coward. He was very insolent one day to MacIver, and the General immediately slapped his face. The *brave* man, however, submitted to the indignity, and nothing came of the blow.

MacIver had many intimate and kind friends whom he met in Servia. First, by his rank, was Colonel (now General) Georges Catargi, uncle to the King. Notably amongst others were Doctor Gorgevitch, Chief Surgeon to their Majesties and Medical Director; Colonel L. Ivanovitch, Chef d'Etat; Major A. Boozovitch, Secretary to the Minister for

Foreign Affairs, and formerly Secretary to M. Christich when Minister at Constantinople; Demeter Todovovic, President of the Gymnasium, a great Servian patriot; and Nicolas Melnikoff, Lieutenant des Lancers l'Heritiére, a young Russian noble who was serving in Servia. There was another friend, whom we have left to the last, at whose house General MacIver was a frequent and welcome guest. This was Monsieur Simon M. Stanisavlevitch, an advocate of Belgrade, who had a charming wife and two very lovely daughters. At the hands of this family he received great hospitality and kindness.

Now that the war was at an end, MacIver, in company of his friend and late commander, General Tchernaieff, was about to make a journey to England, where it was proposed to spend a few months. The celebrated Russian General had with him also, as private secretary, Major Michel Cleudoff. This officer was the son of one of the richest men in Moscow, who had given more monetary assistance than any other individual to the Slav cause. The young major was worthy of such a father, for he was a brave, generous-hearted fellow.

CHAPTER XLII.

GENERAL TCHERNAIEFF IN LONDON—MACIVER RETURNS TO SERVIA—RECEIVES A COMMISSION UNDER THE GREEK GOVERNMENT, WITH INSTRUCTIONS TO FORM A FOREIGN LEGION

THE arrival in London of a man so distinguished as the late Russian Commander-in-Chief of the Servian Army caused considerable interest. General Tchernaieff at once received a number of invitations into society, in which his two brother officers were included. But he accepted few of them. He had come to England to enjoy himself in a quiet way for a few months, and at the same time to get that rest which he needed after the fatigues of a campaign. His purpose was to spend part of the time in town, and the remainder at some retired spot on the English coast, and with General MacIver and Major Cleudoff he first resided at Symonds' Hotel, Brook Street.

Whilst staying at this hotel, MacIver relates an anecdote of the General which illustrates his generous disposition and kindliness of heart. The incident is simple enough in itself, and refers to an old crippled soldier who used to sweep a crossing in Brook Street. This poor fellow had no doubt easily recognised in the strangers staying at Symonds' military men, and more than once MacIver noticed, as they passed to or fro, either for a walk or in a carriage, the ex-soldier brought his broomstick up to the salute. One day General Tchernaieff, too, observed this man, as with military precision he brought his old broom first to the shoulder and then to the salute, and, smiling, asked who he was. MacIver told his late commanding officer that he believed the sweeper to be a soldier who had been discharged from the English army. Upon this Tchernaieff walked up to the crossing, and felt in his pocket for some change, but could find nothing but a sovereign.

"I have got some silver, General," said MacIver, speaking in French.

"It does not matter," replied the General; "I will give him this."

"As you please, General," said MacIver, smiling; "but perhaps he may have fought against you in the Crimea."

"Possibly, but he is a soldier all the same, and is poor," and his Excellency placed the golden coin in the man's palm.

After leaving Symonds' Hotel, General Tchernaieff and his two friends proceeded to the Isle of Wight, and stayed for some considerable time at Tweed Mount, Ventnor. Whilst the famous Russian commander was in this beautiful island, Mr. Robert Coningsby was there on a short visit to his friend MacIver, and wrote another of his interesting letters to a friend in town, which we have seen. It describes a charming duel story, in which a hostile meeting was prevented by an amusing *ruse* on the writer's part. Droll as the occurrence was, however, as it happened in a private house, we feel sure neither MacIver nor Mr. Coningsby would like to see it in print.

After General Tchernaieff's departure from England, MacIver went on to Roumania, but more as an amateur than anything else, as he had no intention of taking part in the war. Having satisfied himself as to what was going on there, he went back to Servia, and remained for some short time.

General MacIver's retirement from the Servian service was of his own seeking. At his special request he was permitted by the King to resign his commission in the Servian Army, as it was understood that he wished to attach himself to General Tchernaieff with ulterior objects. The document which relieved him of his obligations to the country bears date Belgrade, 24th December, 1876, and is signed by the King, Milan M. Obrénovitch, and countersigned by the Chief of the Staff, Miladen Ivanovitch.

It was with regret that he had to sever himself from the friends and acquaintances that he had made in Servia. From the Prince and his charming wife,

the Princess Nathalie, down to the very lowest of
their subjects, he had at all times been treated with
the greatest courtesy and consideration. Of that
august lady, now Queen of Servia, MacIver still
speaks with great admiration and devoted respect.
He has her portrait and autograph, which were
presented to him by her Majesty in person, on his
taking leave. He has also a similar portrait of his
Majesty, which bears the following inscription in the
King's handwriting.

"Au Colonel MacIver ; t'moignage de reconnais-
sance et de sincère estime.
"M. M. OBRENOIVITCH."
"Belgrade, 1-13 Janvier, 1877."

From Belgrade General MacIver went on to Vienna
and to Trieste, and thence took steamer to Cattaro.
On board he made the acquaintance of Prince Louis of
Battenberg, who is at present an officer in the British
Navy, and found him a very pleasant fellow-passenger.
From thence he went to Cettigne in Montenegro, but
finding that Prince Nicolas and his principal Marshal,
Botahvich (who had served with him in Servia) were
not there, he did not remain.

MacIver's next service was under the Greek
flag at the time of the fighting in Thessalia against
the Turks. On his arrival in Athens he was
introduced to the members of the Central Committee of National Defence, and the following translation from the Greek newspaper, *Strength and
Patience*, dated Athens, Thursday, 9th March, 1878,
refers to his presence in Greece.

"Colonel MacIver, who is so well known in the
valleys of battles for his undaunted bravery and fearless character arrived here yesterday. This officer

whose noble ideas of freedom have gained for him the respect and admiration of all sensible people, has served under Italy, America, and Servia, which latter place he has just left, having done his duty nobly to that country. He has arrived here to offer his sword on behalf of the oppressed Hellenes, and in the hope that good results may attend his visit. Colonel MacIver visited us before, but was reluctantly obliged at that time to leave Greece, as the path of glory was not then opened. This good Philo-Hellene on his departure, however, was but waiting the first opportunity when he could prove his love for our country. Colonel MacIver then went to Servia, where he organised the Servian cavalry, and fought as a hero, conquering twice the Turkish infantry at Cigar. Having now returned to Athens, he hopes, with the aid of the Government, to restore the classical mementos of the country with his MacIverian policy of free energy and justice, by breaking the thraldom of the Mussulmanic yoke."

On the 18th March—nine days later—the same paper again refers to the General in a paragraph of which we give a translation.

"The Italian newspaper, *Italian Age*, has received the following telegram which has been sent from Athens on the 10-22 March: 'The revolution in Thessaly is progressing; five thousand revolutionists having assembled on Mount Pillion. The Greeks are much excited, and the Treaty of Peace will not stop the war, and we call on General Garibaldi and on all friends of freedom, so that they may not abandon our cause. The distinguished and gallant officer, General MacIver, is with us organising an army here.'"

After some preliminary negotiations with the Central Committee of National Defence, it was decided that MacIver should form a Foreign Legion, for service against the Turks, and of which he was to have the absolute command. On the 22nd of March he received his commission as General of Brigade from the Committee, which was enclosed in a communication of which the following is a translation. Although these documents are some in French and others in Greek, we have thought it better that they should all appear before the reader in English, and have had them carefully translated.

"Central Committee of National Defence and Fraternity.
"No. 527.   "Athens, 22nd March, 1878.
"(3rd April.)

"GENERAL,

"I have the honour to inform you that the Central Committee of the National Defence have accepted without delay the offer you have made them to raise and organise in Greece a Foreign Legion under your command, to operate against the enemies of the people of the provinces who have risen to gain their independence, and I transmit you here enclosed your nomination as Commander of the aforesaid Foreign Legion. As we have already explained to you verbally, we have also written to the Greek Committees in England praying them to accord you all assistance, and to procure for you the necessary funds to effect the transport of any volunteers from England to Greece. As soon as your soldiers arrive in Greece they will then be supplied with regular funds for their maintenance.

"Accept, General, the assurance of my most distinguished consideration.

"(Signed)   The President,   "P. CALLIGA.

"To the General of Brigade,

"Central Committee of the National Defence and Fraternity.
"No. 526. "Athens, 3rd April, 1878.

"We the undersigned, composing the Central Committee for the National Defence and Fraternity, in the name of this Committee, bestow upon you, Henry Ronald MacIver, the rank of General of Brigade, with full powers to organise and take the command in chief of a Foreign Legion, to operate by land and by sea, against the enemies of the Greek Provinces now risen to gain their independence. You will exert all your energy to fulfil and carry out this mission to the best of your abilities and according to our orders.

"And for this purpose we authorise you to choose and appoint all officers and soldiers to be under your orders. By this present act we pray also all the authorities, political, military, and administrative, to consider the above-mentioned General MacIver, as well as his officers and soldiers, as Greek citizens fighting for the legal defence of the country.

"The President,
(Signed). "P Calliga.
"Members of the Committee,
(Signed) "N. Damaschinos,
„ "C. Scouloudi,
„ "M. Melas,
„ "G. A. Sauz,
„ "F. Meeborhiz."

It will be seen by the above commission that great power was vested in General MacIver. Further, it was fully approved by the Prime Minister, M. Comounduros. Then follows instruction for the organization and working of the Legion.

"Foreign Legion to be formed on the following Basis.

"The Foreign Legion must be formed of three battalions, one English, one Italian, and the other Greek, the latter formed of Greeks inhabiting foreign countries. Each battalion will have at the commencement not less than five hundred men. There will also be a squadron of cavalry, which will serve for the outpost duty and also for vedette, scout, and courier duties; two artillery batteries for mountain duty, and an artillery battery for siege duty; likewise one section of engineers. The Staff will have to be composed of English, Italian, and Greek officers. Each battalion must be commanded by officers of the same nationality as the men who form the said battalion. The medical service will be formed of a Chief Major for all the Legion, and of two assistant Majors per battalion. The ambulance material must be composed of the necessary number of waggons, not less than four per battalion, and the usual number of men attached thereto.

"The officers and soldiers of the Foreign Legion will be amenable to the discipline and rules of the Greek army relative to their entrance on the campaign for their pay, their seniority, and their advancement in the service. The officers and soldiers wounded on the battle field or in service will have right to the same pensions as those in the regular Greek Army. The officers and soldiers after the war will be entitled to be sent to their homes at the expense of the Greek Government.

"If during the campaign, through the failure of communications or owing to the topographical irregularity from the theatre of operations, the commissariat service cannot act, the officers and soldiers will receive the amount of their claims in money instead of its equivalent.

"The commissary officer of each battalion must daily authenticate the strength of his battalion, as well as the amount of their claims, either in matter or in money due to the Legion. A copy of such report will have to be sent daily to the Commander-in-Chief, and another forwarded to the War Minister at Athens. The uniform will consist of a red shirt, blue trousers, cap with white cover, cloak, blanket, boots, and the necessary campaign cooking utensils.

"The passage money of the English volunteers by the boats of Messrs. Pappayanni, will be two hundred and fifty francs, all included, and that of the Italian volunteers, from thirty-five to forty francs. A depot will be established at St. Maure, in order to undertake the organization of the Legion as they arrive, and to attend to their respective corps and equipments."

On the twenty-fourth of March General MacIver was ordered to proceed to England on an important mission in connection with the organization. Ten days previously he had been introduced to His Excellency, M. Comounduros, the Prime Minister, and received instructions to commence operations immediately. Under the special direction of the Minister and M. Melas, he wrote to England, and requested an old brother-officer named Harrington to try and get together as many good and serviceable men as possible. On his arrival in Italy, from Greece, MacIver sent a telegram to this gentleman, advising him that he was on his way to England.

On his arrival in London, he found that seventy-two men already had been engaged, the most of whom had left employment of some sort to volunteer. On the second day after reaching town the General presented himself before the Hellenic Committee, who appeared, or professed to appear, astonished to see him. They informed him that they could not assist his object in any way without proper instructions from Athens; that theirs was not a War Committee, etc., and that they would advise him to write and ask for further instructions. Further, he was told that it would be better he should not call again at the Committee Room, as they were watched by the police agents and spies.

Naturally, General MacIver was perfectly astounded at finding himself left with the responsibility of seventy-two men and officers, without knowing what to do. He felt that his position was a very delicate one, and his feelings towards the London Committee were very bitter. He sent three telegrams to M. Melas without receiving a reply, but still continued to hope that the Committee of National Defence would forward instructions. At length came the following answer from M. Melas.

"Athens, 15–27 April, 1878.

"My dear General,

"I have received your letter, by which you ask that the Committee should write to its correspondents in London relative to the subject of the recruiting of volunteers. You already know that, through the interference of the English Government, a treaty has been concluded with the insurgents and the military Turkish authorities, and that we are now waiting for the definite solution of the question. You will understand then, my dear General, that under these circumstances it is useless for the moment to go on to form a volunteer corps. But I am persuaded that if ever the occasion presents itself that Greece will be able to rely on your generous help and co-operation.

"Accept my sincere salutations,
(Signed) "M. MELAS."

This was the position MacIver now found himself in, with his men out of employ for three weeks, and asking payment for subsistence and remuneration. He settled the matter as promptly as possible, without public scandal, paying the money out of his own pocket.

On the first of May the General wrote to Monsieur P Calliga, the President of the Central Committee of National Defence, at Athens, demanding that he should be released from his obligations to the Greek Government, and received the following reply

"Central Committee of the National Defence and Fraternity,
"Athens, May 24th, 1878.
7th June.

"GENERAL,

"Political reasons, since your departure for England, having rendered impossible the formation of a Foreign Legion, of which you have been named commander by our Committee, your mission is thus entirely terminated, as you have been made acquainted by telegram, and by a letter from Mr. M. Melas. In relieving you from your charge according to your demand of the first instant, the Committee at the same time return you their thanks for the energy that you have shown on this occasion in favour of the Greek cause. Receive, I pray you, the assurance of my high consideration.

(Signed) "The President,
"P. CALLIGA.

"To General H. R. MacIver,
"General of Brigade."

The annexed statement made by Count Louis Pennazzi at the time will explain more fully to the reader the disgraceful way in which MacIver was treated by the Greek Government.

"STATEMENT OF COUNT LOUIS PENNAZZI, MAJOR OF CAVALRY AND CHIEF OF STAFF TO GENERAL MACIVER.

"In order that there may not be any equivocation as to the formation of a Greek Foreign Legion, under the orders of Brigadier-General MacIver, it is necessary that Europe, to whom the formation of the said Foreign Legion has been officially announced, should be informed of the causes which have frustrated its organization; and also that those concerned should be justified and protected in all and every way. I therefore make an exact statement of all that has been done, and as to what has passed relating to this affair.

"General MacIver, finding himself at Athens, and having said that in case of need he would undertake the formation of a Foreign Legion, the Greek Insurrectional Committee of the Government, knowing the valuable services rendered in various countries, and even in Greece, by this distinguished officer, General MacIver, in the cause of liberty, placed themselves in communication with him, to treat on the formation of a Foreign Legion, which was destined to take part in the insurrection of the insurgent provinces against the yoke of the Sublime Porte. General MacIver was presented by the members of the Committee to the President of the Council of Ministers, Mr. Comounduros, who warmly approved of the formation of the said Legion, and ordered the Committee to proceed into all the details of its organization. The Central Committee undertook this charge, reserving, however, the right to form a committee in

England, composed of Greek citizens resident there, in order to collect subscriptions destined for the equipment and arming of volunteers forming the English contingent. The formation of the Legion thus was an understood thing, and all that remained was to regulate and organize the details of same. General MacIver then drew up a statement by which he regulated the strength of the Legion, the conditions of enlistment, and the obligations that the Greek Government (whom the Committee represented) bound themselves to in that respect.

"It was then that a real comedy commenced, of which no one could really explain the last word, and for which Greek statesmen are so famous. At the reading of the statement presented by General MacIver, the Committee answered that they could not bind themselves; that the members had not received any official notice to take any steps in the matter, and that nothing could be done until the President of the Council had by letter authorised them to act in the matter; and that only on their getting this would they take any steps in the case. The same statement was then communicated to the President of the Council by the members of the Committee. What that answer was was never known; but what is sure and certain is, that the same evening that Mr. Comounduros had the statement, he declared to General MacIver, to Commander Count Pennazzi, and to Captain Lazzareto, that all the difficulties had been removed, and that the Committee were ordered to prompt action in the formation of the Legion.

"The day following this interview, General Mac-Iver was presented again to the Committee, to receive orders and to get an Act by which his rank and position would be legally recognised. The difficulties recommenced. They pretended that the consent of the First Minister was not definite; and they then wanted a detailed account of the cost of each volunteer, according to his nationality, asserting that only when they got this would they take any further steps. General MacIver without delay presented the account asked for, calculating it at the very lowest figure for equipment and for transport of the foreign volunteers.

"One would then have thought that all difficulties were at an end; but it was not so. For three days more the Committee put off General MacIver, and at length referred him to the First Minister, this latter again referring him to the Committee, and so on. One said that for political reasons he could not interfere directly in the affair, and the other pretended that he could not enter into the business without first shielding himself against all responsibilities by having the signature of the First Minister. It was nothing more than child's play, and it was only after ten long days of indecision, and after all the European newspapers had published a notice as to the formation of the Legion under the command of General MacIver, compromising him, as well as the other officers, before the public opinion of Europe, that the Committee and the Government, on the urgent remonstrances of the General, put themselves together to take a half step, which left but faint hopes of the formation of the Legion.

"The Government and the Committee in the end decided to pay the expenses and keep of the Legion as soon as they arrived in Greece, but refused absolutely to pay the expenses of equipment or of transport, leaving these to the charge of the committees who could be formed in England and in Italy for the recruitment of volunteers and for their despatch. General MacIver was thus forced to be satisfied with this decision, by which it was very doubtful if good results could be obtained. But in accepting the conditions the General made ample reservations, so as not to be held in any way answerable for the non-success of the project.

"The elements of this organization would have acted not only as a powerful emulation for Grecian youth, but its moral influence would have been incalculable in proving to the enemies of Greece what an ardent sympathy was nourished in Europe for the Greek cause. If, then, this Legion has not been formed, it is owing to the indecision of the members of the Insurrectional Committee and to members of the Government. Such indecision is not to be understood when one thinks with what warmth they accepted the propositions of General MacIver, and with what ardour they pretended to take the responsibility upon themselves of creating the said Foreign Legion.

   (Signed)   " CTE. LOUIS PENNAZZI.
   (Signed)   " CONSTANTINOS LAZZARETO,
           "Captain of the Staff."

"Athens, 5th April, 1878.

Since his connection with the Greek Government MacIver has had no service or employment for his sword. He has simply rested upon his laurels; but, as he is still in the prime of life, we shall no doubt hear of him again ere long, as an active and conspicuous figure in the world's history.

Nearly four years back General MacIver was very prominently before the public as the organizer of a scheme for the exploration and colonisation of New

Guinea. After much trouble and expense, and several months devoted to the maturing and carrying out of this gigantic conception, Lord Derby thought proper to interfere and put a stop to the enterprise. The British and Colonial people, however, are the debtors of the General for having raised this question. The Australian newspaper, *The Melbourne Argus*, commenting upon this in a leading article at the time, says:

"A General MacIver, who appears to have held a commission in the Servian Army, although we suspect from his name and his enterprise that he hails from Columbia, has announced his intention of taking up the island which he considers England has rejected, and of establishing a trading company there on a large scale. Of course it is well enough understood what, in the circumstances of the case, such a trading company means. Accordingly, Lord Derby has announced that if any such attempt is made, the Admiral will be ordered to protect the natives. . . . But what right has Lord Derby so to interfere? He either is in possession of the country or he is not. If he is, he must maintain his right by some effectual occupation; a mere paper claim is, in international affairs, universally admitted to be useless. If he is not in possession, what concern has he in the affairs of New Guinea, or how can he claim to control the action of foreigners in their dealings with that country? English statesmen, however, are seldom pressed with logical considerations. They do not want to take up New Guinea if they can help it, but they are quite clear that no one else shall take it up. They are simply shepherding the island. It is probable that this country owes a debt of gratitude to General MacIver."

MacIver, however, having received no sympathy

from Lord Derby, determined to appeal to the Australian people, and proceeded to the Antipodes on a lecturing tour. Although a considerable sufferer by the failure of his project to colonize New Guinea, he was not disheartened.

After a pleasant passage, MacIver arrived out in Australia in May, 1884, when he found that the New Guinea question was exciting much public interest. He received a cordial welcome from the warm-hearted colonists, and soon made many friends.

With this part of his life, however, we have little to do, as General MacIver is engaged in the production from his own pen of a book in which he will enter fully on his experience whilst in Australia. It will, therefore, suffice for us to say that he visited in turn the different colonies, and speaks gratefully of the receptions accorded to him from many persons of position, and from the members of the Press generally.

But in addition to this, MacIver, whilst at the Antipodes, joined an expedition to New Guinea, where he stayed for a short time. Before leaving England he had publicly stated that he would never return until he had placed his foot on the favoured island, which it had been his purpose to colonize, and that promise he fulfilled to the letter.

The General is most enthusiastic in his praises of the country and resources of New Guinea, and doubtless, when compiling his book, will deal comprehensively with what he saw with his own eyes. The publication, however, has been delayed owing to a domestic bereavement, and thus will not be likely to appear before the New Year, as MacIver—who returned to England from Australia a few months back—is about to leave for America.

In the United States it is his intention, in a

series of lectures, to give his experience as a soldier under the flags of fourteen nationalities, and if these are as well received there as the few which he delivered in Australia, his tour must prove a success.

Before concluding, a few words as to New Guinea: if the General's scheme for colonizing that valuable island was nipped in the bud by the British authorities, the idea nevertheless has borne good fruit; for, undoubtedly, the idea has been the means of preventing the annexation by other interested powers. For this the people of Australasia, and also of this country, owe General MacIver a debt of gratitude, if nothing more.

His is a well-known figure in London, where he has many friends, amongst whom he is much esteemed for his generous nature and manly and straightforward character. His high sense of his personal honour, combined with a somewhat irritable temperament, occasionally leads him into little differences with even his best friends. But he is as quick to forgive as he is to take offence; a friend to be counted upon by those in whom he believes, but a keen hater where he feels that he has been injured.

Yet spite his irritability of temper, and accustomed as he has been for many years to a camp, and to the rough life of a soldier, MacIver is wonderfully tender at heart. Probably in no way is this more strongly evinced than in his chivalrous kindness to women and children.

May he live to serve under more than Fourteen Flags, and to win new honours!

THE END.

www.ingramcontent.com/pod-product-compliance
Lightning Source LLC
Chambersburg PA
CBHW032358230426
43672CB00007B/745